The Past is a Prophet
Creation and the Early Days

John C' de Baca, Ph.D.

Copyright © 2020 John C' de Baca
All rights reserved. No part of this book may be reproduced or transmitted in any form or by any means, electronic or mechanical, including photocopying, recording or by any information storage and retrieval system without permission in writing from the publisher.

Clarity Publishing—Midway, KY
ISBN: 978-0-9728536-0-6
Library of Congress Control Number: 2020908146
Title: The Past is a Prophet
Author: John C' de Baca
Digital distribution | 2020
Paperback Edition| 2020

Scripture quotes are the author's translation from THE GREEK NEW TESTAMENT © 1983, by United Bible Societies

"If I speak the truth, why do you not believe me?"
(John 8:46)

Sin, guilt, and forgiveness are central to Christian doctrine. But startlingly, *The Past is a Prophet* shows them to be just metaphors. Apart from Law they have no existence. And the delightful truth is that God does not hang the Law over us. The true Gospel is about faith apart from works, good or bad. Works neither save us, nor do they condemn us. Our very nature is the problem. The self is the Serpent. We must die to self, and put on the new nature. And we image God. He calls us now, through the Gospel, to follow his lead. The rewards will be of fabulous consequence. We will share in the very life of God!

Preface

Down through the centuries, Genesis has been a sealed book for both theologian and layman. The two accounts of the creation have appeared to be unfathomable mysteries, miraculous and marvelous beyond understanding. For many they are mere myths comparable to pagan mythological explanations of our beginnings, equally imaginative and lacking plausibility. Then, the spread of the theory of evolution has added to that loss of credibility, in the minds of both scientists and churchmen.

If Genesis is fable or myth with no solid basis in history, then the foundation of the Gospel itself is shaken. Christian tradition has always given the events in Eden as the reason for the cross and forgiveness and salvation. Without Genesis the tree of Christianity is pulled from the ground, roots and all. Christian faith is left floating in the air.

If our beginnings are unknown and unknowable, then purpose and meaning for human life go up in smoke. Life then becomes just a quirk of nature, with no solid ground even for morality. To some extent, that idea has taken hold in our Western culture, and particularly in the fields of science. But on the other hand, many people have learned to live with the uncertainties. For many Christians it is easier and more comfortable to just accept the explanations that the churches give, without questioning too much. Science and religion are kept separate. The important thing is to believe. There's no need to rock the boat or question the status quo. Faith is what's important. Faith is a leap in the dark, after all.

And so, Christians have gone their merry way, by and large believing what they are told about Jesus, but only half-heartedly. The doubt remains, always there, nibbling at faith. The Bible is mostly true, as far as the later history it deals with, but maybe it isn't totally accurate about the beginning. Who knows? Just put the question out of mind and go on. Put your faith in Jesus and let those other things take care of themselves. Don't think too much about it.

The Past is a Prophet thinks about it. And it comes up with some answers that will plant the Christian hope back firmly into the ground, and fertilize it.

TABLE OF CONTENTS

Introduction xii

1. **The Invisible Silence** 1
   A. The Caves of Christianity 1
      1. A Better Way 2
      2. The Best Way 4
2. **The Overarching Story** 9
   A. Evolution or Creation? 9
      1. By Design 10
      2. Some Creationist Verses 14
   B. The Word of Creation 18
      1. An Expression of God 18
      2. A Change in God 20
      3. God's Selfie 23
      4. The Plural God 25
3. **The Forming of this World** 34
   A. A Shocking Beginning 34
      1. God Recycled! 37
      2. The Butterfly of Heaven 39
   B. God in the Creation 43
      1. The Real World 44
      2. The True Idolatry 49
      3. Out from the Shadows 54
4. **The True Gospel** 59
   A. Not by the Law 59
      1. True Forgiveness 59
      2. Moving Onward 67
5. **True Beginnings** 70
   A. Clearing the Air 70
      1. All Wrapped Up 70
      2. Dance of the Spirit 71
      3. Nights and Days 73

        4. A Very Slow Dance 74
        5. The Seven Days 75
        6. Six Stages of Development 77
        7. The Source of Light 80
        8. Building a Greenhouse 81
    B. The Earth Comes to Life 82
        1. The Pregnant Earth 82
        2. God's Expression 84
        3. Heavenly Bodies 84
        4. Fish and Birds 86
        5. Rise of the Animals 87
    C. Creation, Not Evolution 90
        1. The Human Creature 90
        2. The Breath of Life 91
        3. The Plural God 92
        4. Then God Rested 93

6. Seeds of the Future 97
    A. Themes and Preludes of History 97
        1. Holiness 98
        2. Israel's Role 100
    B. The Uniqueness of Humanity 102
        1. Imagination and Law 106
        2. The True Gospel of Salvation 107
        3. An Unreal Gospel 111
    C. In the Garden 113
        1. The Creation of Eve 114
        2. The Death and Resurrection of God 115
    D. Events in Eden 117
        1. The Serpent 117
        2. The Temptation 119
        3. The Awakening 119
        4. The Curse of the Serpent 122
        5. The Subjection of Eve 125
        6. The Typology of Marriage 130
        7. The Curse of the Ground 132

7. Paradise Lost 135
    A. Outside of the Garden 135
        1. East of Eden 136
        2. Cain and Abel 138

B. Perplexing Questions 143
　　　　1. The Long Lives 143
　　　　2. The End of the First Creation 148
　　　　3. Forbidden Intermarriages 151
　　　　4. God's Repentance 155
　　　　5. Noah and the Ark 157
　　C. Water Colors 161
　　　　1. The Covenant of the Rainbow 162
　　　　2. Of Human Blood 163
　　　　3. Of Heavenly Eyes and Windows 163
　　D. The Nature of Sin 166
　　　　1. A Sinful Nature 166
　　　　2. To Serve God's Purpose 170
　　　　3. Sins are not Inherited 171
　　　　4. Understanding the Passage 172
　　　　5. Sin Apart from Law 178
8. **Christ in Early History** 180
　　A. The Tower of Babel 180
　　　　1. The Goal of Oneness 182
　　　　2. Heading East 183
　　　　3. The Second Babel 186
　　　　4. The Last Visitation 188
9. **Recycling the Creation** 190

Introduction

Important in the teachings of Jesus were two unexpected, disquieting notes. First, he emphasized that the Jews had not understood the Scriptures. Second, he warned that God was about to reject Israel.

Jesus brought a new and different way of reading God's Word. He used word pictures called parables that were sometimes shocking and offensive. He told stories that held symbolic meanings, and indicated that this was the way God had spoken in the holy writings. He showed that the Father had drawn word pictures of the Son.

The Jews could not see these typological meanings. Incredibly, the Jews crucified their King. They missed not only the bull's-eye, but the whole target. Why did they so miss the mark? It was because the cataracts of literalness clouded their eyes, and loyalty to tradition hardened their hearts.

And alarmingly, the Jews foreshadow Christians. Israel's history foretells the history of Christianity. Jesus' warning is two-fold. It is for the Jews of his own day, but also for Christians of the end-time. Like the Jews, Christians have not understood the Scriptures, and God will reject them too. True to the type, Christians have been blinded by literalism and hardened in their traditions. New Israel will be rejected because, unwittingly, they are hell-bent on repeating the shameful, tragic history of their foreshadowing elder sister. Those who cry peace for the Christian Church are repeating the folly of the false prophets of Israel. Christians will, like the Jews, crucify their king, bringing God's judgment swiftly upon their heads.

Tragically, the churches of Christianity do not preach the true Gospel. Pretending to be scientific, they analyze every word, every phrase of Scripture, quoting one another as if this were the proof of their claims, but they fail to understand the Bible's central truths. Like the Jews, they are blind to the pictures. They will surely reject Christ just as their counterparts did. And they don't even realize this, because they have failed to understand the Scriptures.

The Past is a Prophet is offered with the hope that it will open the eyes of the blind. Christianity's house is being left desolate. Soon she will commit the final abomination that brings desolation. She, too, is filling her cup. It's getting really full. Soon it will spill over.

Chapter One
The Invisible Silence

Some say silence is golden. I say it's not. Gold is never silent. Gold is loud and loquacious, always trying to get your attention. You have to ignore it. If you look its way it instantly shines in your eyes. It can make them bulge out. It can make your heart race. No, gold is never silent and silence isn't golden. Silence is dark and secretive, a cave where you can hide, an invisibility cloak to wrap around yourself. Silence is a hiding place.

The Caves of Christianity

Curiously, when you look closely you can find many Christians hiding there, in the silence, trying to be inconspicuous, their mouth tightly closed lest they open it and be found out. They must not expose their hypocrisy by appearing to preach. It's safer to ease back inconspicuously into the background, and not call attention to yourself. Stay invisible. Hunch down in the pew.

Why? Oddly, Christians are afraid of wagging tongues and accusatory fingers! That's true. They're afraid of tongues and fingers. It's much safer in the silence. So they hide in the hush. What makes them so timid? It's the fear of being found out. They're ashamed to talk the talk because they haven't walked the walk. They mustn't expose their hypocrisy. It might catch the attention of the tongues and the fingers. Better is to blend into the shadows unnoticed and unheard. It's safer when you're unseen. Stay quiet. And if anyone looks your way, smile. But don't say anything. Don't tell anyone about Jesus.

Still, in those dark recesses of silence lurk even darker, more menacing shadows. Among them prowls that darkest shadow of all. Christians must slip away and free themselves from him. They must come out from the caves. And the only way out is to speak. Silence can only be overcome with sound. Nothing else works against it. Muteness can only be overcome by speaking.

The words in us about Jesus, the big ones and the little ones, must be called forth and sent out. They must be spoken. Words come alive as they are communicated. They live in the telling. It's what they're for. It's their purpose. The desire of every word is to be chosen. Is not silence then a chokehold that keeps them from fulfilling their function? Is not silence about the very Word of God then a denial of him? We must come out from the quiet. Guilt and self-recriminations must not hold our tongues. We must free our tongues from their grip. After all, is it not wrong to remain silent when we know we should speak? Shamefully, churches are full of people hiding from accusations of hypocrisy by being silent! They're afraid of the tongues and fingers. They're ashamed to speak openly of Jesus.

Most Christians know that they should testify of Christ. But when the opportunity comes, the H-word immediately slaps them in the face, and pokes them in the ribs, because their lives are not in harmony with the message. They have not practiced what they think they must preach. So they do all they can to make themselves invisible. Ostriches are said to hide by burying their heads in the sand. Christians hide by closing their mouth.

Of course, it's not all their fault, because the Gospel they've been taught doesn't make sense. It's irrational, mythical, and unscriptural. And yes, at times it's even blasphemous. It doesn't match up with the real world, or with the Bible, and it makes God into a monster. The reason many Christians shut their mouths so tightly is as much from honest doubt as from timidity. It's a lack of faith. After all, how can you confidently recommend to others something about which you yourself are unsure, and haven't practiced? Many times it's actually better to remain silent, and leave the preaching to the pastors and the priests. Preaching without practicing is hypocrisy, and proclaims a hollow sermon.

A Better Way

The trouble is, too many Christians don't preach but they don't practice either. The ugly reason for this is that the Gospel they were taught doesn't make sense. Tragically, the churches of Christendom, almost without exception, unwittingly preach a false Gospel. They've become dens of deception. Yes, I'm talking about the mainline churches of mainstream Christianity, the little ones dying in the cities, the big, bloated ones in the suburbs, and the one on the corner of your street. Mostly, they preach in all sincerity, with zeal and great passion. Great passion and sincerity can grow churches, but they don't magically change lies into truths, even when the lies are shouted passionately from behind a pulpit.

Passionate preaching of falsehood remains preposterous and profane. Yes, to remain closed-lipped many times is more praiseworthy than to vomit forth lies passionately and sincerely (Isa. 28:8). Is it not much, much better to remain silent than to puke all over the Lord's table? Christians are caught in a tug of war, ashamed to speak, and ashamed of not speaking. They're damned if they do, and damned if they don't. So they don't.

To draw great crowds, the churches hawk hope and acceptance in various ways. They offer personal peace and happiness to whoever receives their brand of religion. They dangle these as a carrot to convince the crowds that they own the truth. Worship services become pep rallies to animate or shame the people into heightened zeal and audacity for living and proclaiming the communal myths. The more zeal they can whip up, the more people they can attract, and the greater grows their satisfaction and sense of accomplishment. In other churches, the myths take the form of somber rituals proclaimed and celebrated with great dignity and pomp, providing a comforting sense of order and continuity. But lies are lies, even if they attract great crowds of followers. The road to destruction is wide and well-traveled.

Acceptance, hope, and the desire for happiness sell, and the churches swell. But if these are wrapped and sold in a bag of falsehood, it can become a false hope. It will hold ill will toward the truth, and in the end will bear bitter fruit. Whether told dryly or emotionally, pompously or sincerely, lies are lies. Churches built on falsehood, even friendly, growing churches, are built on quicksand even if they're sincere and growing. Sincere quicksand is still quicksand, and can never be a good foundation upon which to build. The more convincing and sincere a lie is, the nicer its clothes, the greater is its deceptiveness. You may wash its face and comb its hair, and even brush its teeth, but a lie is still a lie, even on a smiling face. Even from behind the pulpit in a growing, friendly church.

As more and more people receive it, a lie becomes communal, and is integrated into a people's culture and identity. The boil festers and becomes inflamed. Chronic lies within a community are hard to cure, especially religious ones. So perhaps congratulations are in order, rather than recriminations, to the silent majority. Honest silence is preferable by far to loud lies or false doctrines, however passionately and sincerely they might be proclaimed, and however deeply they might be embedded within Christian culture. Honest, embarrassed silence is much, much worthier than the loud, gold-plated lies told in so many churches.

The Best Way

But silence is just second best. Better would be to find the truth and proclaim it, loudly and passionately. Like John the Baptist, we must be a strong, clear voice of truth in the desert. We must shout a warning. An avalanche of judgment is hurtling downward toward the people who believe that the gates of hell will never prevail against their church. When Jesus said that, he was talking about his church, not theirs. Yes, the sky really is falling. Wrath is building. The pot is already whistling, steaming, belching out its impatient warning.

Meanwhile, the churches wheel out program after program to serve the people and grow bigger. Serving the people is called serving Christ. Their goal is to grow. And the people love being served. The carrot of happiness is strong bait. The churches are unaware that destruction looms, while they eat, drink, and display their obesity. They think that God's wrath will fall only upon pagans and infidels, not upon them. Christianity has rejected the truth and will herself be rejected. Why? Literalism has clouded her vision. She cannot make out the symbolism hidden in God's Word. She can't see the pictures. The churches are blind, and inadvertently preach blasphemy sincerely, passionately, and proudly.

The Holy Spirit is not a genie trapped inside the bottle of literal interpretation. Nor is the Bible just a guide for moralizing, or a magic lamp to be rubbed to let the genie of materialism out. Nor can God be bribed with blind, misguided zeal. So the Bible remains closed to the churches, despite their libraries stacked floor to ceiling

The Invisible Silence

with tomes proclaiming the communal myths, and despite their seminaries spilling over with eager students studying how to regurgitate the myths on cue and more effectively.

The relatively few Christians who study the Bible do so through the colored lens of literalism. They read through the prism of a world-view that harmonizes with their historical traditions. They interpret as they were taught. Without realizing it, they impose their serpentine pseudo-scientific distortions upon the texts, and become ardent in the defense of their distortions. Their hearts are hardened with zeal and conviction and their minds are closed to the truth even while they claim to stand for truth, and believe that they have it. But too many times, what they have is blind eyes and blasphemous lips.

Yes, we are hard on the churches. But should blasphemy be tolerated just because it's sincere, well-meaning blasphemy, or because it comes from a long religious tradition, or because a church is friendly? No, the loving thing is to make the churches aware of their blasphemy. We must speak truth to their face. Truth is the only medicine that will cure falsehood. And it must be given full strength, undiluted. Truth mixed with error is not truth. The truth must be told, even if it offends the status quo.

Not understanding heavenly things, too many churches have focused their gaze on the things of this world. They've turned from heaven to humanity. These churches are engrossed with their own navel. Filling their communion cups with humanism, they serve it generously to the people, come who may, and minister to humanity as if this were service to God. Masters at switching terms, they love the game of substitution. To serve the needy, they claim, is to serve Christ. But the needy are not Christ. Christ is never served through a substitute or intermediary. That would be idolatry. He is not served by serving humanity. Christ is served by serving Christ. An intermediary is an idol. And idols are abominations. A substitute for Christ is an idol, even if the substitute is poor and needy, and stands in line.

No doubt most churches will claim exception, and will object strenuously and passionately that in their service to humanity they are obeying Jesus' commands and demonstrating God's love. But is that so? Obedience to commands makes one a good Marine, not a good Christian. Jesus is not the reincarnation of Moses. He did not give us a new set of laws to break or ignore, or even to keep. He

The Invisible Silence

brought freedom from Law. Putting a Christian label on a can of worms doesn't make it corn or tomatoes. Putting the label of God's love on humanism does not make it the Gospel. Changing of labels is just another form of term switching. It doesn't change one thing into another. It's still a can of worms. And it smells like it when you open it.

You reap what you sow. Garbage in, garbage out. It's silly to sow seeds of humanism and expect divine love to grow. Only the divine Spirit of Christ can manifest divine love. Love is not something that can be substituted. Humans can't love in God's place. You got that, pilgrim? Only God can manifest God's love, thank you. Humans serving humans because of Jesus' commands are not demonstrating his love. At best, their actions testify of it. Or worse, they imitate it. And imitation, guess what, is what Satan does. Without the actuating power of the Spirit, God's love is never present, no matter how many supposed good deeds are done, or how many hungry mouths are fed. Let me repeat. Only God himself manifests God's love, directly and in person, never by an imitation or substitute, or intermediary. Humans cannot love in God's place. A substitute for God, even if it's a loving substitute, is an idol. His love is not expressed by imitating it. Imitation love, like an imitation diamond, is worthless. Imitation love is not God's love.

Human welfare, the good of society, or world peace are neither the highest good, nor the true believer's goals. Apart from Christ, these just present the prettied-up face of humanism, powdered and painted to hide its oozing pimples. The true follower of Christ serves him directly, apart from any intermediary, following the inward leading of the Spirit. Nor is Christ identical with the needy. To serve the needy as if this were service to Christ is idolatry too. Yes, a substitute for Christ is an idol, even if it's hungry, or sick, or naked. You serve Christ only when you serve Christ. And you serve him directly, in direct contact, in communion. Not understanding this, many churches are committing idolatry in the name of Christ! They serve the needy as if this were to serve Christ.

These are serious accusations. Are they true? Their truth is one good reason for this book. Let's say it even more plainly. The central doctrines and practices of mainstream Christianity are idolatrous and blasphemous. There, I said it. And I meant it. The Church is leading the people astray. Perhaps you yourself have been led merrily down primrose lane. If you call yourself a Christian and are a church-goer, you've probably even paid regularly for her lies because it made you feel good. You thought it was the truth.

These statements may offend some people, especially those who have practiced their faith sincerely. But shooting the messenger is not the answer. When the truth offends, the problem is not with the truth teller. Zealots of the churches who are offended with the truth here have a choice. They can either prove these allegations to be untrue according to God's word, or they can verify their truth and accept them. Then, convinced of their truth, they should proclaim it loudly with us.

Reality is not majority opinion. Nor is it personal opinion, not even strong opinion, no, not even your opinion or mine, even if you get very emotional about it, or even if you heard it often in church. Truth is the expression of reality, of how things really are. It's not determined by the size of a church, or how fast it grows, or how friendly it is, or its long history, or how many needy people it serves, or how many programs it can field. Truth is how things really are, regardless of what anyone thinks. A true church teaches the truth, even if it offends, and even if that makes it remain small. If a church or religion does not teach the truth of God's word, it's a false religion, a high place of idolatry. And its devotees are most certainly not walking on the holy ground they seek. A large, populous church that practices idolatry is worse than a small one, is it not? Yes, a small church that teaches the truth is better than ten large and friendly churches that teach falsehood.

We must examine our shoes, to see where we've been walking. Before we can step onto the clean floors of holiness, we must wipe our shoes on the entrance mat of truth. To do that, we must know for sure what God's word really says. It is wise, then, to step back and take a careful look at what the Bible really teaches, taking care not to be blinded by literalism or tradition. We must not try to read God's word with our eyes closed. We must open our eyes and see the pictures. We must read with imagination. We must allow the Spirit to speak while we listen. Then, we must break out of the shadowed dens by shattering the silence. We must speak out. The truth must be shouted from the rooftops, and channeled through the airwaves, everywhere. Yes, it must even be preached in the churches.

The Invisible Silence

But first, we must know the truth. A good place to start is at the start. Isn't that reasonable? A good place to begin is at the beginning, in Genesis. But watch where you step, until we get outside. False tradition lies everywhere. As we proceed, it will be necessary to clear a pathway. We'll need to carefully clear away some of the accumulated falsehoods that lie in our way. We'll need a good, sharp shovel. And boots.

Chapter Two
The Overarching Story

In the beginning is the end. The start tells us about the finish. Genesis portends the future and images it. And the future is many-splendored. So the first book of the Bible is wrapped in a coat of many colors, like a bright, overarching rainbow. From afar, it glows with mystery and enchantment. But as we draw near, the rainbow vanishes. The account sheds its mythical, magical aura of inexplicable marvels and impossible enigmas. We are left with our own, ordinary world of today; no enchantment, no rainbow, and no pot of gold, just reality. But don't fret. Reality has its own enchantment.

Evolution or Creation?

We must spend time with the account, however, and listen patiently to its story. When we do, it opens up to us and begins to share its marvelous secrets. But we must listen very carefully, because it says one thing and means two, or three. The account is both literal and figurative at the same time. It winks at us and smiles as it speaks, telling us about the past while subtly gesturing toward the future, stooping and drawing pictures in the dirt while whispering of heaven.

Despite our efforts at being patient, it sees that we're in a hurry, and skips over vast epochs, over everything that's not germane to our future. It is brief and to the point, and wastes no words. But even with its brevity and symbolism, the creation account is understandable. It makes sense. It is not myth or magic. The world of Genesis isn't wonderland, and our name isn't Alice. At least, mine isn't. Yours probably isn't, either. If it is, well, that's okay.

The account is for real, credible and true. Pristine earth is not a magical land where light shines without a source, where day and night exist even before the sun is created. Stars do not float among the clouds. Nor is there a world without form. Can anything exist without form? The world of Genesis is our own world of today. The account tells us, in its own way, how our world of today came to be, and why. It tells how God formed our world, or rather his world.

But before we can walk through the pages of Genesis and look agog to either side of us upon our forming world, we must first clear away the many piles of orthodoxy that lie everywhere in our path. We must proceed with our shovel of truth in hand. Every step must be carefully cleared. As we approach the first verse, we must shovel away some of the litter. One of the biggest piles of litter that we must shovel out is the idea that creation is the act of bringing something into existence from nothing. That's twaddle.

But if so, the question becomes, how did we get here? What was the creation all about? Does the Bible tell us how we got here, and what God is like? Does it have any rhyme or reason, or is it just a series of anecdotal incidents? Or is it just myth, as evolutionists claim? What is the truth?

By Design

Thinking people often wonder about the meaning of human life. Is there any great purpose for our existence? What will the future hold? What happens after we die? These questions, and others, loom large in the minds of those who read books such as this one. The Bible, of course, holds the answers, but evolutionary science has seemed to undermine its validity. The theory of evolution has created doubt in the minds of many. Nevertheless, while they laugh at superstition and the Bible, evolutionists are superstitious themselves. They have concocted a fantasy world composed of shape-shifters guided by a mindless process that somehow guides the shape-shifting so that it works ever upward. This mindless process, that supposedly operates haphazardly through random accidents, is said to make the shape-shifters ever more complex and smarter. In the evolutionist fantasy, mindlessness has produced mind, by accident. Non-intelligence has produced intelligence. Dead and inert rocks have come alive and learned to think, all by themselves. It makes no sense whatsoever. Denying the biblical God, evolutionists have substituted the Process in his place. Their god is a process called Evolution.

The Overarching Story

Ludicrously, they laugh and turn their noses up at religion while they worship the Process in a nonsensical and baseless religion of their own. But the laugh is on them. An entirely random event or process cannot develop trends. If it is random, there can be no long-term trend. If it can go left or right every time, it will not go left every time, or right. If it does so, it is not random. Something or someone is controlling it. Toss a coin in the air ten times, and it will be heads about half the time, and tails about the same. It will not trend toward more heads the more times you toss it. Try it, if you're not sure. Toss it five thousand times, or ten thousand, or a million times. You'll still get about half heads and half tails. Indeed, the more times you toss it, the closer you'll get to fifty percent.

And yet evolutionists claim that the random occurrences in nature have a general direction, and that it is upward toward ever more complexity. It is completely mindless and random, and yet its trend is upward. That's like saying that the more times you toss a coin, the greater will be the preponderance of heads over tails. Toss it a hundred times and you'll have about fifty percent heads. Toss it two hundred times, and you'll have sixty percent heads. Toss it a thousand times and you'll get eighty or ninety percent heads, and so on. A million times will get you ninety-nine point nine. A billion times will get you a real live human!

Despite themselves, their mindless Process will not work, unless there is a higher power or mind controlling it so that it will indeed trend upward. Otherwise, it would have no trend, regardless of how many random accidents occurred. The evolutionist god must have another god higher up that controls it. That's the only way their Process can work. Randomness does not generate trends. And the more instances of randomness at work, the less likelihood that a trend can develop.

Their fantasy is based on an oxymoron, a random trend. But if it's random, there can be no trend. If it displays a general trend upward, then there is something or someone controlling it. Evolutionists cannot have their cake and eat it too. Evolution is either random, or it is controlled. If it is random, there can be no upward trend. The trend toward more and more complexity that evolutionists claim, is its own rebuttal, a self-contradiction. It smacks them right in the face and then laughs, contradicting their theory that random accidents have resulted in things called humans. Evolution requires design. And design requires a Designer.

Actually, the general trend in nature is not toward greater complexity, but rather toward chaos. The law of entropy laughs and slaps evolutionists in the face as well. It too denies their claims. There must be someone or something beyond nature as we know it that has caused the complexity that we see all around us.

All living things, they say, have evolved accidentally from prior living things, in an unbroken chain of change that began by accident in a nonliving primordial soup. The problem is, it's a chain without any links. There exists absolutely no instance of one being changing into another. No, there is not even one instance anywhere, except in the movies or on television, or in the mirage-filled minds of evolutionists. But because the changes are nowhere to be seen, and no one has ever seen even one such change, the excuse is made that the changes take zillions of years to happen. And yet, the landscape of a few million years ago is barren and lifeless. No matter how far back they go, they still cannot find any links, no, not one. It's a magical, make-believe chain. It has no links. It's a chain with no links, child.

Their fantasy is mythical and magical, even while they claim to disdain myth and magic. No one has ever seen or touched or heard their mindless Process, or smelled him. He's just a theory. All their work, day and night, is based on the need to find evidence that their theory is true, and that their god actually exists. And so they search for him constantly, digging under rocks or in graveyards. Every new skeleton they find is supposed to be evidence of their god's handiwork. But the skeletons say otherwise, and skeletons don't lie. They too, slap the evolutionists in the face.

It's all just wishful thinking. There is no evidence, no links, and no shape-shifting. There has never been a case of one creature changing into another. Shape-shifters don't exist, child, even when you watch for millions of years. The evolutionist Process is nowhere to be found, and there is absolutely no evidence that he exists. And if he did exist, there would need to be someone controlling him, someone able to think and move, and manage him. But if this higher god were mindless too, he would require a god above him, and another above that one, and so on, until you get to the real God. The

The Overarching Story

evolutionist stance has no basis in reality. The emperor has no clothes!

Nevertheless, evolutionists have made a good show of it. The theory of evolution, with its trumped-up evidence, has made a large impact on people. It has cast doubt on the biblical explanation of how we got here. It has made people unsure. There is widespread uncertainty about our beginnings. They have duped the people with charts and time-scales and skeletons. In view of the made-up evolutionist charts and time-scales and skeletons, the Bible account is seen by many as superstitious myth. Nevertheless, despite all their hoop-la and their incongruous and self-contradictory pretense at having purpose, in the evolutionist fantasy there is no real lasting purpose, and no hope for humanity. Nor is there any basis for morality. We have no ultimate reason for our existence. Life is a dead end. We're just an accident, or rather, just the result of millions and billions of accidents under the control (control?) of the great mindless Evolutionary Process.

But if he is mindless and random, how can he control anything? How can he initiate any trends? He himself must be under someone else's control. Otherwise, there could be no trend. In the end, there must be a sentient being initiating the trend. Evolutionists have no answer for this, and so they throw the problem into the infinite and unknown past beyond reach. Of course, we can do as they do, and throw the problem into the infinite past as well. We can theorize that there were millions and billions of gods, each one controlling the one under him. And all these gods must have emerged from the primordial soup. But then the problem becomes, who made the soup? That's the evolutionist position in a nutshell. It's not just a question about the chicken and the egg. It's about the Rooster too. And the soup. So we're back where we started. The whole thing is chicken soup.

To oppose the evolutionist fantasy and to offer hope, creationists offer their own well-intentioned fantasy. But it, too, is magical even while they claim to disdain magic and condemn it. The magical, mythical character of the creationist fantasy is one reason why the evolutionist theory gets so much traction. The creationist interpretation of Genesis is based on a misunderstanding of the biblical text. Despite their claims to the contrary, in the creationist fantasy God has become the great Magician. He made the world pop up from nowhere. Then he makes vegetation, birds, animals, and humans pop up from the ground fully formed, in just six literal days. And the first days and nights, mind you, were before the sun and moon and stars came into being! You have daylight without the sun, and night-time before the moon and stars. What a great trick!

This traditional creationist explanation of origins, accepted as orthodoxy by most Christian churches, is based on a faulty interpretation of the biblical text. It goes against all human experience and plain common sense. The idea of creation from nothing is just as magical as the evolutionist shape-shifting that no one has ever seen. No one has ever seen creation from nothing either. Creationists answer, however, in a manner very similar to the evolutionists. They put the problem out of reach. They come up with the excuse that God did it, and he can do anything. Instead of throwing the problem into the infinite and unknown past as the evolutionists do, creationists throw the problem up at God. He is infinite, you see, and how he did it is unknowable. So both evolutionists and creationists use basically the same tactic or excuse. The evidence for their claims lies in a black hole somewhere, beyond discovery. But the Scriptures do not back them up, nor does experience. No one has ever seen one critter change into another, and no one has ever seen matter created from nothing, nor destroyed into nothingness. There is no evidence for either of these baseless conjectures.

Some Creationist Verses

Creationists sometimes use a couple or three verses that supposedly substantiate their claims. Let's see if they do. Right from the start, we should recognize, however, that the creationist position does not coincide with the Genesis account, which speaks of a re-organizing of the planet, not of things jumping out of nowhere. And we should realize that the biblical references to creation, without exception, mean the transformation or re-forming of that which already exists. Look them all up if you will, tiger. Be sure.

The creationist claim is that, since things that are seen were not made from that which appears, this means that they came out of nowhere (Heb. 11:1-3). But that's not what the verse means. The verse is concerned with faith, as the context very clearly shows.

Faith is the evidence of things not seen. The verse does not refer to the origin of the world, but rather to the agency of its becoming like it is. It's about who or what made it to be like it is. The world was finalized by the word of God, which is unseen. And true faith believes this. It does not mean that things jumped out of nowhere. That would be impossible. It does not refer to the absolute beginning of things, but rather to their re-forming or completion into their present state. The Bible tells us that things came to be as they are through the agency of the word of God, which is unseen.

The word that is translated here as "from," (*ek*) or "out from," also has the meaning of "by." The verse means that things that are seen were not finalized by things that appear. No, they were completed and brought into their present state by the word of God. The verse is promoting faith in the truth that the unseen word of God was the agent of bringing the world to its completion. What's so hard to understand about that? Following is the author's translation of the verse.

"By faith we understand that the ages (worlds) were brought to their completion by the word of God, so that not by that which appears did that which is seen come to be." *The Greek New Testament, The United Bible Societies, 1983.*

The word that is usually translated here by creationists as "formed" or "made" or "framed" (*katartidzo*), does not mean to bring into existence from nothingness. It means to bring something that already exists to its completion or fullness. A quick glance at other passages in which it is used will verify this for us.

Matt. 4:21—mend or repair
Matt. 21:16—prepare, provide, put in order, ordain
Luke 6:40—fully qualify, finish, complete
1 Cor. 1:10—be united so as to be perfected or completed
Gal. 6:1—restore
Heb. 10:5—prepare, ready
Heb. 13:21—equip so as to be complete or perfected
1 Peter 5:10—to perfect, complete

In none of these verses does the word mean to make something from nothing. It means to bring something to its perfection or completion. Nothingness cannot be mended, finished, repaired, qualified, united, prepared, equipped, or completed. The Bible truth is a slap in the face of creationists. Both evolutionists and creationists are red-faced.

Let's look at a couple of other verses that are sometimes quoted. It is true, as Paul says, that God calls things that don't exist as though they did exist (Rom. 4:17). But this refers to future generations and to the coming resurrection, not to a divine magic act. It means that God has the sovereign power to fulfill his word and his desires. His prophecies are certain to occur, his promises are faithful.

In another verse Paul says that God chose the things don't exist to nullify those that do (1 Cor. 1:28). First, it shows that the things that are nullified are existent things. What it means is that new things take the place of old things. The future ever displaces the present. It does not mean that events that happen arise from nothingness. Events, child, even those events that are unforeseen, do not magically appear out of nowhere. In the creation, the world was rearranged by the word of God. It was changed. The author of Hebrews writes here that true faith believes this, that the creation was a reorganization of what existed. True faith does not believe in a magic act of nothingness transforming itself into somethingness! True faith does not believe in false orthodoxy or tradition, but in the word of God correctly understood.

The situation is laughable as well as tragic. Evolutionists embrace myth and magic while denying that they believe in myth or magic. They look down their noses at creationists, whom they consider to be superstitious. Creationists, on the other hand, while claiming that they too disdain myth and magic, answer with their own magical and mythical beliefs based on faulty understandings of the biblical texts. Comically, both evolutionists and creationists claim to disdain myth and magic while they hold myth and magic tightly to their breast with both hands. Both sides ardently seek to prove the existence of their Creator. Both sides claim realism as their method and the support for their findings. They claim that their fantasies are real. They call for everyone to believe in their fantasy with them.

The fight is not between equals, however. The evidence favors true creationism, although not as it is preached in the churches. The truth is rightly reported in the Bible. But the Bible must be understood correctly. We must turn back and read it anew, with fresh eyes. Rightly understood, the Bible can truthfully and convincingly answer our questions about our origins, about life, purpose, and the future.

But we must not read with the beclouded eyes of orthodoxy, religious or scientific. We must read with a desire to know the truth and an openness to receive it, while rejecting what is merely orthodox. Tradition, after all, is not the guarantor of truth. Truth is logical and makes sense, and does not depend on trumped up evidence, whether it is physical, as with the evolutionists, or literary, as with the creationists. True faith is not wishful thinking or, worse, closed-minded zeal, which both evolutionists and creationists display. Nor is truth magical, so we must reject magic right from the start, whether it be religious or scientific. We need to understand what the Bible actually says, rather than what religionists say it says. We must let it speak to us, honestly and openly. We'll need to read carefully without a sack of false orthodoxy over our heads.

We can start right from the beginning, in Genesis. The beginning that we read there in the book of beginnings is not myth or magic. God is not the divine Magician. He doesn't make things pop up out of nowhere.

So, contrary to mainstream tradition, the beginning of which Genesis speaks is not the beginning of reality, or of the solar system or the stars. It's about the purposeful re-forming of the world that was already there. The Bible tells in large, giant strokes how God rearranged the existing world so that it would lead to Christ Jesus. The world already existed. The course of creation of which the book of Genesis speaks was the beginning of our world, as we experience it. It's an account of how God took what was there and formed it into what it is today, and why. And it gives us a glimpse of the future as well. It points us toward the goal and glory that awaits when this present world too is rearranged and the new creation is born.

The account assumes both the existence of God and of the world. Both are present at the creation. The Bible tells us that God is the person or power that made our world become the way it is. He had a plan and a purpose, and that plan and purpose is still ongoing even now. This world's journey is not yet ended. It has not yet reached its grand and glorious goal. But it will. The world is not flying blind. We can see this right from the start. Genesis speaks of Revelation, and vice versa.

So, as we begin, we can accept the existence of the world, of course. But can we accept the existence of a cause of it all? Yes, we can. All physical happenings have a cause. If something occurs a certain way, it's because something or someone caused it to happen the way it did. Our world is like it is because something caused it to be like it is. A causeless physical world or process would be totally illogical and in fact impossible. So we can accept the existence both of the world and of a cause. The Bible calls this earth-ordering cause God, or rather, Gods (*Elohim*).

The Word of Creation

And the agent of creation was his word. That sounds strange. Can a word actually be a causative agent? How? Do words really change things, or are they just puffs of air? The Bible says that the changes that happened in the creation were the result of God expressing his desires. He expressed himself. He spoke. The word of God was the agent of creation. Let's examine this notion closely, and see what it means in its biblical context.

An Expression of God

Words, we know, are expressions of ourselves. They tell who we are, even when we lie. Lies just reveal the dishonesty inside of us. Of course, with God there can be no question of his word being false. His word is true, for it is an expression of himself. God's word is the expression of God. But what does it mean that God expressed himself? Is it just that he made audible sounds, potent and powerful, and the earth obeyed? What language might he have used? In what manner was the word of God the agent of creation? Later, we learn that God's word in the creation, in the beginning, was God (John 1:1-3). So, as we come to these first verses in Genesis, we must read with the understanding that God's word is God. *His word is a symbol of God himself.* That which is expressed is the very Creator. And we know that he's more than a few puffs of air.

His word of creation did not consist of mere sounds, then. Neither was it the verbalization of a human language. It was not Hebrew or Aramaic. If we get this wrong in the beginning, we will miss everything that follows. And that's what the churches have done. They have not recognized the Word of God that was in the beginning for what it really is. They have imagined that God spoke as we do. That is a foundational error that touches everything that comes after, including even the Gospel itself. The truth will be an earthquake upending orthodoxy and turning tradition on its head. So be prepared, tiger.

The truth is that God's word is an expression of himself, of his very own being. God's word is God. And he is not a human tongue. He is not sounds or articulations. The creative word was not of an aloof and holier than thou God commanding from afar a dead and inert earth that nevertheless somehow heard him speak and obeyed. It was God himself that was being expressed. Human language does not express God. It can speak of him, but it can never express God himself. God is not a human language, no, not even English or French or Spanish, nor even a computer language. When the text says that God spoke, that is an anthropomorphism to help us understand. It talks of God as if he were human, to help bring events down to our level. It's a metaphor, child.

It was not a human language that was spoken. It was the Word of God. And all things came about through that Word (John 1:1-3). All things have come about through the expression of God, then. Expressing his word is a metaphor for expressing himself. This world, as it has come to be, is the result of God's expression of himself. And it was not the expression of a literal language. However startling the idea may be to the orthodox mind, the changes that occurred in the creation were changes in God. He was not barking orders from outer space. He was immanent in the action, fully immersed within the changes that were taking place. He was blowing in the winds and swimming in the seas.

In his speaking he was acting. His word and his action should not be separated. His speaking is a way of saying that God was actively involved in and guiding the changes that occurred. Those changes were the expression of God. Startlingly, he himself was changing. That which was spoken was God. To say that God spoke is a metaphorical way of saying that the changes that God was effecting were of God himself. The changes were of God and in God. In the changes that he was initiating, God himself was changing. The Spirit

The Overarching Story

and the world were not yet differentiated. God and the world were yet in oneness.

In the beginning of which the Bible tells, the world was not yet separate from its Creator, (Rom. 11:36; 1 Cor. 8:6, 11:12). Matter and Spirit were not yet differentiated as they are today. That differentiation of Spirit from Matter was completed when God ended his work of making this world the way it is. When the work of creation was finished, the Spirit withdrew temporarily from the world (Gen. 6:3).

Yes, in the beginning God spoke our world into its present state. We should not think that God spoke in the same manner as we humans do, through literal lips that form sounds from the air that blows by them from lungs squeezed by chest and stomach muscles. We must not make God into our image. That's backwards. And it is what has kept the churches from understanding the creation. After all, does not a radio or television speak? Do these have lungs, lips, and tongues? So, if radios and televisions and tape recorders and CD's can speak without lungs and tongues, cannot God do the same?

His speaking is metaphorical, an anthropomorphism to indicate that he expressed himself. He moved. He changed. The Word of God is God. Astonishingly for orthodoxy, God himself, being in the beginning of one identity with the world, was the subject of the processes of creation. When he spoke a change to be, he was changing himself, as it were (Gen. 1:26; John 1:1). His speaking was his expression of himself. The changes that he spoke into being in the world were changes in himself. He and the world were One. The Word of God was the expression of God.

A Change in God

As we've said, this idea of the creation of the world being a series of changes in God as well as in the world can be an earthquake in the orthodox mind. Orthodoxy has made God into a Spirit-only, ethereal, unchanging, and other-worldly being that has always been and who will always be totally separate and different from the world. He is Spirit, while the world is matter. In the orthodox understanding, he was commanding the changes to occur from a safe distance, himself untouched and unmoved by the changes.

In that scheme, he was above the action, merely telling the world what to do, and looking on with satisfaction when it obeyed. God commanded, and the world heard and obeyed. Inadvertently and unintentionally, the orthodox idea of an aloof but articulate God above and beyond the world and separate from it and from all the changes that he was commanding assumes an intelligent, sentient world having the power to act on its own. God speaks while keeping himself holy and separate from the world, and the world hears and obeys. The world becomes an associate, God's fellow companion and partner in the creation.

This idea of the world being actively involved in the creation is true, as we'll see, because the world was not yet separated from God. Creating did not leave the Creator himself unchanged, because God and world were of one identity. The world was an associate because it was not yet separate or distinct from God.

On the other hand, if God was not involved in the changes that were occurring, if he was merely commanding the earth from a safe distance as orthodoxy claims, it denies God's real participation. He merely tells the world what to do, and it obeys. He's the Boss, so the world does what he says. But in that case the world becomes the true Creator! God gives the orders, but the world does all the work. Inadvertently and unintentionally, orthodoxy has set God aside and has put the world in his place. He is no longer the Creator. He is the Boss. The world is the true Creator!

Of course, we know that is not the case. It comes from a faulty reading. The text explicitly and repeatedly says that it was God himself, personally, who was expressing and effecting the changes of creation (Gen. 1:7, 16, 21, 26-27, 2:2, 7-8, etc.). He was involved in the changes. They were the expression of God. And God and his Word are One. He was never an aloof bystander, but an active participant, immanent in the action. In the creation, God himself changed. He is the Creator, the Changer, not just the Looker or Watcher, or Talker. The text says explicitly that the world brought forth the grass and trees, the birds and the fish, and the animals (Gen. 1:11-12, 20-21, 24-25). And in the same breath it emphasizes that it was God who created them. Both God and the world were involved together in bringing about the changes.

Why is it so hard to envision a sentient, conscious world? Is it not because science and orthodoxy have joined together in denying it for centuries? After all, humans are composed of matter. Are we not made of earth? And are we not sentient? Is it then impossible that consciousness somehow should inhere in matter? Must it come as an injection from the outside? The fact of consciousness demonstrates clearly and irrefutably that matter can be sentient. Matter can think. It can feel. If we assume, however, that sentience and consciousness inhere only in our spirit, we must still grapple with the truth that our spirit and our flesh work in conjunction with one another. So then, why is it so difficult to see that this same original hypostatic union of Spirit with Matter can be attributed to God as well? Are we not made in his image?

Can it be that the earth itself was somehow alive and in some degree sentient? After all, it was the earth itself that produced all the living, as God expressed himself. In the beginning, God and the earth were in oneness. Startling, isn't it?

And does not the Bible say that God is everywhere, and in all things (2 Chron. 2:6; Ps. 139:7-12; Isa. 6:3; Jer. 23:24; Acts 17:28)? Is the Spirit not immanent everywhere in the world? Does not the Bible explicitly emphasize that life originated from the earth itself (Gen. 1:20, 24)? Do babies not grow by assimilating the earth? Do we ourselves not live from the earth? The food that we eat, from which we draw life and sustenance, comes from the earth, child. Indeed, the Bible says that God gives life to all things (1 Tim. 6:13). Do all things then not share somehow in God, since it was God himself who is expressed in the huge processes and patterns of our world? Why, then, is it so hard to see that God and the world were One in the beginning? These are questions that we must answer rightly if we would understand the creation.

In the first verses of Genesis, God is of course as yet not fully defined. He is merely named. He exists, just like the world, or rather, in conjunction with the world. Indeed, strangely and unexpectedly, he exists as the world and the Spirit, in oneness. Both are present at the creation. There is much about him that the creation account reveals. Indeed we will later learn that the entire Bible is a revelation of God. So, too, is the creation. Here at the start, the Bible shows that God has expressed himself in the things that happened. The creation account is the report of God's direct and personal involvement in the changes that he was instituting. God was the subject as well as the predicate of creation. Our world is the result of purposeful changes in God himself.

God's Selfie

The first thing the account reveals about the Creator, of course, is that he exists. He is the Existent One. He is alive, and intelligent, and articulate. He has a plan, and a purpose. And according to the first verses in Genesis, the creation is the initiation of that purpose. He is a sentient being that is creative and orderly, and aware. He moves, and communicates, and is interested in our world. He has unfathomable power. He is also relational and communicative, and looks to the future with anticipation. And he changes, for the changes that happened in the process of creation were changes in God himself. All this and more is hinted at and implied in the creation account, right from the beginning.

And he has a will. He wants to reveal himself. And that desire to reveal himself hints that there will be someone to whom he will reveal himself. There will be someone who can reciprocate, with eyes to see and ears to hear. That's us, pilgrim. God had you and me in mind as one of the goals when he began the process of rearranging the world. And that rearrangement was of God himself. He has explained for us what he has done and why, in the words of Scripture. At its core the creation is relational. God wants fellowship with us. He wants us to get to know him. And it will be closer than arms-length. It will be integrative. In receiving Christ we are integrated into the very Word of God, by the Word (1 Peter 1:23). And the Word is God.

Looking at the first verse in Genesis, we can see that the Bible account is about how and why God re-formed the world that was, into what it is today. God took aim, and created. Creation was a reorganizing, a transformation. When it says that the world was "without form," that is not a statement of its physical character. It does not mean the absence of shape or structure, which would be impossible. We must not read with a magic sack of orthodoxy over our heads. The word means waste and empty, futile, useless, chaotic, confused, vain, and void. It means that the world had no purpose or goal. God's creative actions will form it, that is, will give it purpose and direction. It will have a reason for being like it is. And that purpose and goal is Christ. The purpose of the creation is the fullness of Christ, who is the fulfillment of the Word of God. He will be God's full and fulfilled expression, being the reason and goal of the creation.

And the fullness of Christ will involve a radical change in God himself. The fullness of Christ is a new creation, and the goal of this present, foreshadowing one. It will involve the reconciliation of the world back to God (2 Cor. 5:17-19). God's involvement in the creation in the beginning shows that he was looking forward to that change. Matter and Spirit will be re-united into oneness. And that oneness will include us, children, whoever is joined to Christ! There is a divine purpose for our lives, and a lasting future!

Creation is change. Every time creation is mentioned in the Bible, it means the purposeful transformation or reorganization of something in a new way. Creation is the act of transforming or changing something that already exists. It is not a magic act in which something jumps out of nothing and nowhere into something somewhere. Nothing has no legs, so it can't jump. It can't even walk or crawl, or even slither. Nothing can never change into something, no matter where you look or how long you wait, and even if you try to help it. The idea of creation from nothing is completely illogical, nonsensical, and in fact impossible as well as unbiblical. It is magical. And when I say magical, I do not mean it in a good sense. In the Bible, magic is anathema. We must keep orthodoxy from placing that sack over our head. Scrunch it. Tear it up. Light a match to it.

We must keep in mind that creation is the understandable and totally reasonable action of making something new out of that which is already existent. We see it everywhere. We do it ourselves. The creation of our world was not the orthodox nothingness jumping out of nowhere to become something, or nowhere becoming somewhere. It was the formation of our world of today from the prior world. That's what the Bible says. The new creation too, being a creation, will come about by the transformation of this present one. Creation is transformation.

According to the Bible, the creation was not haphazard or purposeless or mindless, then. This rules out blind evolution as the origin of life as it is today, of course. The Bible assumes that God exists, and that he had a purpose in view when he created. Our world reveals the existence of its Maker. And the Bible reveals him even more clearly. The Bible is like a letter explaining the purpose for our world. But it also reveals much about the One who wrote it and sent it.

It says that God spoke the world into the way it is. And words, we remember, are expressions of ourselves. They communicate. They reveal to others who we are, and what our thoughts and desires are. They reveal our inner being. When God spoke, it was a revelation of himself, an expression of who he is and what he's up to. And his words reveal what was in the very heart of God. Those events of the primal past are God's love letter to his beloved, concealed in a time capsule awaiting the arrival of Christ Jesus, who would open it. It would be about himself. The reading would be his revealing. He would be the contents of the letter.

And of course, a letter implies not only that someone wrote it, but it also implies a recipient to the letter. That's you and me, tiger. We need to receive God's Word, which is now Christ Jesus, the expression of God. We need to understand what this world is all about, and where it's headed and why. This is why we need to understand what the Bible tells us. The Bible holds the great code with which we can decipher God's intention for this world and for us. It helps us to know God and to understand why he created. He had us in mind when he created. We were the gleam in the Creator's eye.

This is especially and specifically apparent with respect to the creation of Adam and Eve. Their creation in God's image is a picture of himself. It's God's selfie. So, to the extent that we understand the creation of Adam and Eve, and how they image him, we can come to know even more about God, about the world, and about ourselves. Let's look at the image for a while. Looking at the image of God will show us what God is like.

The Plural God

That image was expressly male and female (Gen. 1:26-27). Together they were called both "him" and "them." Adam together with Eve is called Adam (Gen. 5:1-2). Both together are considered one flesh (Gen. 2:24). There is a melding of singular and plural in describing them. Adam was a singular person and a composite one, a singularity and a plurality. And because he imaged God, we can know that God, too, is a singularity and a plurality. God and the world were One in the beginning, a composite One.

Imaging God, Adam and Eve complement each other and communicate with one another. And they live with one another, sharing life together. These qualities and characteristics are reflections of the Creator. They tell us much about God's intentions for himself and for us as well. The relation between Adam and Eve images the relationship of God and the world. And this latter relationship now includes us, pilgrim, for we are in the world and of it, as well as in Adam. It will be fully realized in the relationship between Christ and the true Church, which is the relationship between God and the world.

God separated Eve from Adam for a while. Then, after being formed into a woman, Eve was brought back to him and they were reunited and were considered as one person again. And this too, their separation followed by reunion, imaged God.

This is extremely significant. It's God saying, "This is what I am like, and what I'm about." Separation followed by reunion into one body is one important aspect of the image of God. It's one way in which Adam and Eve imaged him, a significant and foundational one. It tells us that this is what God is like. One aspect of the divine image, then, is about an original plural oneness followed by separation followed by re-uniting. And that re-uniting is into one flesh or body (Gen. 2:22-24). It is physical. The physical separation followed by re-uniting of Adam and Eve images God. Right from the beginning, God is showing us pictures of himself!

This hints very openly that God and the world were originally a bipartite singularity followed by separation, which will be followed by a reuniting into oneness again. By understanding the creation of Adam and Eve, who were made in God's image, we can understand that in the beginning, prior to creation, God and the world were one Body and Spirit. This truth is one more slap in the blushing face of orthodoxy.

The creation of the first pair was not haphazard, but was a purposeful process intended to reflect upon their Creator. By creating them in the manner in which he did, he was both imaging himself and also hinting at his relationship with the world and his plans and purposes for it. In effect, he was unveiling the future of the

The Overarching Story

world and of himself. The creation of Adam and Eve was a preview and explanation of how the Creator himself would ultimately come to be. It reviewed his past and previewed his future. Their manner of creation tells us about Adam, but more importantly it tells us about God. It was God's confession of what he had done, and why.

Significantly, God was speaking not only in their creation, but also in the manner of their creation. God speaks in pictures as well as in words and deeds. Their manner of creation was a picture that reflected him. It was communicative, so that we could understand. The creation was a series of divine parables.

We must keep emphasizing that in the beginning, God's oneness included the world, for if we miss this bedrock truth, we will miss the whole point of the creation and of the Gospel. The world presently is separated from God for a while. It will be brought back to him in Christ. That is the whole message of the Bible, and the reason for our world. It's the purpose of salvation. And it is an astounding idea, really. We keep repeating it because it's so important and we have been programmed by orthodoxy to reject it.

The creation, pilgrim, was for our sake as well as for God. The truth that Adam and Eve were made in God's image implies that there will be someone able to see the image, to study the likeness and understand and appreciate its significance and beauty. After all, that's the purpose of pictures. Pictures imply lookers. There will come a being that will be capable of seeing the image in Adam and exclaiming, "Wow!" The picture is of God, and gives us understanding of what God is like. There will come a creature capable of knowing God! That's us, tiger!

And this knowledge will become available, first, by looking at the picture called Adam. Then, its greater realization will come about through him who is the greater Adam and the truer image. This will become even more clear as the future unfolds and this true Adam, the Son of Man, is manifested in all his glory. Through this greater Adam we can come to know God directly and personally! He is the Word of God fulfilled, the end and goal of the creation.

So we see that knowing God through Adam in Eden foreshadows knowing God in Christ Jesus. The first Adam foreshadowed the second. Those early events imaged future glories. Right from the beginning, God was employing archetypes that would find their greater fulfillment in Christ Jesus. He was painting pictures. The

Creator wanted us to get to know him, so he drew pictures of himself, word pictures. God has provided us with several selfies.

The image in Adam and Eve hints that God desired companionship. As Eve was to Adam, the world was to God. He was looking to the future, both of the world and of himself. Later, of course, we see that his all-inconclusive purpose was Christ Jesus, who would share in the natures of both Adam and God. In the true Church, the greater Eve, he would draw the world back to the Creator. In him, humanity and divinity would be rejoined into oneness. The world and the Spirit would be reconciled. They would be One, again.

The Creator was looking forward to his reunion with the Body, that is, with all who are in Christ. Christ Jesus and the Church are composed of both the Spirit and the world. And this is how God was in the beginning. Reconciliation would be impossible otherwise. At the creation, God was both Spirit and Body, a singularity and a plurality imaged by Adam and Eve. Their relation to one another imaged God past, present, and future. It reflected how God was in the beginning, how he is, and how he will be. In the fullness of Christ Jesus God is reconciling the world back to himself (2 Cor. 5:17-19). Reconciliation means that God is reuniting with the world. This was imaged by the return of Eve to Adam after she had been completely re-formed.

Adam and Eve were Christ's antecedents, his ancestors. They prefigured him as well. Like the rest of the creation, they were an inkling of the future of both the world and of God. Christ Jesus is not only the Son of Man, but also the end and goal of God's creation, which is God himself in renewed splendor. In the fullness of Christ Jesus the second Adam, God will be fully manifested. And his manifestation, gloriously, will include the saints! That is the Bible message, from beginning to end. It's absolutely astounding and incredibly marvelous, far above and beyond what the churches have imagined (1 Cor. 2:9-10).

Adam in Eden was the first step in the process that would lead to Christ Jesus. And Christ Jesus would be the full and complete image of God, as well as his full revelation and complete manifestation in glory when the Creator's plans are consummated. The creative changes in God in the beginning would lead to his transformation into Christ. Surprisingly, God himself, like the saints who image him, would be a new creation. And his creation is most assuredly not *ex nihilo*! Remember that creation is change, child. The creation of the world was the first step in the creation of God! God, too, is changing. The whole thing is utterly amazing, and breath-takingly beautiful.

God would manifest and express himself fully in that coming one who would be the fulfillment of Adam's foreshadowings. Christ Jesus is the true image of God (2 Cor. 4:4; Coll. 1:15). Our understanding of Christ, then, can help us to understand the image in Adam. In turn, it tells us much about God and his plans. The two Adams sing antiphonally, echoing and re-echoing back and forth to one another. They compete with one another in imaging God. Both Adams are images of him. But Christ Jesus always wins. Adam ends up imaging him.

One thing we know is that Christ united with the true Church is one Body. The true Church does not consist of any denomination or ecclesiastical grouping. It is most certainly not the Roman Catholic Church or the Episcopalian Church or the Methodist or Baptist or any other. These are all just communal ideas and have no real substance or life. The true Church consists of everyone who has received oneness with the Spirit. Together, Christ Jesus and the true Church are a composite oneness, a singularity and a plurality. They carry the one name of Christ upon them, and are the true fulfillment of the image of God first mentioned in the creation account and foreshadowed by Adam and Eve (1 Cor. 6:11; Jas. 4:14). And Christ is God. His name upon the saints implies divinity, not mere ownership as orthodoxy would have it. How different is the truth from tradition! How much grander!

Adam and Eve were an inkling of the One who would be the fulfillment of that primal inkling. Christ Jesus, like Adam and Eve, is both singular and plural. He is the man Christ Jesus and he is also the multitude that carries his name. He is many and he is One. In Christ's oneness with the Church, the Spirit and the flesh are reunited. Composed of all who have received the Spirit, the Church is his Body. The saints are one Body united into oneness in the Spirit. And it's a real body, not just an idea like the churches and denominations of this world.

As we've said, the Church is the Body of Christ (Rom. 12:5; 1 Cor. 12:12-14, 27). In Christ, the Spirit and the Body are One. In

Adam, we see this same relationship, of both singularity and plurality. So we have the two witnesses necessary to establish the fact. The image of God in Adam and repeated in Christ Jesus shows us clearly that the Creator is both a singularity and a plurality of Spirit and Body. We must keep repeating this truth, because orthodoxy has repeated its opposite for centuries, and its error has taken deep root. Orthodoxy has substituted a humbuggery called the Trinity to explain the plurality of God.

When we understand this about God, we are better able to understand what God meant when he said, "Let us make man in our image, according to our likeness." We can understand why he is called by the plural of God (*Elohim*, ie., Gods). God speaks as being both singular and plural, in the same breath that he expresses his desire and intent to make Adam in that same image. And immediately he makes them male and female. We can be sure that the plurality of Adam and of Christ tells us very clearly that this is what God is like. God is not just a singularity. He is a multiplicity (*echad*, a gathering together; Gen. 1:24; Deut. 6:4). And he is physical as well as spiritual.

Theologians and others have wondered for millennia about God's expression of himself as "us." Some have speculated that it was just a semantic anomaly, a sort of "plural of majesty." Others have thought that he must have been speaking to the angels. This is partially correct, as we'll see later. But it will not be as expected. Still others have taken it to refer to a chimera called the Trinity. They have missed the point. First, the passage states plainly that God made Adam and Eve in his image and likeness. Then it clarifies this by emphasizing that the image was in their being male and female.

This too has led some interpreters astray. They have understood it to mean that God is androgynous, that he is both male and female. For them, God is a hermaphrodite. They have made God into a sexual being, an image of man, an idol. They have failed to understand that the image is not about sexuality, but rather about singularity coupled with plurality. It is a composite oneness, as the oneness of Adam with Eve, or as the oneness of Christ with the Church. These both reflect the composite oneness of God, being his image (Coll. 1:15). The oneness of God and the world is what is reflected by Adam with Eve, and Christ with the Church (John

The Overarching Story

10:34-36, 17:21-23; 2 Peter 1:4). God joined into oneness with the world is the reality that Adam imaged and that Christ will fulfill!

Yes, it is of supreme importance that the first quality or attribute of God represented by the image is the composite oneness of God together with the world. The world is included in the oneness of God. This is a startling, mind-boggling and tradition-shattering statement, of course. It's an earthquake that upends the orthodox understanding of God. But we must remember that Christ Jesus, who is the true image of God, is both Spirit and Flesh. He is the union of the Spirit with the Body, the God-man. And the Body, of course, is composed of matter. And that matter that composes the Body of Christ, who shares in divinity, is what this world is made of. It's what you and I are made of, pilgrim. Even now, we share in that of which Christ Jesus is composed. We are the Body of Christ. And our hope is to live eternally, in bodies.

Christ Jesus was made of earth and Spirit joined together as One. So, too, are the saints. God was and will be composed of both Spirit and matter. And that matter will be the world! In the saints, the Creator is reconciling the world back to himself. Wow! Right from the beginning, God is presenting the true Gospel message for us. And it's a reason for us to stand up and shout, tiger.

Yes, Eve was separated from Adam for a time while God was forming her. Then she was brought back to him. And this was in order to image their Maker. Again and again and from different angles we can see that, in the beginning, the Spirit and the world were one God! The "us" of God in the beginning refers to his plural nature, and his oneness with the world. The image in Adam hints broadly of this as well, and hints of his future mode of being. God's future will involve humans, transformed. It will be a new creation made up of transformed and glorified saints. We will be changed. We are the true shape-shifters. And that's the Gospel.

This idea of the oneness of God and the world has ever frightened theologians away, as if it were a step into the pit of idolatry, for it makes the world divine. It is viewed with disdain and horror as the heresy called pantheism. The idea of pantheism is appalling to orthodoxy. And yet, the idea of eternal matter is not at all incompatible with the nature of God. Eternal salvation, which is what every Christian church preaches, is always predicated on eternal physicality. It is true that pantheism is contrary to the teachings of Scripture. But panentheism, the truth that God is both singular and plural, that he is both Spirit and Body, is precisely the meaning of Adam's imaging. More than that, it is the very reason for the creation. It is the center of the Bible message and of the true Gospel and of Christianity itself. There is an empty tomb at the center of the Christian hope.

As imaged by Adam and Christ Jesus, God is a Being composed of both Spirit and (now again) Body. That's how he was in the beginning. He was speaking of himself as a plurality of both Spirit and Body. He and the world were One. God's making man in "our" image hints that both the Spirit and the world together would be involved in the formation of Adam. The primal man, of course, came from the earth, not from nothingness. And he looks forward down the ages to Christ Jesus, its fulfillment and also from the earth. The plurality of God is hinted as well when the text says that the earth itself brought forth the living being when God expressed himself. Life was not injected into the earth. The earth itself produced the living beings, together with the Spirit (Gen. 1:11-12, 20-21, 24-25). The Spirit is the source of life. And life came from the earth. Get it?

Adam would be a composite being, of spirit and flesh. And flesh, in time, would share divinity with the Spirit. Yes, the Spirit would share divinity with the flesh. God and the world would be reunited. The man Jesus said, "I and the Father are One." In him, the Spirit and the Flesh were a single individual, a plurality united into a singularity (John 6:51-58). And he was the image of God (Coll. 1:15). And he didn't have a split personality.

In the beginning, as we've said, to finalize the initial process of creation, God had separated or differentiated the Spirit from the world (Rom. 11:36; 1 Cor. 11:12). Christ Jesus, and every saint who would follow, would be their rejoining (2 Cor. 5:17-19). Reconciliation is not just a return to conviviality or fellowship. Nor is it merely metaphorical. It is a literal rejoining of Spirit with Body. The saints will have bodies in the resurrection, transformed and glorified. And that glory will be the very glory of God (John 17:5, 11, 21-24; Rev. 21:10-11). They will share in the divine glory! They will compose the Body of God, and share in his Spirit! What a glorious homecoming awaits us! Don't let orthodoxy take it away from you, child, or talk you out of it.

Through the process of creating the world and giving it form and direction, God was initiating a process that would in fact transform himself. And this process of transformation was an archetype that would be repeated. Adam in his seed would be re-created in a similar fashion, imaging him. They would undergo the transformation called repentance and conversion. And astoundingly, in creating the world God was re-creating himself! And he wanted his nature and condition as well as his intentions to be known and understood. He was anticipating a being like him, a complement to himself, an Eve that would respond to his love. The first creation was a prefiguring of the new creation. It told the Gospel beforehand. It prophesied.

As if to illustrate and corroborate this, all the trees, grass, birds, and animals were made in such a way that they too would reproduce after their kind. Adam himself, made in God's image, would reproduce after his own kind. And of course this is also true of Christ Jesus, who is reproducing after his kind, multiplying the children of God as they unite with the Spirit. Like the grass and trees and birds, and Adam, God would reproduce a Seed after his own kind. The fulfillment of his plans would culminate in Christ, the Son of Man and also the Son of God (John 17:5, 24). In Christ Jesus and the saints, God is reproducing himself!

And he was hinting of this beforehand, right from the beginning. The image in Adam was specifically male and female. In coming together again, Adam and Eve would reproduce children after their own kind. This was part of the image. It was a strong hint that, in reconciling the world back to himself, God would be reproducing children after his own kind!

Because the manner of the creation is both a manifestation and an illustration of God, it shows that God desires companionship. He wants a being capable of understanding with him, of being conscious and sentient together with him and able to respond to him. He wants to share his life with a being compatible with and complementary to him. He desires a companion able to create, to dream, to communicate with him and create with him. He would share his power and his future. He wants to love and be loved in return. He wants someone like himself. The creation, and particularly the description of the creation written down in the Bible, tells us that God is himself changing, and that we are included in that change, pilgrim. Let's go on, then, jubilantly.

Chapter Three
The Forming of this World

A Shocking Beginning

The Bible is abrupt as it begins, as if we had asked it a question and it is responding. The terse inaugural verse introduces our world of today, where we live. It is not concerned with the vast cosmos, or with time and space. It's not about Venus, or Mars or Jupiter. Nor is it about the absolute beginning of reality or of the earth. Let's repeat. It's not the beginning of the earth's existence. It's a brief, concise summary of how our world as we know it, the way we experience it today, came to be. Its theme is theology, its method is truth, and its purpose is preliminary and prefigurative.

The account does not give a lot of detail, and it leaves out much. What it does say, however, is packed with importance. Its pictures prophesy. Genesis is crucial for understanding our place in the creation, in history, and in the future. Besides telling us how our world of today began, and why, it tells us about God himself. The creation is a revelation of God, as well as a prefiguring of what lies ahead. It hints of God's plans and purposes for our lives, and of his reason for reshaping the world that existed into the way it is today (Rom. 1:20). It readies us for Christ. Is it not important?

As we've seen, its truth knocks the sox off orthodoxy after it pulls the rug out from under it. The first verse of the Bible tells us that God reordered the earth. Look in your Bible and see that creation, every time, means to purposely transform something. Creation is never the impossible and absurd idea that something comes from nothing. That's not how God works. When God gave the world form, he gave it a purposeful design and function. A world without physical form and structure would have been impossible twaddle.

The first verse should be better understood as, "In beginning, God reordered the heavens and the earth." That's what creation is. In every instance in which creation occurs in the Bible, it's a transformation, not a magic trick. It's a reorganization, a purposeful reordering. The creation account doesn't tell us how the world originally came into existence. It tells how and why our world came to be as it is. It has purpose now. It has led to Christ and is continuing on to his fullness.

But many Christians have believed the lie that God's total and absolute holiness keeps him forever apart from the world, as if the world were evil and God cannot touch it without getting dirty. They will readily admit that Jesus was God, but for them the Father is Spirit only. He always has been and always will be. And so the Gospel that they preach lacks the full grandeur and glory that the true Gospel proclaims. Their Gospel is about coming to live in friendliness with God in a happy place called heaven. It leaves God and the saints on good terms, close and sociable, but forever separate from one another. These Christians have failed to see that the true Gospel is about being integrated into the very Godhead. It means to be in oneness with God in the same manner in which Christ Jesus is in oneness with him (John 17:21-23; 1 Cor. 3:16; 2 Cor. 5:18-20; 2 Peter 1:4; Rev. 3:12, 21).

This was God's plan from the beginning. God expressed himself, and our world came to be like it is. We don't know how, or how long it took. The best guess we can make is that the process of creation recorded in the Bible was a lot like the new creation that is now in progress. And this new creation is coming about in a process of development. It's happening in stages, or seven "days" that echo the first days of Genesis. And it's taking its time to do so, but not millions of years.

Neither science nor nominal Church has actually understood the true scriptural meaning of creation. Wanting to keep God's utter holiness intact, the Church early invented the dogma of *creatio ex nihilo*, the magical and unscriptural idea that God created the world from nothing. Biblical creation then became a magical, unexplainable trick that only God could accomplish. "His ways are totally inscrutable, far above mere human comprehension," orthodoxy claimed. The idea had to be received strictly on faith. "Although it seems totally absurd and unexplainable, we must believe it," we were told, "because with God all things are possible." And so the people have not only believed, but they have taken up the sword of anti-evolutionary dogmatism. And rightly so, because evolution is make-believe. It's a house of cards, and the divine wind is blowing. Without God the world becomes, as Shakespeare might say, a tale full of sound and fury, but pointless and purposeless. Evolutionists would take us back to that same dark world that existed before God created. They would deny God's involvement and even his existence.

As a consequence, many churches try to affirm their commitment to the Bible and the reality of God by rejecting and denouncing evolution. But they do it in the wrong way. They answer the falsehood of godless evolution with the falsehood of creation from nothing. They would disprove one lie with another. It's a dogma fight, lie against lie. Ludicrously, they would defend the Bible by misinterpreting what it says. It says that God reorganized the world in six days. How long this was is not known. But it was not the evolutionist's zillions of years nor the creationist's six literal days from nothingness. There is now no way to examine or repeat the initial process, for God is resting from that work. That initial creation is no longer occurring. God's eternal Sabbath is upon us. Nevertheless, the world is chock full of evidence of a Creator. Purpose and organization are evident everywhere in the complexities of nature. And the Bible tells us that God's purpose is Christ Jesus and salvation.

But both evolutionism and creationism would deny salvation. Evolution sets God aside, of course. The creationist denial is more subtle. The doctrine of creation from nothing would deny salvation to the saints, since they too are a new creation. The doctrine thus turns and slaps creationists in the face. But the truth is that creation is purposeful transformation. As a new creation the saints will be transformed, not obliterated. They will be created anew. It's why the Gospel is about repentance, which is transformation. Creation is neither the fierce dogmatism of the churches, nor the fierce dogmatism of evolutionists. It's God's handiwork. And he's good at what he does. He's the best.

It's a strange and ludicrous situation. Scientists reject the biblical account, while the churches unwittingly follow suit, thinking to defend it. We must take care that our defense of the Bible is based on the truth of what it actually says, rather than on a misplaced desire to defend the religious status quo called orthodoxy. Science is

The Forming of this World

not the enemy. Falsehood is. And the truth is, creation is transformation. The new creation is the transformation of this one. And you too, child, will be transformed, one way or another.

We are living today in the Sabbath of the first creation. This world is finished. God is no longer creating it. He's working on the new creation. And he calls us to rest with him now from the works of this world, and to join him in creating the new world of unimagined wonders. The winds of the Spirit are even now blowing across the waters of humanity. New life is springing up from the earth as his word is expressed from the lips of the saints. He calls us now to the same creation story, the God story. It lives in the telling.

Let's go on, then, and see what the account says about the beginning. We must look carefully, then, but not just at the literal words of the account. We must do more than just read a few verses and then moralize about them. We must prayerfully peruse the pictures. The words are eloquent and interesting, but the pictures dance and sing.

God Recycled!

One picture that immediately jumps out and begins to dance and sing is the manner of the creation. Yes, despite the long, dark centuries in which Christian doctrine held that the creation was the beginning of reality, that idea must be shoveled out. We must understand that in every case that the Bible mentions creation, it is the transformation of something that already exists. Yes, every time. Check it out, to be sure (Ps. 45:7, 51:10, 65:17; Isa. 42:5, 45:12, 18; Jer. 31:22; 1 Cor. 11:9; Eph. 2:10; Rev. 4:11, 10:6; etc.). It happens all around us, every day. Indeed, we do it ourselves. We make things. Much of the time we make messes. And our messes are just as much creations as our successes. To create is to make something. It isn't magic. It's work. For six days, that's what God did. He made our world of today. Then, on the seventh day, he rested. That is, he ceased to create. The world was finished. And it was a success. God didn't make a big mess.

He made Adam and Eve. They are echoes of God, premonitions of Christ. So, we have come to understand much about God by looking closely at them. In a sense, we can see God reflected by them. Adam was created from the dust, and Eve came from Adam. In forming

The Forming of this World

them, God used materials that already existed. That's what the Bible calls creation, child. That's what we call it too. We'll go by what God's word says. The creation is his handiwork, which means that it was a process. And processes take time. It happened in a series of progressive steps.

Nor will the new creation issue from nil or zilch. It will come about by the transformation of this present world. And the saints will have a central part in it. Indeed, believers are themselves a new creation. They're in the process of being created, that is, transformed. They don't pop up out of nowhere from nothing.

Things come from prior things, always. That is creation, perfectly logical and reasonable. All the scriptural evidence is on the side of common sense. The evidence is big, and strong, and stands right in our face. It pokes us in the chest so that we won't forget. We must remember. Creation is transformation. Creation is conversion. Don't forget. Creation is purposeful conversion. Creation is conversion. Say it to yourself.

From where did the world originate, then? How did everything start? If the present heavens and earth did not come from nothingness, what was the stuff from which they were made? Are they eternal? One thing is for sure. This world is not the "oops!" of God. It is orderly, and has a purpose. It is good. That is, it pleases him.

Because of this, the world is rational, and creation makes sense. Creation is completely logical. The traditional idea that something—the world!—came from nothing is a childish and irrational invention of narrow-minded medieval minds that could not envision or accept intermarriage between God and the world.

But how did it all begin? That which already existed from all eternity is God. Genesis hints strongly that our world was cut from the Creator's own side, as it were, as Eve was cut from Adam. But this does not refer to the absolute beginning of the planet. It does not deal with eternity, or how the vast, unreachable universe came into existence. It does not concern itself with outer space. Its narrow focus is on our world of today, and tomorrow. The Bible does not say how reality began. It assumes it from all eternity. It assumes the eternity of God.

The inspired New Testament watches and listens, then nods approvingly and agrees. It turns to us and says, "Yes, that's right."

All things of this present world originated in the Creator himself (Rom. 11:36; 1 Cor. 8:6, 11:12; 2 Cor. 5:18). This world originated from God in a way that was imaged by the manner in which Eve originated from Adam. The divinely inspired New Testament interprets the Genesis account for us. It tells us plainly and unequivocally that God himself is the ever-flowing Fountain from which our world flows. And the waters never run dry. They're recycled. Recycling is godly. It's one of the archetypes that God employs. It's how he works. And he has included himself in the process. The creation is a recycling of God!

The Butterfly of Heaven

Now that we've seen creation for what it is, we know that the Creator himself, the Existent One, is changing. He is the divine Transformer, a living, ever-flowing stream, not a stagnant pool. The rippling eddies of history, and especially of the Gospel, are expressions of the Creator. The Genesis accounts, and indeed the whole Bible, were given to us so that we might come to know this. It tells us where he is going, so that we can follow (John 14:5-6). It tells the wherefore and whereunto of this world.

    He's packing up all his things and moving away to a new house. That's the story that the creation account begins to tell. The creation account is the first chapter in the story of God. He's off to another world, a new creation, a new Temple, a living Body called Christ. God intends to move all his stuff over to Christ, making him the Heir of all. And wonder of wonders, this new home will be made of transformed humans, seed of Adam and Eve, reborn as children of God like their older brother. They will be re-created into a new manner of being, metamorphosed like the Father and united with him by their mutual sharing in Christ. They will move into the new home that the Creator is building for himself and all his family in that new world (John 14:1-3). God is doing an extreme makeover of the world, and of himself. He's moving into a new house.

    He has revealed to us this astonishing plan in the Bible because the metamorphosis of God lovingly involves humans. He wants us to know this, and join in. But orthodoxy keeps working against his will, while thinking to follow it. Orthodoxy would keep God forever separate from us by a high fence called holiness. The truth is that the transfiguration of God will include humanity within the divine glory. Marvelously, the metamorphosis of God consists of uniting with the world. As we continue studying, reading carefully and looking attentively at the pictures, we are shown that the fullness of Christ is the goal of creation and of God himself. Christ Jesus is the bright, multi-hued Monarch Butterfly of heaven.

As the beloved Heir of God, he will be God's completed transformation. The divine Christ is the new creation of God! He will be a corporate Person with a living, Spirit-filled body composed of all who receive him and who are themselves received in turn. This growing body of Christ is the new house and temple in which the Creator is going to live in holiness, wrapped in a rainbow.

As would be expected, the Father's children resemble him. They repeat his story. And their testimony has an unexpected and delightful twist. They repeat his story not only with their word of testimony, but with the pattern of their lives. They are learning to live out that pattern, to be like God. Like their Father, their word and their actions should be one and the same. They should not merely speak the truth, they should live it. Just as the Word of God is God, the word of every saint should be that saint. The saints must learn their role as co-creators with God, speaking the new creation into existence (1 Cor. 3:9; 2 Cor. 6:1). Like God, they are telling their own future to come forth!

Here is the truth of the matter. God is creating himself, changing into a new Body. And the saints are made in the image of God. We too are a new creation. God is transforming us. And this transformation comes about through the same word of God, as we live and testify in the Spirit. As the Spirit lives and testifies through us, we are taking part in the work of creation, working together with God (1 Cor. 3:9; 2 Cor. 6;1). In a very real sense, with God's help we are creating ourselves! This is part of the image of God that we share. We are building our future house, like God, working together with him. So, the sensible thing is to build with gold, silver, and precious gems rather than with hay and straw, is it not (Matt. 7:24-27; 1 Cor. 3:9-15; 2 Tim. 2:20)? Like the Father, and like Christ Jesus, we too undergo metamorphosis. We are a new creation. And the Gospel story that we tell in word and deed images and repeats the story of God. Our lives in Christ should replicate God's own story.

What is that story? It's a tale of conversion. It's about change, about death unto new life. Christ Jesus is the very image of God. He displays the God pattern. Every saint receives Christ and is converted. United with Christ, every saint is changed into a new creation, to await a new body. That is the very story of God, children. He too, is undergoing conversion. He has received Christ through the cross and is eagerly awaiting his new Body. Yes, the lives of believers are the abridged version of God's own story. Like Christ Jesus, their lives echo God's plans and purposes for this creation and the next, and for himself. Conversion is at the center of creation. Indeed, it is creation. Believers are living testimonies of the Creator, echoing motifs that repeat both the creation story and the Creator's own story. Believers too, like their Lord, will be metamorphosed, to flit like butterflies from glory to glory in the garden of God!

Their lives enact the Gospel, which is the same divine story. They become living testimonies of God, imaging the divine history, mirroring the origin and manner in which the world came to exist, how it continues, and where it is going. And they tell us why. Their purpose mirrors the divine purpose. Presently, there is a division, a differentiation between God and the world, which will be healed when the Spirit and the transformed creation come together again. Matter and Spirit will be rejoined, in Christ. That is the overarching plan for all of history and the whole creation. Christ is seated upon the throne of glory around which all the butterflies of heaven will gather.

The Gospel is the story of God, told in the story of Christ. It's the greatest story ever told, because it's the greatest story that can be told. No other is so all-encompassing, or as beautiful. It starts with the Creator, creating. And that's how it ends. And the end is imaged in the beginning. It will be glorious and beautiful beyond description. The whole thing is absolutely fantastic.

The lives of the saints tell and retell this fantastic tale. It's a tale of change, and it touches every level of reality. Creation changes the things that exist into something new and different. Creation is an artist taking a chunk of clay and shaping it into a little figurine. The chunk goes out of existence, while the clay continues, now in a new form. The clay has been changed into a figurine. That is creation. It's what God does. It's called recycling too. The divine Artist takes little chunks of clay from the earth and forms them into little figurines called humans.

In a sense, the chunks of clay go out of existence so that the figurines may exist. Always, things go out of existence so that new things can take their place. The present is erased, but the future is written already. That is creation. It happens wherever we look. And even if we close our eyes, it still happens. A generation comes, and a generation goes. The present gets up and leaves so that the future can sit down for a while. All of reality follows this same archetype. It's the pattern of life from death. And it images God. This same pattern is also at the core of the Gospel that the saints should preach and enact in their lives. In the saints it begins with repentance. Change touches everyone. It's an archetype that images and includes God.

It's everywhere, all the time. We ourselves are being pulled along in its ever-flowing stream. That which we were yesterday, or a moment ago, has floated away, and yet we are still here. Even the change called death doesn't destroy all being. Life overcomes death always, everywhere. There is always a future. Existence is forever because God is forever.

This victory over nonexistence is what in fact constitutes creation. Creation is a change from glory to glory. All of reality, everything, shouts this Gospel archetype to us everywhere. It's the shout of victory, the archetype of triumph. The Gospel is all around us, wherever we look. Victory over death is echoed in all things. The bells of creation everywhere toll God's eternal lordship. Every moment angel voices are singing the infinite glories of the God of all creation. Can you hear them? Look around you, and listen closely. Tap your foot and sing along with the music.

The story of Jesus turns the volume all the way up and repeats this same song of victory. Jesus' story of triumph over death is the epic story of all creation. The process of creating transforms reality. And creating is what God does. He forms new reality according to his will, by expressing himself. So that we might understand, his expression is also called his speaking. Creation happens through the Word of God (John 1:1-3). And his expression results in being over nonbeing, in victory over death. And that is also the Gospel story, and our own (2 Cor. 3:18). All creation joins in singing God's story and glory. It's ringing all around us. Wow! Isn't that something? Are you listening? Better yet, are you singing along?

We can see that the Gospel of Christ, which succinctly tells the whole history of the creation and the story of God, is hinted and prefigured already from the beginning, in the creation account. Genesis speaks of things with which the Gospels and the Revelation agree, and repeat. They all tell the same Gospel tale. They sing, and the song is antiphonal. The beginning sings to the end, softly, in anticipation. And the end sings back in fulfillment, a little louder.

Genesis holds the DNA of the world. Orthodoxy has twisted and scrambled it, though, and has ended up with a surrogate Christ and a wholly other, untouchable God. If we run off without hearing and understanding what Genesis actually says, we will end up the same way, at the wrong destination and with a false Gospel. We will faithfully but foolishly worship a Frankenstein in the place of God.

We must set aside magical inventions and medieval fantasies. We must go back to the beginning and start over. We must understand Genesis before we can understand the rest of the Bible. We must restart the engine of understanding, then take the right road and head in the right direction, with our headlights on bright. And we must stay on course.

The road we take will lead to our new home in the full majesty of Christ. Our new home is the throne of God! If we end up anywhere else, we have taken a wrong turn (Rev. 3:20-21). God is preparing a place for us in himself (John 14:1-6). The fullness of God is our destination and everlasting dwelling place. The creation's goal, and ours, is God, happy to have us back. Any other destination is a dead end.

God in the Creation

God is in the creation. He is not just an ethereal, totally other Spirit hovering above it. Although presently the Spirit and the world are differentiated and separate to a certain extent, that was not always so. And it will not be that way forever. God and the creation will unite once again, at the consummation of all that is written. The road to Christ was laid right from the beginning. Now we must walk it.

The Real World

Our road begins with the very first verse. The heavens of Genesis are not the spiritual world, or the place of eternal bliss to which believers hope to retire. Neither are they the vast reaches of outer space. The heavens of Genesis are the atmosphere that encircles this earthly globe. They are the dense, gaseous expanse that envelops the earth (Gen. 1:20). There are thick clouds everywhere, lots of them, unbelievably dense and dark, doorkeepers denying entrance to the light. But in the darkness, the Creator will speak. He will call for the darkness to dissipate.

The world is more than just the casual and indifferent work of his hands. He put his heart into his work. The creation is the divine Artist's heartfelt and passionate expression of his very being. It's the beat of his heart (Ps. 19:1-3). It's a work of art, a painting, a sculpture. It's a love song, for God is love. This world is an expression and transformation of God's very own self. Its infinite profusion and variety is the articulation of God. It is his expression, for it originates in him. It was torn from his side, so to speak.

Does this mean that the world is divine? Christians shy away from that notion because orthodoxy has shooed them away like a flock of pigeons. It challenges her doctrine of creation from nothing. She calls it pantheism, a pagan idea like witchcraft or idolatry. With an expression of shock and disgust, orthodoxy jumps about and waves her hands wildly, to scare the people away from entertaining such a thought. Then she smiles secretly, thoroughly pleased with herself, for she thinks to have protected the utter holiness of God.

"This world is not God," she frowns, shuddering, shaking herself from the thought. "No, only God is divine. Certainly, God is both immanent within the creation and transcendent over it, but he is nevertheless wholly other, entirely different and separate," she insists. Translated, this means that God is in the creation, but he isn't. She nods yes, but says no. Half of her face smiles, while the other half frowns. "God is immanent, but he is also wholly other from it," she insists repeatedly, as if she had two tongues, each contradicting the other.

Then she settles back smugly with her arms folded, as if the self-contradiction were proof of its truth. She presents it as evidence that God is far above and beyond us. It exalts him and verifies his grandeur. Ordinary reason doesn't apply to him. "See," she smirks, "he is far beyond human logic," and the proof is her nonsensical, self-contradictory claims. "If we could explain him, he would not be God," she says, smugly, thinking to honor him, believing it is a compliment. The truth of her claims is their irrationality!

"God is beyond reason, far above human understanding," she repeats. The inanity and absurdity of her claims is her proof! And amazingly, the people are awed and bedazzled by this mumbo-jumbo. "What an awesome God," they cry! But orthodoxy, not God, is the one beyond reason. Do two plus two equal six because it's so absurd? No, absurdity proves only falsehood and foolishness, child. Self-contradiction and nonsense are assuredly not the proof that a statement is true.

She has shooed the people away from the true God, portraying him as nonsensical. Is that not blasphemous? Thinking to reject idolatry, she embraces an idol of irrationality made up of pious-sounding words, an unknowable god, kissing its toes and singing its praises in full-hearted flattery. Then she leads the people in prayer. But will an idol god made up of empty words instead of stone answer them? Child, child, will you pray and pour your heart out to an idol, fervently and in full expectation of being answered?

Why should we run from the bogey man of eternal matter, from a divine physicality in the past, if that is the future toward which we aspire? We long for the resurrection of our material body, in which we expect to live forever, do we not? In doing so, we acknowledge that matter is perfectly compatible with eternity. True, the Bible does not teach pantheism. This physical world is not all there is. But neither does it teach that God is wholly other than the creation, or beyond reach or reason. Nor does it teach us to run away from him. The ultimate proof is our Lord Jesus, fully divine and fully human. And being human means that he was physical. Why should we fly away from Christ Jesus like a flock of scared pigeons? Is it not blasphemy to teach that God is beyond physicality, above and beyond reason and good sense?

The Scriptures begin with God transforming the world into its present state (John 1:1-3; Coll. 1:16-20). He was there within it, in its very heart, immanent, expressing himself, forming our world in ways that pleased him. In his mind was a set of blueprints. This world is a preliminary model of his dream home. And he likes to work with repeated patterns. God's presence in the heart of the world in the beginning hints that he will live in the heart of the new creation too. And we are the new creation! God will live in the throbbing heart of his new Body. That's the Gospel, people. The first creation is a figure of the second. The past is a prophet, and freely preaches the Gospel to everyone who will listen. God will live in our hearts! Like the new world that he is building, this present creation didn't exclude God. It held him tightly in its very bosom.

And he is eager to tell everyone who will listen about his new home, and show them pictures of it. They're moving pictures, with surround sound. God does not hide in the silence. As he spoke this creation into being, his word was realized. It became as he had ordered. It lived. It held the presence of God. In God, word and action coincide perfectly. And both are dynamic and unopposably potent, for they are expressions of the Creator himself.

As God spoke in the primordial mornings, what he said came to be. God's speaking, however, is an anthropomorphism, a way of portraying God in human terms. In the creation, the Word of God was a statement of God himself (John 1:1-3). God's speaking was God's acting. Words of confession express who we are. The creation, being the expression of God, reveals the heart and mind of the divine Poet who rhymes it. Our world is the first line in a poem of God. The second line is even now being spoken into being. Unlike our own words, God's words are never pointless or powerless, or false. They are one and the same as his actions. His words become reality, for they are true. They materialize. They live. God spoke our world to be, and it is. And he's speaking the new world into being as we speak.

His word is never just an echo in the wind. It takes form (Coll. 1:17; Heb. 1:3). History is the expression of God's creative word performing his will, materializing in events as it has been commanded. As God speaks, his Spirit-empowered word fulfills itself, sometimes at once, sometimes as prophecy. Always, the word of God is true. It happens.

But creation is not all outflow, never a one-way street. That which exists is recycled, like a river that is gathered back up into clouds to return and again sprinkle the hills and valleys. Recycling is one of the archetypes that God employs. In the fullness of time, the divine Word began the return of this estranged Eve back to her divine

Adam. The Word became flesh, a special flesh, jump-starting the world's return to God, putting in reverse its primal separation. The reconciliation began. The Word of separation became the Word of reconciliation.

Jesus became the firstfruits of the new creation, the first human to be reconciled with the Creator (Rev. 3:14). This means that both the outflow of God's word, and its return, are the embodiment of the divine will. The Word has ever been present in the world, sweeping back and forth in the ebb and flow of events, pushing here, tugging there, patiently shaping the happenstances of history in accomplishing the divine plan, readying the world for the eagerly awaited reconciliation (2 Cor. 5:17-20).

With a twinkle in its eye, the Bible chuckles delightedly as it tells us that God is physical as well as spiritual (1 Cor. 15:44). It points to the heart of history and to an empty tomb. Christ Jesus is unarguable proof that the expressed Word of God can merge with materiality, and that it does so. It can become embodied, tangible and touchable (1 John 1:1-4). Christ Jesus was the Word made flesh, touchable flesh. In him, Spirit and body became One, again (John 17:5). And he is God's future, as well as our own. The future involves God's metamorphosis into a renewed embodiedness, a living Temple.

The idea that God is forever disembodied, a wholly other Spirit, is not what the Bible teaches. But it's what many churches teach, inventing a false definition of God's holiness. Then, with the unscriptural idea of a wholly other God, they have failed to understand the nature of idolatry. They mistakenly hold on to its meaning within the Mosaic Law, as if that Law were still in force. Limiting the definition of idolatry to that which is from the Law, the churches have not fully recognized its prefigurative nature. They have not understood that all the Law has been annulled, all of it, including the old idolatry. But, holding to their understanding of idolatry as given in the Law, they keep it binding, as if it had not been annulled. It's as if the churches would continue to sacrifice sheep and goats. But the old idolatry, like the rest of the Law, was just a shadow.

To avoid idolatry, misguided Christians long ago decided that the natures of God and of the creature are completely incompatible with one another. But they mistakenly took idolatry to be that which is

The Forming of this World

defined in the Law. Idolatry in the Law foreshadowed something even worse, and more prevalent.

God is Spirit, they declared triumphantly, as if this would keep him from also being embodied (John 4:24; 1 Cor. 15:44). Nevertheless, the man Christ Jesus was perfectly divine and perfectly human. Denial that God shares in physicality, and that physicality shares in God, denies the true Son, as well as the true Father. It manifests the spirit of Antichrist (1 John 2:22-23, 4:15-16).

To foist this untouchable and unknowable God on the people, orthodoxy separated the Father from the Son, while winking and smiling and claiming that they are not really separate. Then she separated them from the Spirit, still winking and smiling, claiming that the Spirit is not separate from either the Father or the Son. And voilá! She pulled from her magic bucket a three-headed, impossible abstraction that she named God the Trinity! God is three Persons, indivisible yet distinguishable. And the pretended proof of her claims is their irrationality and illogic!

So, although the three are one and indivisible, they are yet three, and they each (each?) have different functions or manifestations. Only the Son became flesh. The Father is somehow still totally separate from the world even though Christ was flesh. God is indivisible, but divided. He is One, yet Three. And our failure to understand how this can be, is to the glory of God. It shows that he is way beyond our puny ability to understand, you see.

What a great trick! They are One, yet they are Three, at the same time and in the same place, and also in different places at the same time. They are one God in three Persons. Only the Son, not the Father, is embodied, because God is Spirit. Orthodoxy has seemingly avoided idolatry. Then she bows, and the audience stands and cheers.

But the Bible is not a gong show. Christ Jesus was without question both divine and human. The claim that the world did not originate from within God because creature and Creator are incompatible, is itself incompatible with the Bible and with the truth. If Christ Jesus was divine, then embodiedness is perfectly accordant with divinity. God has a body. The Bible boos orthodoxy's theatrics off the stage. Her theatrics are unconvincing. God is not a good joke to tell on Sunday mornings in church. Nor is he an impossibility.

The Bible does not hold Spirit and matter forever separate. How could our spirit interact with our body if there were no point of contact? There is a oneness to us, even though we are both spirit and flesh. And that is what God is like. He is not forever separate from the world. God is building his Temple. It is possible to know God physically (John 14:7-10; 1 John 1:1-3).

The True Idolatry

The present separation between God and the world is healed in Christ. He is the suture that pulls both sides of the wound together. To imagine a wholly other God in order to keep him holy and separate from the world and thus avoid idolatry, as orthodoxy does, is to shake one's head and say no to Jesus' entire ministry of reconciliation. It means to turn one's back on the Gospel and stomp away from the whole course of creation, from God's plan of the ages, and from reality itself. Is it not madness?

Jesus received the Spirit beside the Jordan at his baptism, which is a symbol of death and resurrection. His story is God's story. God, too, received Christ! The Spirit received the flesh, and vice versa. There's an empty tomb in the heart of the creation shouting that God is now embodied. The resurrection of Christ Jesus into the eternal glory was certainly not an act of idolatry! And what's more, we worship him, do we not? We worship an embodied God. At least, we should.

The Church cannot keep God forever only spiritual. Christ Jesus is not a ghost. When she denies the true Gospel of reconciliation and tells lies about him to his beloved Bride-to-be, it's like spreading lies to break up two lovers. And the more urgently and convincingly the lies are told, the worse is their odiousness. But nothing can separate the saints from God's love, no, not even the oft-repeated and sincere lies of the various churches (Rom. 8:38-39). God yearns for his beloved. He has made wedding plans.

These issues are not peripheral, or unimportant. How does your own church stack up? Does she preach the real biblical God who has a Body, or is she telling the traditional lies about him passionately and sincerely? Have you yourself bravely gathered up courage and sincerely but erroneously proclaimed the communal lies of your tradition? Or, have you been hiding silently in the hush and shush?

Preaching the falsehood of a Spirit-only God in order to avoid idolatry is itself in fact a subtle but pernicious form of idolatry, for it incites worship of a false and bodiless God. And it denies Jesus' work of reconciliation. The false God of orthodoxy is not the true God of Scripture. Does it make sense to try to avoid idolatry by committing it? Does it make sense to try not to get muddy by wallowing in a mud-hole, even if you are sincere?

"No it doesn't," someone might object, "but God forbade us from worship of any created thing, which would be idolatry." Well, sorry, but that's not exactly true. He forbade Israel, not you and me, from making images to worship or serve (Eph. 2:11-12). They were not to make or serve images of God of anything in this world. Then he sent them the man Christ Jesus. Huh? What? Yes, they crucified him because he claimed to be God in the flesh. God in the flesh, get it? He was the true image of God, in the flesh.

No doubt someone might object by quoting Romans 1:23-25 to me. It says that they worshiped images and served the creature instead of the Creator. They substituted idols for the living God, and that was idolatry. But remember that this was after the Flood, during the time when the Spirit was separated from the world. Today, the Spirit and the creature are no longer totally separate. Today, the Spirit has in fact united with the creature, first in Christ Jesus and then in the saints (Matt. 10:40; Luke 10:16; John 13:20; 2 Cor. 5:20; Gal. 4:14; Phil. 2:5-11). It is still true that we should not worship the creature outside of Christ, for the world separated from Christ is still separated from God. But this does not apply to our worship of Christ Jesus. It is most certainly not idolatry to worship our Savior! Christ Jesus has been transformed and glorified, and received into the Godhead (Matt. 28:18; Acts 1:9, 2:23, 5:31; Rom. 8:17; Phil. 2:9-11; Heb. 1:1-5; Rev. 3:21). Jesus is Lord. He sits on the divine throne of highest majesty. He and the Father are now completely One. And he is extremely worthy of praise and worship.

In the Law, idolatry is the making or serving of an image or any other thing and serving it as if it were God, or a stand-in for him, his vicar (Ex. 20:1-5). Idolatry is the worship of a false god, or the attempt to worship the true God through a man-made representation, an image. Imagining a Spirit-only God and worshiping that image is idolatry, people! Inventing an impossible God with three heads is idolatry as well.

The attempt to worship God through an image of him assumes a separation between the worshiper and God, which requires an intermediary of some sort, an idol. The image becomes the intermediary. But the only intermediary between God and humans is Christ Jesus, because he is both human and fully and completely divine (Rom. 8:34; 1 Tim. 2:5; Heb. 7:25, 9:24). He has been received into oneness with the Father.

And he has a body. There's an empty tomb to prove it.

What the churches have done is to worship a human invention, with their idea of a wholly other, Spirit-only God, unmoving and totally separate from his creation and his created ones. In keeping God eternally separate from the creation they are putting distance and kind between him and his children. God is their invention, and they seek to worship their invention. With the best of intentions, they have nevertheless tried to worship God by worshiping a human construct rather than the true God of Scripture. In the eyes of the Law, then, they are guilty of idolatry. While claiming to abhor idolatry, they are swimming in it. Sincerely.

To their credit, they rightly trust in Christ to bring them into God's presence. Trusting in Christ is the Gospel call, and is the true path unto salvation. But Christ does not take us to an idol, a human construct, but to the true Father. And he does not merely take us to the Father's presence, but rather into his very being (John 14:1-3). Because of his great mercy, and because he does not take our sins into account, believers who receive Christ experience true salvation even when their idea of God is idolatrous. Otherwise, if the Law were in force, orthodox believers would be convicted of idolatry!

Nevertheless, idolatry in the Law is just a shadow of the true and greater idolatry of trying to serve God outside of Christ, separated from him (Heb. 10:1). Separation from God is the true sin that is healed only by receiving Christ, and walking in the Spirit.

Here is the truth of the matter. The Law's foreshadowing lesson about idolatry was that God desired to be worshiped directly, never from afar or through a manmade intermediary. It looked forward eagerly to the indwelling of Christ in the saints, when they would serve God in oneness, with no distance or separation between them. There would be nothing and no one to take his place or substitute for him. This was the lesson in the Law. Take that to heart, dear one. He would live in the saints, and they would live in him (John 17:21-23).

The Forming of this World

Worship from the outside, in separation, is but a shadow of true worship. True worship is service, child, not flattery from afar in order to obtain his blessings. Yes, Old Testament worship, like Old Testament idolatry, was just a shadow. And it has gone the way of all shadows wherever the light shines. True worship is fulfilled only in Christ the Son, in oneness with the Spirit. All the Law has been annulled, child, all of it.

The Law was a lesson that helped us learn about Christ Jesus. The lesson is still valuable. It shows us clearly and emphatically that we should not worship the things of this world. But Christ Jesus is not of this world. He is holy. He has been transformed and received back into the Godhead, bodily. God has a body, child.

True idolatry, then, is not the act of attributing an original divinity to the creation, or seeing God revealed in nature, or anticipating a literal, physical reconciliation. Instances abound in the Bible of God revealing his presence within nature, such as in fire, winds or clouds, or lightning, or voices, or in manifestations of angels, and so forth. All of God's dealings with humans are within the creation. The best example, of course, is Christ Jesus himself, whom we do worship. Jesus Christ is Lord. He is God, and he is embodied.

No, we don't worship the world, or anything in the world apart from Christ. We worship God in Christ, who is One with God and the coming fullness of him. God is becoming embodied once more. This present world is not God's final purpose or expression. It's just a prototype, a sacrificial model in the creative process of forming Christ, in whom alone the Father is well-pleased. True idolatry, then, is to worshipfully serve anything in this world, or in heaven itself, apart from Christ. The only instance of a human fully integrated into the Godhead yet is Christ Jesus. Idolatry, then, is to serve whatever is not of him, or to try and serve God outside of him. True worship is to walk in the Spirit.

Christ is served directly, with no distance in between, no separation, and no substitute. He is the truth of God, his full revelation and genuine manifestation (Acts 4:12). To know God, we must know Christ. To worship a Spirit-only God from afar, separated from him as in Old Testament times, is just a shadow of true worship. It is left-over worship, part of the Law which has been repealed. And it denies Christ Jesus and the Gospel. It is the true idolatry against which the Law remonstrated. Now the Law has been superseded. Christ Jesus is the very purpose of the creation, and is the only full manifestation and revelation of God worthy of worship.

So, once more, how does your church stack up? Is she worshiping from afar, as if God were still far above and separate from his children? Is she unwittingly committing idolatry, while thinking to avoid it? If she is, should you not tell her and instruct her in the truth? But be careful, for they will try to crucify you.

Christ's coming fulfillment is God's will and eager desire. The goal and direction of our lives should be to do God's will, which is to serve Christ in the new creation. That is true worship, and nothing is more important. But we must do it in direct contact, in oneness with the Spirit of Christ who lives and moves within us. We must be united into oneness with God. Otherwise, it is not true worship. Separation from God is not true worship, even when we elevate him high and away from ourselves with the most pious-sounding, flowery flatteries.

Christ is the new tent of meeting in which God and humanity are being reunited. To serve anything or anyone else religiously in the place of Christ Jesus is true idolatry. To worship a forever disembodied, nonphysical God from afar rejects Christ Jesus in order to worship a false God of Spirit only, the God still separated from the world, the Old Testament God, the shadow of him. It's a case of the true idolatry toward which the Law pointed.

As we can see, the truth turns the tables on tradition and orthodoxy. The accusers become the accused, and are found guilty. Those who worship a wholly other, Spirit-only God are the true idolaters. They unwittingly commit idolatry even while they claim to avoid it. Their idea of God is the Old Testament God, the inchoate God, the God of the Law. But let me repeat. The Law has been annulled.

Christianity, which is the new Israel, was foreshadowed by fleshly Israel. And fleshly Israel's downfall was idolatry. Like Israel who prefigured them, Christianity too has unwittingly fallen into the same snake pit. And like Israel, they do not realize their calamity. They fiercely defend their idolatry.

True worship, we repeat, is service. Our service of worship should not be through any intermediary, any intermediary whatsoever, including distance or separation. That would constitute idolatry. God is worshiped/served only in Christ, in unity with him. The central significance of Christ is new life in union with God. God wants us to serve him directly, merged into oneness with himself, he in us and we in him (John 17:21-23). That is the only true worship, and it happens only in Christ. Other than Christ, any intermediary between God and humans, anything in between, even if we worshipfully call it God, is an idol. A false God is an idol, child. True worship must be in the Spirit and of the truth (John 4:23-24). True worship is to walk in sweet communion with Christ, listening to the melodious lyrics of his voice within us, gladly doing his will as our own, singing and keeping harmony with him in the rhythmic cadences of the new creation.

Whether made of stone, or words or ideas, whatever draws us away from the true Christ, or whatever comes between us and Christ, is an idol. True idolatry allows the things of this present creation to intrude between the worshiper and the Spirit. God will be expressed fully in the newness of the fulfilled Christ. We must live for the future, and the future has arrived. It is Christ Jesus. And he is the rejection of this world for the next. He is the holiness of God, the fulfillment of the Creator's purpose of metamorphosis, the great joiner, our august example and guide, and the evolving fullness of God (Coll. 2:8-9). And the saints, everyone who has received Christ, are part of that evolving fullness. Yes, child, catch your breath and let's move on.

Out from the Shadows

The reconciliation of God and the world is accomplished only in Christ. The doctrine of an unchanging, wholly other God distorts his picture into a disfigured caricature. In contrast, the new creation will be the loveliest, most elegant expression of divine artistry. To paint together with God in the new creation is true artistic expression. Drawing others to his beauteous fullness is true worship. True worship is a living testimony working together with God in creating a divine work of art, a new world of exquisite beauty.

The living testimonies of the saints constitute their brushstrokes on the canvas of God's painting. It is their worship. They must speak and live Christ. They must embody him. Any other worship is false worship. They must not smear the mud of idolatry on God's canvas. The doctrine that God is too high, too far, too different, too holy, beyond understanding and forever separated from us, is the mud of a false Gospel that arrogantly paints the face of a false Father, and a counterfeit Christ, into God's masterpiece. God lives in your heart, child, if you are a believer who has received Christ.

Life outside of Christ is separation from God and is the true sin. Idolatry under the Law foreshadowed this great truth. Let me repeat. Life separated from Christ is the true sin that brings eternal death. Christ is literal reunion with God in the renewed oneness of the creation with the Creator. The true Gospel is reconciliation (2 Cor. 5:17-20; Coll. 1:19-22). Let me repeat. The true Gospel is reconciliation, physical as well as spiritual. It is not mere congeniality. It is a literal union into one Body, the removal of the true sin of separation from God. In Christ, God and the believer are made One. Denial of the Creator's metamorphosis into embodiedness that gathers in the saints is a false Gospel. Don't be fooled, dear one.

God's strong desire is to transfer all that he has and is into his new home in the Son. There's a big moving van parked in the driveway of this world, and God is packing all his stuff into it, getting ready to move. If we don't want to be left behind, we should put all our stuff into the van too. But God doesn't want to take any junk with him. We need to leave our junk behind. Anything that is not compatible with the Son is junk. Throw away your junk, child, all of it.

The Creator will be embodied again. His uniting with this new Body is reconciliation. Reconciliation is irrefutable evidence that God was at one time united bodily with the world, but became separated. Reconciliation would not be possible otherwise. You can't return to a place where you've never been.

The original separation of God from the world constitutes his holiness. Eve was separated from Adam for a while, and then reunited with him. Similarly, the corporate Christ is the literal reconciliation of God and the once-separated creation into one divine Body (Coll. 1:19-22). Gloriously, the saints will constitute that living Temple of God's delight.

In sum, the rejection of God's embodiedness, preaching his total separation and absolute difference forever from the created world, is a false Gospel. It fabricates a distorted picture of God, an idol, and presents that deformed image for worship. Denying the true creation, it must invent the further foolishness of creation from nothingness in order to hide its nakedness. Idolatrously, when the churches deny the real, physical reconciliation of the world with himself that God is accomplishing in Christ, they totally misunderstand the Gospel, and make reconciliation merely metaphorical. Orthodoxy has denied God's true Gospel epic, and has substituted a hellish horror story in its place. But true believers do not worship Frankenstein. They worship Christ, embodied (John. 14:7-10).

We must understand that whatever opposes Christ, the real Christ, is satanic. This includes false doctrines of God. Be thankful that God is merciful, child.

The Creator of this world desires us to worship in the Spirit and in truth (John 4:23; Phil. 2:10-11). The Spirit of truth is Christ (John 14:6). And no lie is of the truth. Doesn't it make sense then, to worship the real Christ of Scripture, the living and growing embodiment of God? He is the shining Light that has chased away the shadows. The day has come.

One of those shadows was Judaism, all of it. Christ does not make us hop, skip and jump to the Law. Offerings of lambs and goats and oxen are not the pathway to heaven. Shockingly, God's revelation of himself in the Old Testament and in Judaism, like the other things of the Law was just a temporary shadow too, merely a prefiguring of the future. Always, the end is patterned in the beginning. The past is a prophet. Startlingly for many, the revelation of God in the Old Testament is just a foreshadowing of Christ Jesus in his fullness.

Yes, dear one. Christ Jesus is the Heir of God. All that the Father is will be transferred to the Son. But there is an astonishing, mind-boggling consequence of this truth that orthodoxy has overlooked. A testament, including heirship, does not take effect until after the death of the testator (Heb. 9:16-17). The heirs do not receive their inheritance until then. Jesus' death is the precondition by which his followers become heirs of the kingdom (Rom. 8:14-17). But even more startling is that Jesus himself is the Heir of God! The Son does not receive the inheritance until the Father has died! Jesus is the full and genuine image of God. The cross, then, is the story of God. It pictures the death of God!

Death is a separation between spirit and body, as shown at the cross. And for Jesus, it was temporary. It was just three days. The death of God, then, which was imaged at the cross, is just a temporary separation between the world and the Spirit. After three "days," or dispensations, Body and Spirit will be reconciled. This is the true Gospel (2 Cor. 5:17-19).

Christ is the reality that the whole system of sacrifices and offerings of Judaism prefigured, and what the history of Israel foretold. He is what the revelation of God in the Old Testament hinted at, and what the creation story whispers. All the heads in the Old Testament are turned toward the Son. Every seeing eye looks toward him. Every prophetic finger points to him. All its stories speak about God's Heir. The whole Bible urges us earnestly to the Coming One. God will be revealed fully in Christ, and only in Christ. He is the complete fulfillment of God's Old Testament shadow. He is God's future, the reality and realization of the new creation, and the fulfillment of the old.

Believers who worship in the Spirit and in truth do not worship the God of Israel as he was revealed in previous ages. The God of the Old Testament is the inchoate God, the shadow of God, the type or picture of his coming glory to be revealed in Christ Jesus. All the things of the Old Testament were the overture to the grand symphony that was to be played in the Son and Heir.

Yes, the Law and the Prophets were shadows. The entire religion and kingdom of Judaism was a shadow. Judaism was a shadow kingdom, a dark realm of types and figures. The Jews actually walked in darkness, along with the rest of the world (Isa. 9:2; Luke 1:79). In God's providence, first came the shades of night, the Old Testament, and then the light of day. Our charge as true believers is to worship God in the light of Christ Jesus, not in Yahweh or Elohim or Jehovah, or any other name (John 5:22-23; Acts 4:12; Phil. 2:9-11).

Even now, God is not yet revealed in his fullness. The body of Christ is still growing. The new creation is still a work in progress. It's still evolving. We've seen his ads and billboards, and now we look forward to his personal appearance. Christ is coming soon.

However, like Israel who prefigured them, Christians will quite unexpectedly be repudiated when the Lord returns, just as his first coming brought the rejection of the Jews. So it is written, so it is drawn. And so it will be done. God does not say the truth in words while drawing false pictures. The pictures are parables. They preach, and they prophesy. The types and figures in the Bible are just as valid and reliable as are the jots and tittles, the consonants and vowels. The figures speak. And what they say is true, for God himself has drawn them with the indelible ink of his divine pen.

It is a serious mistake in hermeneutics, in interpretation, to read and apply the Old Testament as if it were merely literal, or on a par with the New Testament, or as a well from which to draw moralizing platitudes. Christ Jesus interpreted the Scriptures typologically and Christologically. He read them as shadows and promises of himself, fulfilled and superseded when he came. He knew how to read with understanding. He himself, he explained, was the true Bread, the Light, the Sabbath, and so forth. In fact, he even identified himself as the Father (John 8:58, 10:30, 14:7). It was very God who was present in Christ. It was Emmanuel. And he showed us how to read. The way to read the Bible is to study the pictures to find Christ. The Bible is an invitation to receive Christ, identify with him, and then to follow him, to do as he did and be as he is.

But we have to look for him, rather than for moralistic platitudes about how we should try to behave. That's Judaism reborn, not true Christianity. Our behavior is the outcome, not the basis or goal, of our relationship with God. The goal of the Gospel is not good behavior, child. It is oneness with the Christ Spirit. A new nature, not meritorious works as in Judaism, is the true Gospel. It's not about laws, rules, or etiquette. It's about conversion, a bona fide, literal change in nature. It's metamorphosis into a new creation. Let's look at the true Gospel a minute. But we'll need to keep our shovel in hand to keep clearing away the accumulated traditions as we've been doing. It's a little tedious and repetitive, but it's good exercise, and it will help us to remember.

Chapter Four
The True Gospel

True sinfulness is not what we do. It's what we are by nature. God's holiness consists in his temporary separation from this world. Then, because we are in and of this world, we are separated from him and unholy. This natural separation from God is the true sinfulness that sin in the Law symbolizes. And the only counter to separation is reunion. We need the super glue of the Spirit to affix us back to the Creator. The first step back toward God is to receive Christ. Full reconciliation will come when we are received back into the Godhead at the Consummation (John 17:11, 21-23).

Not by the Law

True Forgiveness

Someone might argue, then, that we are punished for something over which we had no control. We are punished for being part of the creation. That is another error that comes from orthodoxy. Remember that the Law is done away with. And with it went punishment. And the Law of Israel, in which punishment for sin existed, never applied to non-Israelites. Just as salvation does not come from works, neither does condemnation come from works. Our deeds neither condemn us, nor can they save us. It is all God's doing. Salvation is according to God's long-range plan. It is based on his desire to create for himself a new Temple in which to live. His plan from the beginning was to save those who would receive him. Others would have their day in the sun, and then they would return to the earth from which they sprang, like the other animals. Horses and pigs and chickens die, too. It's not because they sinned, but because they are not included in the new world that God has planned. Face it. God did not plan for every human to be saved. Eternal life is not for all the animals. This is God's world, child, and he calls the shots. He does not owe salvation to everyone, or to anyone. Are we to judge God (Isa. 64:8; Jer. 18:2-6; Matt. 27:7-8; Rom. 4:8, 9:21; 1 Cor. 13:5; 2 Cor. 5:19)?

Neither do we die because Adam sinned. We die because we inherit his nature. To escape death and live forever we must partake of the tree of life, which is Christ Jesus.

This over-arching story of separation and reunion is the truth of the Bible and the heart of the Gospel. But it is not the most popular story. The prevalent Gospel among the various churches is forgiveness of our behaviors called sins, which are defined as transgressions of the Law. But the Law has been annulled. And it never applied to Gentiles. It was a covenant between God and Israel. The true Gospel preaches grace. Grace takes a broom and sweeps up the Law and its sins together. Indeed mercy, forgiveness, and love all take up the same broom. The true Gospel gathers up the Law and throws it out the door.

The churches, however, espouse the traditional, prevalent Gospel. They bring the things of the Old Testament back inside. "God's Law still applies to every human because, although we Gentiles were never under the Law of Moses, there exists an unwritten but universal Law of God that we all have broken," they claim. Because the churches could not find a law in God's word to throw over us, they invented one! They imagined a universal law that no one has ever heard or known. To make their Gospel work they must have a law for which God forgives us. Without Law, there can be no forgiveness for transgressing it. Like the Athenians who built an altar to the Unknown god, they have built an altar to the Unknown Law (Acts 17:23)!

The traditional Gospel that the churches preach is forgiveness of the punishment of our awful, unlawful behaviors called sins, which are transgressions of God's Law. We are forgiven because of God's mercy and love, through Jesus' sacrifice on the cross. It leaves the Law still binding, even while claiming that it has been annulled. Its annulment means then only that we can be forgiven for breaking it. It remains binding on everyone except those who receive forgiveness in Christ. Orthodoxy preaches that mercy and grace are God's relenting to impose the Law's punishment upon us. That is, we are forgiven for having broken the Law. And that Law is the Ten

The True Gospel

Commandments. It's Judaism taken back out from the dust pile and shaken to remove the dust, and then thrown all over non-Jews. In Christian orthodoxy, incredibly, God forgives us for breaking a shadow that was never over us. Gentiles were never under Israel's Law. And shadows, of course, cannot be broken. Traditionalists declare that Judaism has been superseded, while nevertheless putting their neck under its yoke in order to rejoice for God's forgiveness (Deut. 22:10; Gal. 5:1). Or else, they invent an imaginary law to place around their neck. They must have forgiveness for breaking a law that does not exist. Does that make sense?

If the true Gospel is forgiveness for breaking God's Law, then it means that the Law is still in force. Inanely, the whole world has become guilty for having broken the Mosaic Law, although it was given only to Israel, and only since the time of Moses. Or, all are guilty for breaking the Unknown Law! Only, we can escape punishment because Jesus already suffered its punishment in our place. Jesus was punished for breaking the Law, although he didn't break it. God pretended that he broke it. He pretended that Jesus was us. Yes, Jesus did away with the Law, but we still must not sin by breaking it. This means that Jesus must have only pretended to do away with the Law. The Law just pretended to leave. It went out by the front door, then sneaked back in through a side door when no one was looking. The whole Gospel has become mere pretense and imagination. It makes of the cross a charade in which God, Jesus, and believers pretend that the Law has everyone by the neck. And then vast hordes of people pretend they are saved by pretending they are joined to an imaginary thing called the Catholic Church.

For Protestants, repentance becomes sorrow for our having broken the Law, and a resolve to change our behavior and stop breaking the Law. So we receive Christ, in order to be forgiven for having broken the Law, and to receive help in keeping the Law. And we read the Bible in order to moralize from it, to find principles by which we can order our behavior and keep from breaking the Law. It's all about works, based on the Law, even while it pretends to be free from the Law. It is a kind of grace, that's true, but grace under the Law. It preaches condemnation, by the Law, followed by forgiveness of that condemnation, ever in relation to the Law. The whole system is based on make-believe, and leads to behaviorism, a religion of works, a clone of Judaism. It's based on the Law even while it denies this. It's Judaism dressed up in fancy new clothes. But its shoes are way too tight.

Works religion is like trying to change the evil thoughts in your head by dyeing your hair, or getting a haircut. It doesn't work, even if you shave it all off. Try it, and see. Neither can you change the evil desires of your heart by wearing a corset. It doesn't change the nature of what you are. Try it, and see.

The true Gospel, on the other hand, sets aside the Law, for salvation and reconciliation are not works-based. Because the idea of sin and punishment is so ingrained in traditional Christianity, we must repeat here that the Gospel is not about behaviorism. The Law was just a foreshadowing. Behavior should issue from our changed nature in which the Word of God expresses himself in us. True religion literally unites people with the Christ of true repentance, which is genuine conversion. True conversion is transformation into a new creation. Metaphorical religion leads people to something called repentance and conversion, but which is merely sorrow for one's actions called sins. If it goes no further, it remains only a change in attitude or behavior, often quite temporary. True biblical conversion does not leave the supplicant still separate from God or enslaved under an imaginary Law. True salvation is to receive and serve Christ in a real conversion. And that means a real transformation. It means freedom from Law. And it means a new creation. Get it? Conversion is a new creation.

Does this mean that anyone who receives Christ through repentance of sins is not saved? Happily, no. Reception of Christ saves, whatever the motivation. Christ promised to receive everyone who would come to him (John 6:37). Nevertheless, truth is a better basis upon which to preach salvation than is metaphor. Metaphor says that salvation is "like" this, while truth shouts, "This is it! I've found it!"

Despite her denials, mainstream Christianity is behavior-based, stuck in the mud of metaphors, trying hard not to commit sins. The Bible has become a text for moralizing. Christianity has become a kind of recycled Judaism. But Judaism was a religion of shadows, a realm of darkness. The Law of Israel, the Ten Commandments, was really a mélange of veiled pictures. They were not spelled out and were easy to overlook. And that's what the Jews did. They missed the figurative nature of the Law, and saw only the literal. They read

The True Gospel

the words, meticulously, but ignored the pictures floating above the words.

Now Christianity has taken the Law and put it back into the Gospel. The churches are still mired in legalism. Salvation is taken to mean God's relenting to inflict the Law's punishment on us, because he punished Jesus in our place. The Law is still seen as having jurisdiction over us. Orthodoxy thus serves the Law, even while claiming grace and freedom from it. Indeed, many churches think grace to be God's enabling of the believer to keep the Law! That will not happen, child, until the Consummation, for the Law is a picture of life in Christ. This bears another look.

The startling truth is that the breaking of the Law, called sin, is just a shadow picturing the deadly condition of separation from God that brings eternal death. The Law in the Old Testament was just a shadow, child, so its offspring are shadows too (Heb. 10:1-4). Alarmingly for many, this means that forgiveness of sin under the Law is then just a shadow too, just a figure. It pictures reunion with God, which is literal, physical and spiritual reconciliation. That's hard to accept, isn't it? We've grown up with the notions of sin and forgiveness, always in relation to the Law. The churches have preached it for a long time, and have been very sincere and convincing. Many believers have died for the doctrine. Multitudes have been saved by it.

Nevertheless, however strange and alarming it may appear, forgiveness of sins is just a picture in the Law, just a shadow. The Law was the heart of the old, Mosaic covenant that God made only with Israel. And that prefigurative covenant has been annulled (2 Cor. 3:5-11). It has been superseded and replaced. The reality that forgiveness in the Law pictured or foreshadowed is contained in the new covenant, available to all people. The new covenant is life in oneness with God, and therefore free from sin, that is, from estrangement from God. Forgiveness of sin under the Law was a prefiguring of that oneness and freedom that we have in Christ.

That's hard to accept and yes, forgiveness of sin is what all the prophets, Jesus, and the apostles preached. But the abrogation or annulment of the Law that Jesus accomplished automatically brought with it pardon of sins. Did you get that, child? The followers of Jesus preached pardon from sin through the cross. After the cross the Law is no longer in effect. It means that in Christ the wrongs that we have done and will do will not condemn us. And this is totally apart from Law because Jesus did away with it. In annulling the Law, Jesus did away with sin, for sin is the transgression of the Law. And the Law was only over Israel anyway, as a picture. In annulling the Law, then, Jesus made forgiveness of sin available for everyone, everywhere. The Law, and the sin involved in breaking it, is no more. The consequence of annulling the Law was forgiveness of sin. No one, Jew or Gentile, believer or nonbeliever, is under the Law. No one is guilty of breaking the Law, then, or condemned by it, even when doing things prohibited by it called sins. This is what is meant by forgiveness of sin. The Law was just a picture symbolizing being in Christ or in the world.

The truth must be stated clearly, emphatically, and repeatedly. The truth is that our salvation has nothing to do with the Law. Law has no jurisdiction over us. We are not saved by keeping it, nor are we condemned for not keeping it, whether believer or nonbeliever. Salvation is available to all. Nevertheless, only those who receive Christ will escape the coming judgment, which will involve the destruction of everything that is not of Christ. Humans outside of Christ will be destroyed, not because they broke the Law, but because they never received Christ (John 3:18). They remain in the world separated from God, which is the true sin that sin under the Law prefigured. This world, pilgrim, is on its way out.

Yes, the abolition of the Law did away with sin. That is, it brought forgiveness. Forgiveness of sin is the result of abolishing the Law, because without the Law there is no sin. The reality that sin and forgiveness in the Law pictured is our natural estrangement from God that results in death, and reconciliation with him that results in eternal life. And reconciliation is not based on Law, but on God's grace through faith. Forgiveness is the absence of the Law's tentacles.

Sin is transgression of the Law (1 John 3:4). Where there is no Law, there is no sin (Rom. 4:15). Where there is no sin there can be no forgiveness for transgressing it. That's why salvation is not based on the Law. We are not under Law. No one is. We are under grace (Rom. 6:12, 18, 22, 8:2). Christ has brought freedom from the Law and from death. Freedom from Law makes true forgiveness of sin available to everyone, Jew and Gentile.

There is forgiveness, which was under the Law and was a mere shadow, and there is true forgiveness, in Christ. True forgiveness came with the cross, because it repealed the Law. Salvation is now available in Christ. In receiving Christ our wrong behaviors are not counted against us. That's what forgiveness under the Law pictures. Freedom from sin, from Law, is the true forgiveness foreshadowed by forgiveness in the Law. We should not subject ourselves, then, to the shadow that is Law (Gal. 5:1, 13). Shadows cannot save us. Nor do they condemn us.

Law is weak and powerless. Transgression of the Law invoked punishment. But punishment has no power whatever to heal or undo sin. It is meant as a deterrent, and as a teaching mechanism. It has no moral quality, nor does it fix a wrong or heal a hurt or injury. Punishment for sin fixes nothing. Even the hot fires of Hell that orthodoxy invented fix nothing. Punishment has no power over the past. Its outlook is only for the future. Punishment does not atone for sins. Punishment is the consequence of transgressing the Law. Where there is no Law there is no sin and no punishment. And there is no Law in force today because Jesus did away with it through the cross. And there are no hell-fires awaiting unbelieving sinners either, for the same reasons. Believe it, child.

God forgives the wrongs that we have done when we receive Christ. His forgiveness, however, is not the abstention from inflicting punishment for transgressing the Law. It is the overlooking of who and what we are, and what we have done, looking forward to our coming change. We are not saved on the basis of what we have done in regard to the Law, but rather for what we can become. We will be changed, and given a new nature. The Law is a lesson for us to study so that we can know about life in Christ. But we must repeat here that it has no authority over us, and no jurisdiction.

Salvation is based on God's grace and mercy. It's based on his loving plan and purpose. It comes through faith because we are free. In order to receive Christ we must believe in him and trust him and his word. Forgiveness of sins is an object lesson, a teaching mechanism. Sins are not counted because they don't exist (Rom. 4:8; 1 Cor. 13:5; 2 Cor. 5:9; Coll. 2:13). Sins were eliminated when Jesus annulled the Law. Where Law went, sin followed. Jesus threw them both out the door, and slammed it shut. Then he bolted it. Law cannot touch us, tiger.

It's true that all have sinned, that is, they have done things contrary to the Law (Rom. 3:23). But only Israel was ever under the Law's authority. God does not save us according to our behavior, nor does he condemn anyone according to behavior. Forgiveness of sins is based on God's love and comes by receiving Christ. It does not come by punishing anyone. Nor is it escape from the punishment that the Law required. Indeed, the Ten Commandments do not threaten punishment, because they are prefigurative of life in Christ.

As we've seen, God's long-range purpose is to grow a Body in which to live. It will be composed of everyone who receives oneness with him in Christ. And he wants them to serve him well, of course. The Law's lesson is how to live in the Body. The members of his Body must not fight among themselves. They must not harm other members. The hand, for example, should not make a fist and strike the face in anger. Sins are all those actions, behaviors, and attitudes that will be improper for the members of his Body, because they are members of his Body. The Law was a foreshadowing lesson on how to live in Christ. It was a foreshadowing of life in Christ.

The Law is a teaching tool (Rom. 3:20, 7:7). The saints should live in harmony with the intent of the Law, not because they are under it, but rather because it is a blueprint for their future life in the Body (Rom. 6:1-2, 15). The Law is a series of pictures of life in Christ. We must understand its symbolism. Breaking its commands is not what condemns. Condemnation actually is a legal term, a metaphor to symbolize the truth that, apart from Christ the whole world is destined to destruction. The behaviors that the Law prohibits, called sins, are the reason why. These behaviors are inherent in human nature. We are self-centered and incapable of doing God's will. So we are unsuitable for serving in the Body. This is why we must be changed and given a new nature capable of doing God's will rather than our own. Otherwise, we will be destroyed along with the rest of the world for the same reason. This world was never meant to last forever. It was merely a preliminary incubator to birth Christ Jesus and the saints.

Because sin and punishment are so ingrained in orthodoxy we must emphasize and keep repeating that true sin is our condition of being separated from God, and therefore from life. Jesus took away the sin of the world by opening the door to reconciliation with God (John 1:29). He became sin by becoming human, not by taking our behaviors upon himself (Rom. 8:3; 2 Cor. 5:21). It is true that sins are actions and behaviors contrary to the Law. But actions neither save nor do they condemn. They result from what we are. They are merely the symptoms. The root problem is not what we do, but rather our nature that causes us to do what we do. We are sinners by nature, and that is why we do things unsuitable for living in the Body (Rom. 7:14, 17:20). Salvation involves receiving a new nature and healing that separation. And eventually, we will be changed into beings capable of doing God's will willfully.

The early Christians early realized that the Law of Moses was not binding upon either Jews or Gentiles (Acts 15:1-29). They soon saw that the Gentiles were never under the Law of Israel. The churches should preach forgiveness for what it really is, a foreshadowing fulfilled by receiving Christ and in him freedom from the consequences of being estranged from God and life. The reality it points to and longs for is literal oneness with God. True forgiveness of sin means reconciliation based on conversion, that is, on a real transformation.

A grouping of shadows called the Law, which have all been repealed, should not be mistaken for the bright light of reality in Christ. Forgiveness of sins in the Law is just a foreshadowing, a lesson, a tutor to lead us to Christ. The true Gospel is reconciliation, and the Law is just a picture of it, just a shadow. The true "I AM" of God is Christ. And in him, the Law has no force. So, the true believer should abstain from doing those things that are contrary to Christ not because the Law has authority over him or her, but rather because it is a standard for life in the Body of God. In Christ, Christ has authority over us. This is why the New Testament exhorts us away from sin. Its reality is life in Christ. Are you in Christ, pilgrim? If so, should you not, then, abide by his leadership?

Moving Onward

Reconciliation means that this world issued from divinity and will be returned there, transformed and re-created in loving reunion with the Christ Spirit (John 17:5, 22). Believers who receive the Spirit of sonship will be exalted and glorified, and literally share in the divine nature as does the first-begotten Son (2 Peter 1:4). Christ in his fullness is not just a man called Jesus. He is a vast multitude, numerous as the sand of the sea, uncountable as the stars of heaven, and glorious as the Shekinah of God (John 10:34, 17:22; Coll. 3:4; Rev. 3:21).

The glory of the Gospel is not just the fact of eternal life. Far more important and glorious is the quality of that life. We will literally share in the divine nature, people! How awesome! It is foolish to exchange our real, glorious freedom and standing in Christ for subservience to the Law, especially to an unknown, invented and imaginary one. The Law is not our taskmaster. It is our servant, charged with showing us about life in Christ.

It is senseless to exchange our true physical union with God for an imaginary conviviality that churches falsely call reconciliation, but which only means that God is no longer angry with us and will not punish us for breaking his Law. We must learn the lesson of Esau, who sold his birthright for a bowl of soup. Or remember Lot's wife. Our birthright is oneness with God!

God's anger and jealousy are just metaphors and are figurative, as is his wrath. They're teaching tools, anthropomorphisms, as are condemnation and forgiveness. They are part of the system of Law given the world as a lesson to study, as a figure of the reality that came with Christ. The Law, all of it, is a lesson pointing us to life in Christ. It spoke for a while of Christ and then became properly silent. Legalistic condemnation and forgiveness are just as shadowy, and just as annulled, as the sacrifice of bulls and goats and lambs. Believe it, child. Do not be afraid. Salvation is by faith, by reception of Christ, not by works. And neither is condemnation based on works. This means that it is not based on sins! The only action that will condemn you is to reject and never receive Christ. Eternal death comes from lack of faith, which keeps one from receiving Christ.

No doubt someone will find offense with these claims, for the metaphors are dearly beloved. Christians have grown up with them. The Law is like family. But why should believers become angry for being shown that the pictures they've been kissing all these years are just pictures? Wouldn't you rather hold tightly to Christ himself, rather than to his picture?

We must not be duped by the orthodox sleight-of-hand, by substitution of the figurative and metaphorical for the real. We must not put the Old Testament on a par with the New Testament. The errors of orthodoxy must not fool us, and its furious antics must not chase us away from the truth. We are not pigeons, even if sometimes we coo. We must not be led down the wrong road by their detour signs. The right road will lead us home to the Father. Hellish tales of terror, and threats of eternal torture, must not frighten us or deter us. Forgiveness for Law-breaking should be understood for what it is, just an illustration that leads us to its reality, which is reunion and re-assimilation within the Godhead. The true Gospel of Christ is neither a child's fairy tale nor a horror story. Nor is it a re-run of Judaism, which is all about breaking the Law and being forgiven for having broken it. God is love. The true Gospel is reconciliation. And it begins in Genesis. Let's go there once more.

Chapter Five
True Beginnings

As we've seen, there was a lot of misguided orthodox nonsense that needed to be shoveled out before we could proceed. It was a bit tedious, but now that we've done that, we can walk once more through the account in Genesis. But watch where you step. We'll keep our shovel handy as we proceed.

Clearing the Air

All Wrapped Up

When God began to create, the Bible says, the earth was formless and empty, a vain and purposeless place. There is no article in the text, no "the" to the beginning. It's not about the beginning of reality or of our planet. It's about how God began restructuring the already existent earth into its present shape and condition. The "in beginning" with which the Bible begins, refers to God's plan to transform and organize the world into what it is today, with the purpose of its leading to Christ Jesus and the Gospel and the new world that he had in mind. It's the beginning of his work, not the beginning of time and space and the universe. The first verse could be stated as, "In beginning to work his plan, God transformed the heavens and the earth."

And nothing can be formless or empty. That's impossible. The earth had a form, otherwise it could not have been "empty." Neither could it have been empty, which would be impossible as well. And the waters had a "face" or surface. It just wasn't like it is today (Gen. 2:4-6). The description of being waste and empty and without form is not just a physical description, then. It is a hint of something more, of something spiritual. It's a shadow, like the other things of the creation. The Genesis accounts are, in fact, a description of how God gave it form. To give it form meant to give it purpose. The world, as it was, had no purpose or goal. He formed the earth into what we see around us. Giving it its present form implies that it was given purpose. The world is not just a toy that the Creator is playing with. The creation account is a condensed report of how God purposely and designedly took charge of things and reorganized them, with a specific goal in mind. Later, we learn that his goal was Christ and the saints. The world as it was, needed to be changed. It needed to be aimed.

As he began to create, it was as if the earth were fidgeting in her sleep, tossing and turning under three blankets. The first blanket covering the fitful globe was a primordial sea called "the deep." On top of this, helping to keep it warm, was a second blanket, a thick cloud of vapors and gases (Job 38:8-9; Ps. 104:5-9). These incredibly dense vapors did not let light penetrate down to the surface. Darkness lay heavily upon the face of the waters, for the atmosphere that covered them was thickly shrouded in vaporous mists (Gen. 2:4-6). So it was dark everywhere. And above the clouds another blanket had developed, a frozen layer of water that would surround the entire globe, enclosing it in a bubble of ice, called a firmament. When the Creator began his work, the earth was dark and nebulous. But it was there.

Dance of the Spirit

And the light would come. The Spirit of God was present, gusting freely in hurricane winds that danced across the face of the waters. The Creator was dancing in the dark. Soon he would draw the curtains aside and let the light in. The heavens that are mentioned here are not outer space, for birds will fly in it later. These heavens are the atmosphere, dense and nebulous, that lay heavily over the deep like a warm blanket. But the sky would soon become brighter, prefiguring the spiritual brightness that would shine to lighten the spiritual darkness later.

This first day was an archetype and a promise. God would employ basic, archetypal patterns right from the very beginning. The shades of night would be followed by times of light. First would come darkness, but the day would follow, always. First would come promise, then fulfillment. Events would prophecy. They would take the form of archetypes or patterns, and would be accomplished, for they were prophetic. Night followed by day would be one of these archetypes that God would employ everywhere. Darkness would be first, but it would give place to the light. God was painting in chiaroscuro. The darkness would create thankfulness in the hearts of those who would one day be enlightened. It was a portent, a foreshadowing of the true Light of the world (2 Cor. 4:6).

The second pattern was wrapped up in the first. Events would happen as types and figures of the future. The creation would bulge with promise. Past events would foreshadow future events. In the shadows would be hints and whispers of things that would be revealed in the light. This principle of prefiguring was another pattern that the master Creator employed from the beginning. The creation, as well as later events, would prefigure and point to God's ultimate plans and purposes. He would hint of the end right from the very beginning. Early things would be a foreshadowing of later things. The past would prophesy.

The archetypal creation of this world foreshadowed the new world that would come in the daytime of God's glory with the passing of the night and its shadows. This world of Genesis began in the dark, but the light of day soon broke in (Luke 1:78-79). Likewise, the true and greater day of the Lord would break in magnificent brightness with the passing of the night. The first days would foreshadow the last. First things would be promises that God would keep.

Yes, this first dark and shadowy world of beginnings would in time receive the sunlight at God's command, an event that prefigured a coming sunlight that would shine upon another darkness, a spiritual one. Genesis foreshadowed the day of Christ and the Gospel. Events of the first creation foresaw these greater marvels to come with Christ. And they will surely come. The events of Genesis are both meaningful and prophetic. God's word and action are inseparable. He speaks in pictures and events as well as in actual words. The events of the creation are prophecies, God's message for the future, showing the end from the beginning.

In these primal scenes, the Spirit was fluttering like a great bird, hovering over the earth, as if it were flapping its wings over the waters. Those powerful pinions fanned the dense atmosphere into unimaginably violent storms that whipped across the face of the wind-tossed deep. The gales of God pushed and pulled powerfully at the waters, gathering them into mountainous waves that rose and fell with uncontainable energy. The Spirit was moving over the wildly churning deep, dancing in the winds, zestfully twirling across the face of the waters. And within these sweeping, swirling, hurricane winds of creation was God's echoing voice (Gen. 3:8-10). He was expressing himself. He was himself changing with the earth, wet in the waters, whirling wildly in the winds.

Those sweeping gales were God's resounding command for the darkness to step aside and let the light enter (Eze. 37:9-14). Obediently, the mists would fade. As the dancing winds swirled and spun to the music of creation, the air would start to clear. This was not the beginning of light. It was already there. God's "Let there be light" meant that the light of the sun would begin to penetrate the mists. And soon the earth would awaken and peek out delightedly from under its blankets of clouds and water and would rise, getting ready to meet the coming daylight. Surprised and disgruntled at being set aside by the rising earth, the seas would huddle together as if to discuss the situation. Land and sea would be separated.

Nights and Days

The sunlight overhead quickly took advantage of its opportunity. It nimbly began to slip in between the dense clouds being whipped and torn by the mighty blasts of God's breath. But the darkness would not leave without a fight. It was slow and heavy, while the light was agile and quick. They were evenly matched. They fought endlessly, tirelessly, round after round after round. The match is still ongoing. They're still chasing each other around the orb of earth.

Importantly, the Bible does not say that the rounds of darkness and light were normal 24-hour periods. Hours had not yet been invented. No one wore a wristwatch yet. The Hebrew word for day (yom) means to be hot. The word for night (layil) means a twisting or twining. Neither of them means a 24-hour period. The earth was spinning, pirouetting around the sun. God and world were dancing. Were they slow dances? Were they fast?

A Very Slow Dance

The days of creation consisted of one period each of darkness and light. But the days are not ordinary. They are periods of unknown duration consisting of darkness followed by light. A day of creation consists of a period when things are inchoate and undeveloped, followed by their transformation into a new and different state of completion. This pattern or archetype of darkness before light, of latency followed by fruition, is important to remember. We can see it everywhere in God's handiwork and in his dealings with humanity. There's always darkness before light (Gen. 1:1-3). That's how our world began, and how it will end. The bright, effulgent radiance of God himself will chase away the present shadows (Rev. 21:23). Night precedes the day, always. First there is latency, then fruition. First there is prophecy, then fulfillment. There is Adam, and then the new Adam. There is the Old Testament, then the New. There is this world, and then the new world. This archetype is God's signature.

The text allows for an unspecified number of literal days within the sequence of events that constituted a day of creative development. We should understand the days of creation of which the Bible speaks not as ordinary days, but as unspecified periods of darkness followed by light in which new, purposeful changes occurred, always by divine expression.

The first days of Genesis are creation times, periods in which things were changed from what they were into what they became. They are not the absolute beginning of things. The days are long, giant strides toward colossal changes. They repeat the archetype that is manifested in all creation, which is darkness unto light, of latency unto realization, which constitutes one creative day (2 Tim. 1:10). This archetype is the way in which God works. It anticipates the Gospel. The days of creation, days of the past and of things physical, are hints and shadows of brighter days that would come, the days of the Gospel and of spiritual transformations.

But there is an even greater truth hinted at here. God's manner of creation reveals him. His handiwork bears his signature. His working in prefigurings and prophecies reflects himself. He is the Creator. And creation is change. He initiates change both in the world and in himself. Every change in the world is a change in the divine

Changer. The archetype includes the Creator himself! The consummation of this world's history will involve a change in him.

This is why Christ Jesus is called the Heir of God. He will be the end result and realization of God's metamorphosis. The creation's prefigurative nature tells us that he too is evolving. God, too, will be transformed! That's shocking and disconcerting, isn't it? But the truth of the Bible is that God is transforming into the fullness of Christ. He is both the subject and the predicate of the creation. The unchanging God of orthodoxy is not the God of the Bible.

The creation was his work toward a new self. He would have a new body, imbued with the Spirit. He was changing clothes, so to speak. He would dwell in a new temple. He is the Creator. And creation is transformation. In Christ, we are awaiting a new God!

The Seven Days

Because God works in archetypes, the days of creation hold important clues about the future. He repeats himself, in ever more marvelous manners. Since these first days of Genesis are the days of creation, they prefigure the days of the new creation, that began to lighten at Jesus' baptism, and that broke openly at Pentecost. Both Genesis and Revelation speak about seven days of creation. The new repeats the old in a new way. The creation is a poem that rhymes.

The seven seals in the book of Revelation speak in symbols about the days of the Gospel, the seven days of the new creation. These seven days of the Gospel correspond with the days of the first creation, which prefigured them. Genesis tells us about the Revelation, and vice versa. They rhyme with one another, and they sing, antiphonally. Events of the seven seals in Revelation are the fulfillment of that which the seven days of the first creation in Genesis prefigured. They are the light that follows the darkness, fulfillment of the promises hinted at in the beginning. And the last seven, the Gospel days of our lives, are not literal 24-hour periods. They're stages of development. That's what creation is. It is reorganization, and it takes time.

As should be expected, there is a rough correlation discernible between the two creations (Gen. 1:1-2:3; Rev. 6:1-11:19). For example, on the first day of Genesis, the Spirit was moving over the face of the waters as God called for light to shine upon the darkness, separating the two. In the first seal of Revelation, correspondingly, a rider goes out to conquer in the name of Christ. He rides in the Spirit to light the spiritual darkness, bringing a separation between believers and unbelievers, between the children of light and the children of darkness (Ps. 18:10; John 1:4-5, 9; 2 Cor. 4:6). In the first seal, as in the first day of Genesis, the Spirit moves over the dark and turbulent face of the waters, shedding light wherever it goes. In both Genesis and Revelation the Spirit is present, gusting and blowing (Acts 2:2; Rev. 6:13). The Creator is a master poet, and he works in parallelisms like Hebrew poetry.

The second day brings a separation of the waters, and the second seal correspondingly brings spiritual warfare, which is a separation between peoples, also called waters (Rev. 17:15). The separation is between the waters above, and the waters below. Then, the third day of Genesis brings the growth of vegetation, while the third seal talks of wheat, barley, oil, and wine provided daily to God's people (Rev. 6:5-6). Yes, the days of Genesis and Revelation rhyme, roughly but discernibly.

The fourth day is strange and mysterious. It's about rulership. The sun, moon, and stars appear on the fourth day, to rule over the day and the night, and to be for signs and seasons. During the fourth seal in Revelation Death and Hades are revealed as God's dread agents. They are given dominion over the fourth of the earth, which is a symbol of the Christian world of the End-time. That they are given dominion means that they ride under divine authority. Ever so subtly, what this fourth seal says is that heaven rules. Death and Hades, and the wild beasts of government, ride only by divine sanction (Rev. 6:8).

The moon and stars appear and rule after the sun has set. The sun is a symbol of Christ Jesus (Mal. 4:2). The moon and stars symbolize the saints. What we see here then is that Zion and the saints hold dominion after the Sun has set. This hints very subtly of the death of Christ and of those who follow him, followed by resurrection and dominion after death. The Gospel is hidden even here, in the fourth day of God's creative work.

On the fifth day, the waters and the air teem with living creatures under God's blessing. Correspondingly, in the fifth seal God's martyrs proliferate at the altar, the place of blessedness. Its lesson is again that God's blessing comes through death. There will be an abundance of souls teeming in the waters and in the air, in the world of humanity and in the world of the spirit. Salvation will be both physical and spiritual.

Then, on the sixth day, God makes humans in his own image. They prefigure him. Humans, too, will be changed in the new creation that will come. The first Adam will be changed into the second. In their creation God employs the same method that he uses in all his work, which is darkness before light. Then he sends them on their way, saving them through the Flood, which finalizes his work on the first creation. Correspondingly, during the sixth seal the end arrives, and God's creative work comes to an end, for the Gospel has run its course. A special, chosen group of humans have again been made into God's image and have entered into safety in the ark of salvation. They have passed through the flooding waters of humanity and have survived.

Finally, on the seventh day of Genesis, God rests. In the seventh seal, God finalizes his work as the kingdom of God arrives, and he begins his eternal rest. As these comparisons show, in some days the rhyming is not very close, and must be stretched somewhat. Like Hebrew poetry the correspondences between Genesis and Revelation are repetitive and rough, but discernible. They say the same thing in a different form. Give the days of Genesis a shave and a haircut, put a suit and tie on them, and they would look almost civilized. We could invite them over for supper. We could invite them to church with us.

Six Stages of Development

The days of the creation held unknown numbers of literal days. They were periods in which various creative developments occurred. A literal 24-hour day would seem to be too small to hold all the life forms jumping out everywhere. Normally, the trees would not only have had to flower and be fertilized, but then they would have had to produce their fruit, which would then have had to ripen, drop, be buried, and grow another tree that would itself repeat the whole process countless times. Did God create countless numbers instantaneously, or did he create a few of each kind so that they would proliferate? The text does not say. However, since God and the world were still One, it is entirely conceivable that the world could bring forth in countless numbers as well as in smaller groups. The same thing is true with respect to the grass and other vegetation, the fish, and the animals.

When Jesus healed the blind and raised the dead, it did not take years and years to happen. It was almost instantaneous. The apostle Paul says that we will be changed "in the blink of an eye" when the last trumpet sounds (1 Cor. 15:51-52). The new creation will appear almost instantly. Miracles recorded in the Bible did not take jillions of years. Likewise, the miracles of the creation did not need to happen over vast periods of time either. But how long did they take? The Genesis account clearly states that the miracles of creation happened in "days." Many interpreters take that to mean 24-hour periods. The account, however, does not specify a literal day. It just says that a day consists of a period of darkness followed by light. But we do not know exactly how long these periods were.

We must remember that Genesis deals with the transformation of the heavens and the earth into their present state. Creation ended when the heavens and the earth were formed into how they are today. At what point in the creation did this happen? To answer, we must look at the two accounts. In the first account, which begins at Chapter 1:1 and ends at Chapter 2:3, the earth is at first waste and empty (Gen. 1:1-2). This same emptiness is repeated in the second account (Gen. 2:5-6). Then the second account goes on to describe in greater detail those events that happened with respect to Adam and Eve and others during the sixth day. All that happens then up until the Flood occurs during the sixth day.

During this sixth day God created the animals. He created Adam and Eve. He formed every beast and every bird and brought them to Adam, who then named them all. God planted a garden in Eden, and put Adam there. He created Eve, who was enticed by the Serpent. They were cast out of the garden, and later had children. Their first child Cain built a city. Men began to multiply prodigiously, and lived for centuries. Fallen angels cohabited with human women. Noah built an ark. Then came the Flood, which ended that world and brought this world into its present condition. The heavens and the earth were finished (Gen. 8:22). And this all happened on the sixth day. From this we can see that the days of creation were longer than a single 24-hour period.

Did the birds and the fish reproduce each after its own kind in such prodigious numbers as to "swarm" in the air and in the seas in just one normal day (Gen. 1:20-21)? The creation was awesomely marvelous, but did it happen in just a few hours? The text says that God commanded the birds and the fish to be fruitful and multiply (Gen. 1:22). So their fruitfulness would reasonably be according to the nature of each. It was by natural processes. And they were in existence in prodigious numbers up until the Flood. Did God create just two of each kind, as when he brought the animals to Adam (Gen. 2:19-20)? The text does not say. But if the sixth day lasted for centuries, is it not reasonable to think that the plants, fish, birds, and animals came to proliferate over a long period as well?

The sixth day continued until God rested from his work of creation, when he then withdrew and the Sabbath began (Gen. 6:3). Up until the Flood, during the sixth day, humans had been multiplying. It took more than a few hours! And Adam died on the sixth day as God had warned, the day in which he ate of the fruit, and yet lived 930 normal years (Gen. 5:5).

Indeed, the whole period in which God made heaven and earth is called a day (Gen. 2:4). Clearly, the days of the creation were not literal 24-hour days, just as the seven days of the Gospel are not literal 24-hour days. Nevertheless, the days of creation follow the same pattern of darkness unto light, of a literal day. The pattern of night unto day beats like a metronome throughout the account. And it's still beating today.

When God was done, he rested. The Sabbath began. The Sabbath is a figure or foreshadowing of life in Christ. It is not just a day, but also a place of rest, prefigured by entering into the Land of Promise (Deut. 3:20, 12:9, 25:19). The true Land of Promise and of true rest, of course, is Christ (Heb. 4:1-10).

However, the creation was the transformation of a world that already existed. What was the world like prior to the creation? Was there some sort of cataclysmic event that made it "waste and empty?" Scientists claim that there were plants and animals long before humans came to exist. The Bible does not say. What it says is that, when God began the work, the earth was waste and empty.

The Earth already existed. When he separated the waters, they already existed. When he separated the land from the waters, they were already there. When he created the light, it already existed. The sun, moon, and stars already existed before the creation. Then, is it possible that when God "made" the plants, animals, and birds, they were already existent? Was the creation merely their proliferation or their re-emergence? Were the basic building blocks of life already present when God transformed the earth and sky? The text does not say. But neither does it deny this.

The Source of Light

The light had a source. Light in the abstract, without a source, does not shine in the days of Genesis. Nor does it illumine our hearts today. The creation was not a magic act. God himself called the light of the new creation the light of day, that is, of sunlight (Gen. 1:5). Should we contradict him? When God began to form our world the sun was already there, watching and waiting. The light of day was the light of the sun. God's creation of the heavens and the earth means that he transformed them into their present state. And the heavens of Genesis are the atmosphere, not outer space (Gen. 1:20). God had plans for the world. He would transform it so that it would accomplish those plans.

The original darkness was caused by dense clouds that kept the curtains of the sky shut tightly around the earth so that the sunlight could not enter. Now, under God's articulate winds, the sky was lightening. God was drawing the curtains aside, and the eager, virile light was entering and shining all around. Soon the steady march of literal days would break through. Sunlight would illuminate the darkness daily.

The clearing of the skies prefigured the future. The gales of the Spirit are blowing in our own day of the Gospel, chasing away the dense clouds of spiritual darkness, letting in the sunlight. The voice of the Spirit is sounding. God is drawing back the curtains of ignorance and false doctrine that cover our globe. He's illuminating the heavy hanging darkness with the fruit-bearing brightness of his truth. This great Sun of our salvation is shining his virile rays into our desolate world, and the earth is bringing forth the living beings, the children of God, made in his image. Yes, the Creator is even now calling forth the eternal daylight by the dancing winds of the Spirit (Luke 1:78-79). His voice can be heard sweeping across the face of the many waters. The Gospel is moving in the world through the word of God taking effect in the hearts of believers. The Spirit is moving in the world, bringing a new creation into being.

And with every new soul saved, God is changing. The Body is growing. With God, speaking is doing, as it is with him who is called the Word of God. In the beginning, this is how God must have spoken as well, expressing himself inaudibly but with power, within the changes that he was initiating. The creation was an expression of himself. And as he expressed himself, he changed. The word of God is powerful indeed. It creates its own truth. It happens because it is expressed. It is creative, for it is the expression of the Creator. Creation is what he does. It's his nature. The creation, this world, is the expression of God. He spoke it into its present state.

Building a Greenhouse

With the events of creation God was drawing pictures of the Gospel. At God's expressive and compelling word the waters began to separate, as if they were two peoples, children of this world below and the children of heaven above, two generations (Dan. 2:39-43). A great gulf appeared between the upper and lower waters. The lower waters still roiled and raged, but much less now, and gathered themselves into primeval seas. The upper waters blanketed the clouds, shivered, and froze into a bubble of ice enclosing the earthly globe high above the face of the deep. God had formed a greenhouse over his watery world. He was getting ready to plant. But he needed some good soil first. He needed a hotbed. The fields had to be readied for planting.

This ice bubble that encased the earth is also called a firmament (*rakiah*) as if it were something solid, hammered out and spread across the heavens like a sheet of gold beaten out by a divine hammer (Job 26:10, 37:18; Prov. 8:27-29; Isa. 40:22). Between the two bodies of water, in the expanse of atmosphere called heaven, the winds still twisted and turned as the Spirit swept across the foaming waves.

As we've noted, the Spirit is moving over the waters in our own day, speaking the words of the new creation that separate the nether waters from the upper waters, the living from the dead. It is happening today through the faithful preaching and dying of the saints (2 Cor. 5:20, 6:1).

That first greenhouse is gone. The great bubble that encircled the globe melted away and brought the great Flood as the work of creation came to a close. The windows of heaven opened, and poured out their contents upon the children of wickedness in the days of Noah.

But before the firmament melted, inside the greenhouse the earth was blanketed with warm, humid air. It was cloudy, but becoming ever more translucent. God called the ever-clearing expanse heaven. He was speaking his will into existence, eloquently, poetically, and prophetically, in the winds of creation. It was good. Yes, it was good. Life was about to emerge.

The Earth Comes to Life

As we approach the beginning of life on the Earth, we'll need to keep our shovel in hand. As we've seen, there's a lot of false tradition lying all around. That's okay. We'll shovel it out as we go. Just try not to get in the way of the shovel. Stay on the path. There will be some surprises along the way, so be ready.

The Pregnant Earth

The dancing and spinning was making the earth dizzy. It convulsed under the cataclysmic forces that surged and blew, reeling under the varying stresses and changes in temperature that were playing across its entire girth. It writhed and twisted, cooling unevenly. And it began to swell in places, pushing the land up into great mountains from under the waters, bulging as if the planet were pregnant (Ps. 104:1-9).

The surprised waters gathered themselves together as if to consult on how to push the upstart land back down (Gen. 1:9). But the land rose too high, even for those mighty waves. They could not cross the strong barrier of God's commanding word (Job 38:8-11). They must concede the territory. Their boundaries had been set. Later, in Noah's day, they would make one last, all-out effort to take back the land, but they would be driven away. The land would rise even higher, thrusting its mountain peaks upward into the atmosphere called heaven.

The land, for its part, was now progressively receiving the bright, penetrating rays of the sun. It pushed up from under the waters, emerging from under its warm blanket, stretching, delighted in its newfound freedom, basking in the sunlight. The earth bulged, and writhed in labor pains.

Then wondrously, at God's command the earth brought forth numberless varieties of plants. Vegetation everywhere pushed up from the ground looking for space and sunlight. Here we must clear away a large shovelful of tradition. Listen closely as the Bible speaks. It leans over to us, and tells us firmly and emphatically that the origin of plant life as we know it is the earth itself. The text says clearly, emphatically, unequivocally, that the earth itself produced a profusion of life, as God expressed himself (Gen. 1:11-12). The bulging earth was infused with the vitalizing, invigorating, living Spirit of God (Gen. 2:5-7; John 20:22)!

Now think carefully. If the earth gives birth to life, then the earth has to be alive, the earth itself, not just the plants and animals that emerged from it. Indeed, they draw their life from it even today (1 Tim. 6:13). God was expressing himself in the primordial winds (Eze. 37:9-10). He expressed himself through the waters as well, and in the land that now was so copiously birthing the herbs of the field, and the trees that would bear fruit each after their own kind. The Spirit-filled Word was everywhere, pulsing with life, expressing the will of the Creator in the stupendous changes that were happening (John 1:1-3). And it was good. How could it be otherwise?

God was not a drill sergeant looking down sternly from space and barking orders at the earth from a distance. He was in the thick of the action, immersed in the waters, blowing in the wind, and pushing up plants now from within the moist soil that was teeming with life and vigor. The whole earth everywhere was vibrantly alive with the Spirit of God. The music was loud, and the dance of creation was upbeat and jumpy. The Creator was in the groove, singing mellifluously within the processes of development, calling forth the six waves of creation.

And the earth was eager to comply with his directives. It gladly began the process of bringing forth new life forms to sprout up and grow upon it. The Scriptures tell us explicitly that life is the product of the earth (Jer. 23:24; Acts 17:24-28; 1 Tim. 6:13). The earth itself gave birth, and one day it will give birth again (Isa. 26:19, 42:5).

And this second birth, too, will be perfectly executed by the divine Word. It, too, will be the expression of God.

As this world evolves, the Creator is expressing himself, *ehyeh asher ehyeh* (Ex. 3:14). Because of the Creator's immanence in all things, the impassable chasm between living beings and the so-called inanimate world is a mirage of both orthodoxy and science. All living things extract their life from the earth. The plant kingdom is earth's offspring. Earth birthed the plants, and she sustains them. The living earth is of the very substance of God, torn from his side, as it were, and infiltrated by his life-giving Spirit (1 Kgs. 8:27; 2 Chron. 2:6; Ps. 139:7-12; Isa. 66:1; John 1:3-4; Acts 17:28). Since the Flood, the Spirit has been partially separated and differentiated from the world, but there will come a man fully re-infiltrated by the Spirit, who will begin the re-union of world and Spirit.

God's Expression

The text tells us that God spoke his will into existence. He expressed his plans and desires for the earth to bring forth the grass, and trees, and flowers. But we must remember that his speaking is an anthropomorphism, a metaphor for the creative expression of his very own self. He is the Creator, the Transformer. We mustn't think that he spoke with literal lips, or a literal mouth, exhaling from literal lungs through a pair of vocal chords. We must not make God into our own image. He spoke within the creative process itself. Creation was the Word of God expressed. The Word was God in the beginning, even as he is today (John 1:1). As the creation developed, it was through the very Word of God, the divine expression (Coll. 1:16-17; Heb. 1:3).

God did not hide in the invisibility cloak of silence. He spoke. He expressed himself, and the earth produced vegetation. The emergence of plant life was a giant step forward in God's metamorphosis. This is why it was good. It would lead to the Son, in whom the Father is well pleased, for he is very, very good.

Heavenly Bodies

As the atmosphere cleared, the heavenly bodies appeared. They had been there all the time, watching from the far regions beyond, hidden

True Beginnings

by the dense clouds that covered the world. The creation account speaks in the language of appearances, and describes events in metaphorical, human terms. The appearance of the sun, moon, and stars in the sky is exactly that. It's their appearance. Obviously, the stars cannot literally float in the atmosphere around the earth. But they can appear to be there. We still speak in this manner today. We say that the sun rises or sets, and that the stars come out at night. The wind blows, and lightning strikes. Lovers still stroll beneath the moon and look up at the stars, rather than sideways or down.

That is the sense in which the Bible says that God made the sun, moon, and stars, and placed them in the heavens. We remember that the heavens here are the atmosphere that covers the earth like a blanket, itself enclosed within a glasslike bubble of ice called the firmament. God did not place the luminaries and stars literally in the atmosphere. He "made" the sun, moon, and stars by clearing the air so that those luminaries could be seen. This is an account of how our present world was formed into its present state, not a story of how the universe came to be.

When the text says that God made the heavenly bodies and placed them in the sky on the fourth day, it means that he now made them visible from the earth. Had you been there, you could look up and see the celestial luminaries, yet dimly, through the frozen windowpanes of ice that encircled the globe. They are like mighty monarchs, each with its own kingdom and territory, the sun to rule the day, the moon to rule the night.

God expressed himself, and it happened. The winds still blew, softer now, as God spoke the divine will into existence. God was dancing on the waters, singing in the winds. And the ground was adding its strong base note to the music. The rhythms of creation were shimmying and shaking throughout God's growing world (Gen. 3:8). Even the stars, watching, could not help but tap their feet and sing with delight (Job 38:7).

Plant life was now present in profusion. Vegetation did not precede the sun. It was already there, throwing its penetrating rays at the Earth, peeking inquisitively into God's greenhouse. There was never the traditional nonsense of daylight before the sun.

God had called the light day, and the darkness night, when he had separated them, long before (v. 5). Evenings and mornings are normally the rounds of darkness and daylight chasing one another around the world. Normal, ordinary days are caused by the earth's rotation with respect to the sun. But these are not ordinary days. They are the earth-changing, heaven-clearing days of creation when life is bursting out all over the place. As the clouds cleared and opened the door wider and wider, more sunlight entered. The greenhouse was working as planned.

The days of creation were archetypal stages of development that followed this same sequence reflected in earth's relation to the sun. And they were shadows of the future. In the future, when earth evolves out of the present darkness into the eternal day, it will happen from its relation to the true Sun in the true heaven, already present above us, and watching. The pattern revealed in Genesis will be repeated. Its promises will be fulfilled.

The luminaries of Genesis are shadows too. Foreshadowing is the pattern and function of this world. It's the archetypal pattern. The present creation is a foreshadowing of the second. We're living today in a world of shadows, looking for the dawn of a new day. Our present world speaks prophetically and longingly of a better and brighter one. Always, the past speaks of the future, and says good things about it. The past is a prophet. The end is told from the beginning. The sun in all its brightness is a symbol of the great Sun of righteousness himself, who rules the day and shines his life-giving light into the world. Indeed, his glory is what makes the day. Like the earthly sun, he was already present when the days of our world began.

The moon is a figure of Zion, the kingdom of God that rules past death, staying up until the shining dawn of our salvation. And the stars also appear, symbols of the sons of God, the uncountable hosts of the saved, shouting joyfully at the delightful unfolding of God's awesome creation (Ezra 3:11; Job 1:6, 38:4-11; Ps. 19:1-6). What bliss awaits the saints when these foreshadowings are realized!

Fish and Birds

The next day brings with it teeming schools of fish and flocks of birds swarming everywhere, multiplying in the power of God's word of Spirit and life. Again, we are told that they originate from this planet itself. Life originates in the waters as in the land, abundant and vigorous. The waters, the air, and the land are alive, then, truly and wondrously alive. They are infiltrated by the very Spirit that causes existence and that gives life (Jer. 23:24; Acts 17:28). Schools of fish dart here and there in the waters. Birds trustingly cast themselves into the air's open arms, and the air faithfully catches them in its sustaining currents. This fifth day finds fish and fowl teeming upon the prodigal, life-giving earth.

They are fruitful, and multiply exceedingly, nourished and empowered by the Creator's Spirit-filled word of blessing (1:22). Like the grasses, trees, and flowers, they too hold within them the seeds of their own succession. They reproduce. They repeat themselves. The Creator likes patterns. He likes repetition, ever similar but never exactly the same. He's a poet.

As we've seen, he himself is included in the archetype of darkness to light, of shadow to fulfillment. He is changing from the prophetic, prefiguring God of the Old Testament into the full splendor of his revelation that is not yet manifested. And here, he made the world of living things to image himself, employing another pattern. In creating the living things, he placed one pattern within another. The new pattern here is that everything reproduces after its own kind. The creation rhymes. In the beginning, God was already hinting of the Son, the Seed of his own succession. God was revealing himself past, present, and future. The creation is a revelation of God (Ps. 19:1-3; Rom. 1:20). It is his confession, his "I AM THAT I AM."

Rise of the Animals

At God's word, animals pulled themselves up from the mire, wiped the mud off, and began to leap and crawl all over the land. These are not dinosaurs. They are the animals and creeping things of our world of today. Their ultimate origin was the earth. The account does not say how they came about. It neither affirms nor denies that they came about through a process of development. What it denies is Darwinian evolution. It affirms that all the land creatures in our world of today originated at the Creator's command and under his direction and control, in one day. It was through the expressed Word of God. This does not deny the existence of dinosaurs. It ignores them. It jumps over them across the boundless ages, and lands right here beside us. It tells us how the world of today came to be as it is.

Throughout the creation account, the Bible never goes into minute detail. It paints with a giant's brush, broad, sweeping strokes. Its emphasis is on pattern and process, on sequence and development. It repeats the archetype of darkness unto light that constitutes a day, of pregnancy unto birth, of latency unto fruition. Its accent is on the createdness of life, which means that life originated in a process of development at God's command through his purposeful generative expression. And significantly, it arose from the earth itself.

This shows that God was immanent within the creation. He is not an alien in outer space looking down on the world. He is within it, of it, and changing with it (Acts 17:28). The proposal that God created from afar by fiat, as if speaking as humans do, misunderstands the divine origin of the earth and the nature of creation. It misunderstands how God speaks. Speaking does not require lungs, lips, and tongues. Do not our telephones, radios, and televisions speak to us?

The biblical accounts explicitly, emphatically, and repeatedly present the creation as the stepwise, progressive changes that God was causing to occur in the earth as he expressed himself. The creation was God's Word becoming reality. God does not remain silent. He speaks within the processes of change. And he never gets in too much of a hurry. He takes his time, and does things the right way.

However, the process did not happen as the Darwinists would have us believe. We don't know how long the creation took, but we have a hint of it in the creation of Eve. Her creation did not take millions of years! Neither did the creation of Adam take millions of years. Adam lived 930 normal years. His first son was born when he was 130 years old. We can be absolutely certain that the creation of Eve is less than that. The creation of our world was not the long, drawn-out chain of affairs that scientists would have us believe.

Creation is transformation. It happened stepwise at God's command and under his control. Because all things are created, everything has arrived on the highway of change. The Bible does not say how long it took the animals to arrive, except that it happened in one creative day, the sixth. And that day was centuries long.

The creation account is how our world, as we see it today, came about. The days of creation were not literal 24-hour periods. They were epochs that followed the archetype of darkness unto light, of latency followed by fruition. It was a long, stretching parade of literal days rumbling down the road like motorcycles coming to a rally, each adding to the roar of creation that God had begun. And the loudest and best was still to come. But it wasn't billions of years. Our world as it exists today is not that old.

The true theory of creation is totally rational. Scientists reject the biblical account of creation because the mainstream, traditional churches have misunderstood it and have told them the wrong story. On the other hand, Christians properly reject the Darwinian theory of evolution because the scientists have told them the wrong story as well. Their theory of God-less evolution, of inert matter coming magically to life all by itself, and then of one life form magically changing into another, has no basis whatsoever in reality. There are no intermediate species, child. There are no links, no, not a single one. Darwinian evolution is a chain with no links. There is no chain. It's a theory with no evidence. Godless evolution, and creation from nothing, are both of them unbiblical and wrong.

Importantly, the Bible says clearly and emphatically that God commanded the earth itself to bring forth living creatures, and it obeyed. The earth itself gave birth, at God's command. The process was not Godless. Neither was it the Darwinian hooey of countless minute changes.

Biblical creation and divinely guided transformation are one and the same. The words are like John Paul Jones. Whether you call him John or whether you call him Paul, it's the same person. If you send John away Paul goes with him. To deny that creation is transformation is to deny the Scriptures. And it denies the true Creator. Is it not silly to deny creation while trying to prove the existence of a Creator? In our striving to disprove ungodly evolution, we must not deny Scripture. What we must deny is the God-less so-called scientific theory of evolution. Churchmen and evolutionists exchange volleys across one another's bows, thinking to score direct hits. But they never connect. Each is mistaken, and thinks that the other party is the one in error. It's silly. And it's tragic.

The animals originated from the same earth from which the plants had emerged. They came from the earth. And when they die, they return to it. This is the manner in which God creates, developing new things from already existent things. And it takes time. Creation was a process. It had to be. Even instant oatmeal takes a minute or two to prepare. And our world is certainly more than a bowl of cereal.

Creation, not Evolution

The Human Creature

The Bible says that God created Adam from the ground, and Eve from Adam. Again, the exact process is not given. No one knows how he did it. Let me repeat. No one knows how he did it. The record says only that Adam was created from the dust of the earth, and that the other animals were created from the dust of the earth too, all on the same day. It doesn't say that Adam came from the other animals. It does say, though, that he was one of them. Adam and Eve were animals (Gen. 2:7, 7:15, 22). Yes, child, they were animals. And you and I are their offspring!

With Adam, creation was still occurring. The Sabbath had not yet arrived. God was not yet finished. He would not rest until he had created a woman. Correspondingly, he will not rest until he has created a Bride for himself from the greater Adam's side. He will absolutely finish the new creation. The Bride of Christ will be fully formed before God rests in the eternal Sabbath. Isn't that reassuring?

In a special creative event, God put Adam to sleep, and created a bride from his side. God took special interest in the origination of Eve. She prefigured the Church and Zion (Eph. 5:31-32). Her offspring would be Jesus would be called Christ. Perhaps it took only a few minutes, or perhaps a few hours, or just a few seconds. The text does not say.

Her formation from Adam was a typology looking backward over her shoulder toward the Creator, from whom the world originated. Just as Eve was separated from Adam, the world was separated from God, for they were made in his image. It also looked forward, since she was the prefiguring of the Church. The creation of Eve was a skillful brushstroke on the portrait of God's self-revelation. She was part of the divine image, and a hint of the coming light. As prefigured in Eve's reconciliation with Adam, reconciliation with the world into one Body will complete God's intention for the world.

That is why the Spirit became flesh, human flesh, in the great, great, great, great, great, great, great—etc.—grandson of Adam.

It is interesting that God created humans, ancestors of the Son, from the earth on the same day that he directed the earth to bring forth the other living creatures. A living creature, or living soul as some Bibles have it, is merely an air-breathing animal. That's all. And that's all Adam was, an air-breathing animal, like the other beasts and the birds (Gen. 1:20-21, 24). Until the creation of Eve, there is no indication that God created Adam in a process different than the way he created the other living creatures (Gen. 2:19). But Eve came from Adam, just as the true Church comes from Christ Jesus. Adam sprang from the soil and water of the planet, breathing its air and eating its fruits and veggies. He was dust, like the other animals, and to dust he would return, like them (Eccl. 3:19-20). Adam shared the same origin and life as the rest of God's very motley menagerie. The breath of life in his nostrils was the same as that of the other beasts (Gen. 6:17, 7:15, 22).

And he would share the same destiny, were it not for the marvelous plan that the Creator had in mind. God had a special destiny lined up already for the line of animals called humans. With the passage of time would come one who would not pass away with time. He would fully share the nature of the Creator himself, as well as that of Adam.

The Breath of Life

Our shovel has been handy. Here, we'll need to use it again. Adam shared many biological characteristics with the other animals. One of these shared characteristics, as we've mentioned, is the breath of life (Gen. 1:30). All the animals and birds are living souls, every one of them, those that chew the cud as well as those that chew tobacco (Gen. 1:20, 24). In this, Adam was not unique. He shared the same spirit of life as they did, the very same one. That's what the Bible says, however much orthodoxy may rant and rave (Eccl. 3:18-21). Yes, we are animals, pilgrim.

Then what sets humans apart? Among other things, God gave Adam imagination and the capacity for language. And he gave him the Law. With these came the ability to envision abstractions, to anticipate and plan. He could create possibilities in his mind, and then put them into effect. Like the Creator, he could create! He could empathize, and therein share in another's thoughts and feelings. Adam was free to make choices. When the time came, his offspring would be capable of freely receiving Christ, and sharing the Gospel message. Their speaking would then become the power of creation. The image in Adam would find its fruition. Adam would be like God! He would know good and evil (Heb. 5:14).

God is the Creator. His word is creative. It makes things happen. It is truth even when it speaks of the future. This is why he calls his saints to speak the truth. Speaking the truth images God. We must learn to speak the truth past, present, and also future, like God. We must not hide in the silence. Indeed, our speaking can be creative, when coupled with the power of faith. Speaking the truth of the Gospel involves all of this. In proclaiming the Gospel the saints image God. Prophecy spoken in the Spirit is creative, for it will certainly come to pass. God's plans for his children set them apart from the rest of the menagerie. We are to be a complement for God, as Eve was for Adam.

God gave Eve to Adam, torn from his side, a being responding to him who shared his nature and who yet was differentiated from him. Together they were Adam's completion and fullness. And they imaged their Creator. God had a special role for them. Their race would culminate in Christ Jesus. That's what set them apart and made them special. And it's why God called the creation so very good.

The Plural God

We can all shake hands and agree that Adam and Eve were made in the image of God. That's clear enough. But did Adam have three heads? He and Eve were of the same flesh, and metaphorically, prefiguratively, became one body again after their separation (Gen. 2:24). Two separate human beings were counted as one. The two together are called Adam. They were a composite oneness. The Creator, then, must be a composite Oneness. And if you count the spirit in Adam and Eve, they are three. Is God a Trinity, as the churches claim?

Without their spirit, both Adam and Eve would have been zombies. They would have been non-persons. Each was composed of a body and a spirit. If you count their spirits, they would have been four, not three. Take away either their body or their spirit, and the individual is gone. Adam and Eve were only two persons, not three. And together they were counted as one, imaging God.

The two of them being counted as one flesh foreshadows not the Trinity, but rather the oneness of Christ and the saints. They foreshadow the oneness between God and the creation when the world will be reconciled back to God. When this happens, again they are not counted as two, or three, but as one. Body and Spirit together will constitute the oneness of God. It's a composite oneness. God's oneness in fact hints of the Gospel. The word (*echad*) by which he is identified in the Shema, in the "Hear, O Israel," has its root in the idea of uniting or gathering together (Deut. 6:4).

Like Adam, God was originally one Person, composed of Body and Spirit. Because of that complexity, of that duality of Body and Spirit, he could speak of himself as "Us." When he separated the world from himself in the process of creation, this plurality was made even more manifest. After the creation he would be juxtaposed with the world, face to face with it, two entities that shared commonalities and who yet were separate and different from one another. Body and Spirit had been differentiated. But they were complementary, each to the other. In Christ, they will come together again (Eph. 1:22-23, 4:15-16; Coll. 1:18). The world is an Eve being prepared for her eagerly waiting Husband.

God's plural invitation to create humanity in "our" image actually prefigures the Gospel call. God invites us to work with him in creating the new man in his image. This is the saints' present labor of love. The new creation is a joint effort. The saints are working together with God in creating the bright new world of tomorrow by preaching and witnessing in the Spirit. Eden's foreshadowing scenes of long ago will find their fulfillment in the bright sunlight of the long-awaited morning. And the day will linger, lovingly, as long as the divine Sun shines his everlasting light. Doesn't that make you want to jump and shout? Go ahead. Do it. I'll wait.

Then God Rested

On the seventh day, God rested from all his work on this first creation. It was finished. This model world was done. The prototype looked good. So he placed it proudly above his worktable, and began preparations to build an even better one, modeled after the first. It would follow the same pattern, but would be much better, with the kinks all ironed out. The new world would be free from sin and rebellion. In fact, he would use the material from the old world to build the new one. No need to let it go to waste. He could recycle it. That's how God creates. He recycles things. Creation is a re-cycling.

God's rest means that creation is not happening in this present world. Scientists look for it in vain. This world is finished. However, God is not idle. He's creating a new world. And it too will not arise from nothingness. Creation is change, not magic. Believers are being converted into a new creation as we speak. The winds of creation are blowing over the face of the waters. God is creating new life made in his image (John 20:22). He is breathing the breath of life into whoever receives him!

God once spoke through the creative, divinely expressive winds of the Spirit. His Spirit now speaks through his faithful people. Their Spirit-filled testimony in word and deed is the mighty breath of God, the voice of many waters powerfully calling forth the longed-for glories of the new world now being formed in the Son. Their message is Christ, the growing fullness of God. God once more is expressing himself, and the new creation is taking form. The saints are co-creators with God!

Creation is happening all around us. The new world is evolving and taking form in our own era. The seven days of the Gospel will run their course during this original Sabbath of God's rest, which began when God finished his creative work on this world. Because he's still resting from that labor, but working on the new creation, we're living in that original Sabbath, which has endured since the seventh day of Genesis began. This first Sabbath will go on forever.

This present Sabbath has its echo in the seventh seal of the Revelation (Rev. 8:1-11:19). The seventh seal holds seven days within it, hinting that the present Sabbath in which we are living holds the seven Gospel days. Joshua's seven-day siege of Jericho pictures the current Sabbath as well, in which the seven days of the Gospel happen (Josh. 6:1-5). On that last day, the seventh, Israel marched seven times around Jericho. The seven occur within the seventh. So there is strong evidence that the seven days of the Gospel run during this present seventh day in which God is resting from the original labors of creation. It is strong evidence, as well, that the seven days of the first creation were not short 24-hour periods. The seventh day of Genesis holds within it the seven days of the Gospel, as well as the untold numbers of ordinary days that have come and gone. We're now living in the original Sabbath of this world, preparing to make the jump into the next world. True Christians are high-jumpers.

God sanctified this long-lingering day from the other six days of creation by setting it apart. Holiness consists in the manner in which a thing is treated, not in something that infiltrates a thing. God hallowed the seventh day by treating it differently from the other days. We must keep it holy in the same way, by resting along with God from the works of this creation. Whoever does not rest in Christ is profaning God's Sabbath, which began at the Flood. The true lesson of God's Sabbath is not indolence. Work is not somehow evil. The lesson of the Sabbath is a call to cease with God from the dead works of this dying world. It's already created. It is finished. Why should we continue to work on it? The Sabbath day is a call to holiness, to separation from this world. It's a reflection of the Sabbath that began when God rested. And it foreshadows a greater rest, a greater holiness. It foreshadows the faith-rest in Christ.

It's not an excuse for laziness. Work is not evil, but laziness is not righteousness or godliness. God is still working (John 5:17, 6:29). It's just that he's no longer working on the prototype. He's now working on the new world. The Sabbath is a time to rest from the things of this world, in order to place our full attention and energies in helping build God's new project. God has called us to rest with him in the Sabbath of this world, but also to work with him in this new endeavor.

The flesh will be rejoined with the Spirit. The world will be reconciled with its Creator. God's invitation draws its arms around the saints, and gathers them in to his Sabbath of rest. They must keep this ongoing Sabbath holy by dedicating it to creative worship. True worship is to serve God in Christ in the new creation. That is their holy, priestly service. It is lawful for God's priests to work on the Sabbath. Indeed, work on the new creation is their sacred duty and their sacrosanct privilege.

The Sabbath of Genesis, then, is not a literal 24-hour day. It's the time in which we are now living. We can see, then, that the other six days of the original creation were not literal 24-hour days. They were periods of night followed by day, recurrent archetypes or patterns.

Work on the new creation, like the original that foreshadowed it, will involve six days or time periods too. The Gospel will run for six days. They are periods of darkness followed by light. They are times of transformation. And purposeful transformation, we remember, is creation. The Gospel times are creation times.

The sixth day of the Gospel will continue until the birth of the new world in all its magnificence. The true and greater seventh day will then burst out openly from the present darkness into the dazzling brightness of eternal light. It will watch, ecstatically, as the saints make the jump from this world into the glories of the higher estate. The coming eternal Sabbath is eternal rest in Christ from the restrictive and moribund things of this present world. It will be life set free to live in the divine creative expression. We will be holy because he is holy.

But what, exactly, is this holiness to which we are called?

Chapter Six
Seeds of the Future

Creation did not end when Adam and Eve were formed, during day six. God wasn't quite done. He didn't just walk away when he had formed the primal couple. History had to lead to Christ. God had a marvelous future in mind. Human history must develop according to the Creator's design and desire. Nothing must turn it aside.

Day six was coming to a close, and God still needed to make a few minor adjustments on his world, and on the human couple. Like a skilled photographer, he must carefully pose the human couple. The different poses would be foreshadowings, lessons for generations yet unborn. Human history must continue as he had planned, and yet with the utmost of artistic license.

World history is a play that's already written, but only the broad outlines of the plot are given, and it has very few stage directions. It consists mostly of ad-libs. The actors and musicians pretty much make up their lines and the music as they go along. They must improvise freely. But the main theme cannot be changed. The divine Playwright has written it into the script. The theme of all history is the glory of God in Christ. He will be the star of this epic presentation. Every actor and actress, every stagehand, all the musicians and singers, the dancers, everyone everywhere must further this main theme.

Themes and Preludes of History

So, even after he had created Adam and Eve, the Creator continued to walk among the trees in his garden, planting seeds of destiny. These flowers of the future would grow and reproduce profusely, each after their own kind. Some of them are still growing even today. When fully mature, they will fill the Creator's garden with the perfumed fragrance of Christ. One of the loveliest of these budding blossoms is the sweet rose of holiness. But he did not plant it until the six days of creation were at an end. He needed to wait until the last moment, just prior to his leaving. It would be the final planting.

Holiness would be his departure. It would come at the end of the sixth day, and would begin his rest. Holiness would happen as he walked away from the world, when the work was done. It would be his sanctification. He would leave for three days. Holy, holy, holy is the Lord. But the sweet flower of holiness could not be planted until the Creator was finished posing the primal couple exactly right.

Holiness

In the Old Testament, holiness meant to be separated from the ordinary course of life unto a special place or role. For example, the temple utensils were holy because they were set aside for use only in the temple service. Any other use was prohibited. They had no special power infiltrating them. They could not dance and sing, or dip by themselves. The spoons, lavers, and tongs of the temple held no magic. They were holy by being dedicated to their special use in the temple. They were treated in a special way.

Likewise, the temple itself was holy. Nevertheless, it had no power of its own. It was just a building. Like the utensils, it could not dance and sing either. Its holiness consisted in its special usage, separated from the ordinary and mundane unto the service of God.

The nation of Israel was called to be a holy people too. Their holiness was their special place, unique among the nations, in service to God, and his special presence among them. God dwelt in a special way in their midst. Unlike the temple and the utensils, however, they could dance and sing. But their song and dance tended to be not very holy.

The name of God was holy as well, but not because its sounds or letters held any special power. It is not magical. Nor is the name of Jesus a magical incantation (Acts 19:13-17). God's name was holy because the people did not pronounce it in vain, dishonestly, or jokingly. It was separated from ordinary, everyday usage. They kept the name of God holy by the special, extraordinary way in which they treated it.

That is how the literal, normal seventh day of the week in Israel was holy. It held no special power, no magic. Like every other day it

Seeds of the Future

was sometimes sunny, sometimes cloudy. The birds did not sing lovelier on Saturday. The flowers did not bloom brighter. It was and is just an ordinary period of darkness followed by daylight. Its holiness consists in the manner in which people treat it. They must keep it holy by desisting from ordinary work and dedicating it to the service of God.

Likewise, God sanctified the seventh day of creation and made it holy by resting in it, thereby treating it differently than the others. He did not instill any magic into it. He made it holy by resting from his work. Saturday follows the pattern set by the seventh day of creation, nothing more and nothing less. Israel was called to treat it holy by treating it differently than the others. That difference is what its holiness consisted of.

And surprisingly to some, even God's holiness is not a power. It means that he is set apart from this world. The Spirit was separated from the Body at the Flood, when Gods' work was done. His separation from this world is the true holiness of God. He is set apart so that he can work on the new creation. He quit one job to take another. We must be holy like him, separated from the things of this world. We, too, must quit our old jobs, to work on the new one.

We cannot overemphasize this. God is no longer working on this creation. It's finished. Been there, done that. He's working now on building his new Body. God is a bodybuilder. The true Sabbath is not abstention from work. Laziness isn't holiness. Holiness is rest from the works of this world in order to work on the new one. The Sabbath is upon us. We were born in it. We were born to rest. Let's get busy, then, and rest with God while working on the new creation.

God's true rest, of course, is in Christ (Heb. 4:1-11). We must keep the Sabbath holy by resting from our worldly labors, while working in Christ. God's day of rest is not a literal, 24-hour day that follows Friday. Nor is it a time of indolence. It's the peace and quietness of faith. It's salvation by grace. Most of all, it's oneness with Christ, which is literal separation from this world. Whoever does not rest in Christ is breaking God's true Sabbath, however lazy they might be on Saturday, or Sunday, or any other day. In Christ, we have work to do. We are co-laborers with God, working together on a most magnificent temple never before seen by human or angel eyes (1 Cor. 3:9).

Israel's Role

When God ordered Israel to keep the seventh day holy, it was not because the day had any special power or character, then. There is no special perfume called "holiness" blowing in the wind of the seventh day. Smog fills the air as much on Saturday as it does on Monday, or any other day. Nor did Israel have any special power to inject into the day. It meant that they should rest from their usual and ordinary work routine, like God, and dedicate the day to his service. And this was because God had rested on the seventh day of creation. They were to follow God's example. Child, they were to be like God!

Like little children, they would put on their Father's hat, big as it was, and his shoes, big as they were. In keeping the Sabbath, they would do as their Father did. They would be like him. Yes, Israel was to be like God! They would image him in holiness. Israel, too, like Adam and Eve, was an image of God. And that prefigurative image looked forward to Christ Jesus, who is the true image of God (Coll. 1:15). And astoundingly, the saints share in that true image. They are the true Israel, his true firstborn, meant to be like God (Ex. 4:22). In Christ, the saints too become the true image of God. They become holy, separated from this world like he is.

The Law, being a shadow, was a clear hint that God's people should become like him. It hinted of the Gospel. The Law, like the creation itself, was prefigurative. It ever pointed to Christ. In Christ, it has become reality. The whole religious system of sacrifices and offerings, of kings and prophets, all God's dealings with them showed that God's plan was for humans to become like him. They were to become a godly, holy nation, a living testimony of the Creator. But here too, as in Adam, the image in Israel was not in their genes. The Law was not a lesson in biology. It was Typology 101. They were an anticipation of God's true Israel.

Like Adam and Eve, Israel was to become like God in their knowledge of good and evil as well (Gen. 3:22). This meant knowing what was and what was not his will, and it was presented to them in the Law. Obeying the Law meant doing God's will, which is good. And of course God's will is Christ. The Law was a prefiguring of Christ. Disobeying meant not doing God's will, which is evil, and symbolized that which is not of Christ. When, like Adam, they broke the Law, it symbolized a rejection of Christ. Then, centuries later, when they literally rejected him for Caesar, they were themselves rejected. The foreshadowings in the Law were fulfilled.

The Law, and their knowledge of good and evil through it, was just a shadow of the true knowledge of God's will. The true knowledge of his will, and of that which is not his will, is gained through the inner voice of the indwelling Spirit. In the Old Testament, knowing good and evil meant knowing the Law. But it was just a shadow of knowing Christ, who is the Law's fulfillment, and the good and perfect will of God.

This is of extreme importance. The Jews were figures. They were foreshadowings. Israel was a re-run of Adam, a second witness. And like the primal couple, they did not keep the Law, and so they were cast out of God's presence. The only way back into Paradise is to get past the flaming sword of God's Word of truth. They too, like Adam and Eve, were given the Law in order to show them their spiritual nakedness, and their need of a Savior, a Messiah. The Law would point them toward him. So, what happened?

They missed the point, being blind to the Law's typological character. God's commands became ends in themselves, dead ends. They became morality plays. Complying with the rules, they thought, was all God expected of them. So they played the role, perfunctorily. They recited their lines, and nothing more. They could read the words, and memorize great chunks of them, but their eyes were closed to the pictures. They missed the underlying meaning of the Law. So, when the word was fulfilled, they crucified him.

Like the churches of today, whom they foreshadowed, they meticulously investigated every verse. They saw every tree up close and magnified, but missed the forest. They killed the sacrifice, but did not partake of it. Even though they looked eagerly for his coming, they were ill-prepared to meet their Holy One when he came. Instead, incredibly, they crucified him on the false charge of blasphemy for claiming oneness with their holy God. They crucified the one endowed with the true knowledge of good and evil. And so they lost their special place within God's favor. They were cast out, and lost their holiness.

And appallingly, they were foreshadowings of Christianity. The churches of the End-time, the prideful new Israel, blinded with orthodoxy like their older sister, will commit the same abomination. They will kill the true saints for claiming to be the divine Children of

God, co-heirs with Christ and participants within the Godhead. Despite their aims and claims to the contrary, the churches of Christianity still hold humanity firmly separated from God. Their Gospel is of salvation into God's presence only. They stop short of fusion within the divine nature itself, keeping humanity forever separate from God. Holiness then becomes separation from the world but also from God. And, like the Jews of Jesus' day they think they are doing well and honoring God as they wait for their Messiah. But keeping humanity separated from God is the work of Satan, the anti-God principle. When Jesus returns, it will be judgment and condemnation upon Christianity, not blessedness, just as it was for the Jews earlier with Christ's first coming.

The Uniqueness of Humanity

In disobeying God's Law, Adam showed the incapacity of ordinary, self-centered humans to do God's will. Humans ever seek to do their own will. Because of this inability, this innate self-orientation, the human animal is not suitable for service in the divine Body. To demonstrate this, to open his eyes to his inadequacy, Adam was told not to eat from a certain tree. It was likewise with Israel. They were given the Law for the same purpose, to demonstrate the incapacity of ordinary humans to keep it. They too, like Adam, disobeyed.

But unlike Adam, this did not open their eyes. They kept them tightly closed, thinking that this showed them to be faithful. Because of Israel's incapacity to do God's will, they are unsuitable for the Body and cannot live forever. Judaism must surely die, in the day they eat of the tree. The tree in Eden was a figure of the cross, and this other tree brought the death of Judaism. Nevertheless, the Jews will one day receive Christ. But in doing so, they must die with him. That's what baptism in the Spirit means. It means death with Christ, in order to live with him (Rom. 6:3-6).

In Eden God had planted a garden full of good trees and pleasant. In his garden were two special trees that prefigured the cross. The fruit of one tree would give eternal life. Notably, however, Adam never ate from it. The lesson was that humanity would not live forever. His race would perish. Eternal life was not for carnal humans, the servants of the Serpent. Animals, even those we call

Seeds of the Future

humans, even those we call Jews, are not the inheritors of heaven. Adam must be clothed upon with Christ. He must receive a new nature. The old nature must be shed.

The fruit of the other tree was the knowledge of good and evil. But in the day that Adam ate of it he would surely die. And we know the rest of the story. He ate, and he died. The problem is, he lasted several hundred years after he ate, before he died. Did God lie to him?

No. As we saw earlier, the days of Genesis are not literal 24-hour periods. Adam ate the forbidden fruit on the sixth day. That's when he lived, and that's when he died. He was created on the sixth day, and he died on the sixth day, hundreds of years later. Put that in your hat.

It also meant that the human race, prefigured by Adam, will not outlive the sixth day of the present Gospel times. Fulfilling Adam's destiny, humanity will surely die on the day it partakes of Calvary's tree. But, as in Eden, the day is not a literal 24-hour period. It's the day of the Gospel, of the cross, and it has gone on for over two thousand literal years. Adam's shadow is long indeed. It reaches all the way to the end of human history. Eden's forbidden tree portends death to carnal humanity. Take that to heart, dear one. Adam will surely die. The race will go out of existence. Humanity is heading toward extinction. Star Trek is pure imagination, nothing more. Sorry.

Adam would die like the rest of the animals. But he was unique among the beasts because he was given the Law. He had the choice of obeying or disobeying. To obey meant doing God's will, which was good, and to disobey meant doing evil. By disobeying, he came to know the difference between good and evil. It was not a fall. It was knowledge gained. That bears repeating. But, we won't. Just remember it. Adam understood now that good meant doing God's will, which would produce his wellbeing. Good was God's will, revealed by the Law, while evil meant disregarding it, and getting into trouble, big trouble. But he didn't fall. Well, I repeated it, anyway. It's important.

This tree too, like the tree of life, was symbolic. Good and evil revolved around God's word, foreshadowing the Word. Obeying it meant good, while disobeying it meant evil. It foreshadowed the tree of Calvary (Heb. 5:14). To eat the fruit of the cross means to receive the Spirit, and then to know God's will directly, inwardly, as the Word dwells in us. It means to acquire the true knowledge of good and evil. Good, we recall, is God's will, while evil is that which is contrary to his will. Receiving Christ is the only way to gain the true knowledge of good and evil. It does not come by obeying the Law of Israel.

By the way, we do not learn evil when we receive Christ. It is inherent in our nature as humans. What we learn is the distinction between good and evil. We are naturally self-oriented and ever seek to do our own will. We consider our own lusts and desires to be good. We learn the true good, which is the will of God, only by denying ourselves and receiving Christ. It opens our eyes to our true character, which is ever inward-oriented, ever seeking to do our own will. That is the true evil, humanity's basic and universal problem, for in doing our own will we reject God's will. We cannot serve two masters.

This is the bedrock reason to receive Christ. It makes us acceptable for the Body. In receiving Christ we learn to do God's will, and to deny ourselves. At least, that's what we should learn. Self-service, then, is the true evil. We must understand that human nature itself is the Serpent. In serving the self rather than Christ, we serve the Serpent!

Upon receiving Christ we begin to walk in the Spirit, which teaches us to do God's will rather than our own. It's a walk in holiness, of separation from the things of this world. True evil is to walk in the flesh. You can tell where someone's been walking by looking at the soles of their shoes. Same thing with a church. Has she been walking on holy ground, like she claims? What's all that humanism, then, all over her shoes? Why do we need a shovel to walk through the churches?

When we partake of the fruit of the cross, we become like God. We become images of him, knowing true good and evil (Gen. 3:22). We become his children, and share with the Son in his nature, yes, the nature of God (2 Peter 1:4). The tree in Eden spoke of the tree just outside of Jerusalem, and in Paradise.

Partaking of the fruit of the cross entails death to the carnal man. It requires a denial of the pleasures of human carnality, of service to the self, which is the Serpent. The health and wealth Gospel comes straight from the Serpent's mouth, then, dripping with true evil.

Denying self-denial, it promises and encourages abundant life in the flesh, claiming the cross as its basis, as if the cross were an invitation to hedonism. It makes of the cross an excuse for Serpent worship! And it implicates God in its blasphemy. It is humanism. But the true Gospel is a call to take up the cross. Its focus is heaven, not this world. Humanism is rebellion, the refusal to keep this present Sabbath holy. It's a rejection of true holiness.

To receive Christ means that we surely die with him, in order to surely live with him. The Law was given to Adam in order that humans could come to know God's will, which is good. At first this knowledge, being through Law, was shadowy and prefigurative, awaiting its fulfillment in Christ (Gal. 3:24-27). Knowledge of God's will came according to the universal archetype, of night before light. At first, it was dark. God's mysteries had not yet been revealed. Now the daylight of understanding has come. The fruit of the cross is delicious and good, and able to make one wise. But the warning still sounds, that it involves death. We must each take up our own cross.

Receiving Christ is not a fall, however, just as there was no fall in Eden. It is the doorway into true knowledge of good and evil. The movement of creation guided by God is ever forward and upward. Adam did not fall backwards. He opened his eyes. It was a step toward Christ. The divine Photographer was posing his subjects in such a way that they would prefigure Christ Jesus (Heb. 5:14).

The pair from Eden was unique and different from the other animals by their capacity to know God's Law, that is, God's will. Correspondingly, reception of the Spirit of Christ makes believers different from other humans. It makes them special. It makes them holy, partakers of the divine nature like Jesus, and able to know the will of God, directly and personally. The knowledge of true good and evil makes us like God, images of our Father (Gen. 3:22). That's shouting ground! The desire to be like God is not evil, child, so long as it goes beyond imitation. True godliness is expressed only by God. To be truly godly, you must have Christ within you, and let him live through you. True holiness is never apart from Christ. We are holy only because he is holy within us (1 Pet. 1:16).

Godliness is the purpose for which humans were created and for which they are saved. Adam was purposely posed in God's image and likeness, in a pictographic, foreshadowing way. He was a precursor of Christ. Adam and Eve were given dominion over the other creatures, and the children of God are correspondingly given dominion over the whole of God's new creation (Heb. 2:5-8). The teaching of Genesis, not understood until the coming of Christ, is that humans are unique from the other living creatures in their capacity to become children of God, and to know then God's will (John 1:12; Eph. 5:17). Adam, Israel, and humanity in general may have access to God's Law not because it holds authority over everyone, but so that we can recognize our need for a new, holy nature capable of doing God's will rather than our own. The Law is meant as a lesson to be studied, not as a taskmaster condemning us all. It points us to Christ and life.

Imagination and Law

The capacity of salvation starts with the uniquely human ability to understand and be motivated and governed by abstractions called laws and rules. Laws and rules start us on the path to understanding good and evil, and to learn to master our self-centeredness. They show us that there is a standard of behavior outside of and greater than our own wishes and desires. They prepare us for the realization that God's will is greater and worthier than our own.

Laws awaken in us the capacity to live in relation to one another, and especially in our relation with God. Laws, and in particular the Law of Moses, are actually a prefiguring of life in Christ. They teach us to love one another. We are members of his Body, and must learn not to harm one another. Laws are one of the bases of civilization as well. But they are abstract, intangible, and imaginary. They have no substance. You can't actually touch, break, or keep any of them. They're just communal ideas, accepted as if they were real. They awaken within us the idea of good and evil.

The knowledge of good and evil is one of the sweet-scented seeds that God planted in Eden. It's an ever-blooming grandiflora rose that will flower in the Gospel times and beyond, in the greater Paradise. It blooms in our capacity for abstract, metaphorical thinking. We can imagine things, and determine our behaviors by these imaginings. We can dream, and follow our dreams, even when they are unrealistic or illusory. We can describe to others our plans and hopes. We can construct entire worlds, and show them to other humans in books or movies. This ability to manipulate hypothetical, metaphorical ideas is the basis of law, government, science, and religion. It makes us capable of receiving salvation. It makes us capable of learning God's will. And to do God's will is the ultimate purpose for which humanity was created.

When God gave Adam the Law, it engaged Adam's capacity for abstract thought. It was a mental event. He was warned that when he crossed the invisible fence God had placed around that certain tree, he would die. Sure enough, upon eating of the fruit, he died. But it didn't happen immediately. What happened is that he realized his inability to do God's will. His own will had full control. He was in big, big trouble.

Disobeying God and eating the fruit did not kill him, however. It was not poisoned fruit. God had planted the tree, and it was good fruit (Gen. 2:9). Adam was not immortal before he ate from the tree. He was mortal, for he could die. That's what being mortal means. It means you can die. Even had he not eaten the forbidden fruit he would have died. Immortality would be gained only by eating of the tree of life. Eternal life was not taken from Adam in Eden. He never had it, because immortality is only in Christ. It is not the natural state of any animal. Adam died because he was denied access to the tree of life.

God drove the newlyweds out of the garden, toward the east, to fulfill their mortality. The man of the flesh will not live in Paradise. He must work the fields of this present unholy world until he returns to the ground. Vanity of vanities, humanity must die. But there is hope. From death, a certain kind of death of a certain one, the lovely flower of immortality will sprout one day. Adam's story will continue in his seed, and will follow the universal archetype of death unto life, of darkness unto light, which is the Gospel. The Light will triumph over the darkness. The Son of Man will conquer death, and will rise from its cold clutches. God recycles everything.

The True Gospel of Salvation

The true Gospel and plan of salvation is based, of course, on what is real. It harmonizes with reality. Otherwise, it would be a discordant theme. The truth is that humans are alienated from God because of their creatureliness. They are separated from God by being in the world and of it. The first Sabbath began with God's separation from this world, remember? In our carnality, our worldliness, we cannot do God's will, for we are self-oriented, immersed up to our eyeballs in this world. So he provides us with his Law, symbolizing his will, which no one can keep, revealing to us the incapacity of our self-oriented nature to do his will. But it also hints that we should be like him. We need help. We're like babies with dirty diapers. We need to be changed.

Law manifests our soiled nakedness called sin, and the sentence of death because of our human animal nature incapable of doing his will. Adam was not meant to be the final product. God created us so that he could have a Body to serve him. Understandably, he wants a well-coordinated Body that will serve him well. That is, after all, the reason why humans were created. They were created to do God's will, not their own, by sharing in the Spirit and serving in his divine Body. But Adam was just the first step in a two-step process. The goal of the creation was Christ, the second and true Adam. The first one was a shadow, just the first step. Humanity transformed will become the Body that God is now building. God is a Body builder.

God's Law presents to us the idea of good and evil. Keeping the Law represents doing God's will, which is good, while breaking the Law represents not doing his will, which is evil, also called sin. And like all the other animals, we naturally want to do our own will. We are self-oriented. Our natural inclination is inward. The Law tells us that we are under sentence of death because of this human, animalistic nature. Knowledge of sin, of not doing God's will, moves us to seek salvation, to receive union with Christ and to be re-clothed by being changed into a new creation, with a new nature ultimately capable of doing God's will. Then, upon receiving Christ, we begin learning to do God's will by walking in the Spirit. The Law is a teacher that shows us how bad we are (Gal. 3:24-27). It finds us guilty, like a well-lighted mirror that reveals the mud all over our face, so that we can wash and be made clean.

Sin and guilt in relation to the Law are abstractions, however. They are just metaphors that teach us about our need to be re-clothed with Christ and in him to eventually be given the full ability to do God's will. Yes, child, both sin and forgiveness are imaginary constructions of the Law. And Law itself is an abstraction, an idea flitting in and out of our consciousness, and written down so we

Seeds of the Future

don't forget. Sins in the Law are just ideas. You can't literally keep them or break them. Sin is a symbol of our natural separation from God and eternal life. Forgiveness symbolizes being given a new nature by being reunited with God. We must not confuse the metaphorical with the literal. We must not confuse Law with grace and truth. The metaphors, the shadows that are sin and forgiveness, are not the reality. The reality is our natural alienation from God, which is the true sin, healed by true reconciliation when we receive Christ.

In saying that sins are not real, we are not denying that a real, physical action has taken place. Perhaps a person has been murdered, or a home has been burglarized. But they are sins only because the Law forbids them. Sins are transgressions of a law. Where there is no law, there can be no transgression of it, and therefore no sin (Rom. 4:15, 5:13). And where there is no sin, there can be no forgiveness of it! Actions by themselves are not sins apart from laws. Sins under the Law were just shadows, object lessons exposing human self-centeredness and pointing to the natural separation from God that results in death.

And child, only Israel was given the Law. Non-Jews have never been under the authority of Israel's laws. No Gentile is guilty of breaking any of the Ten Commandments! Gentiles were never under the Mosaic Law, or in the covenant that God made with Israel. The Law is a lesson to be studied, to learn of our need of transformation, and a foreshadowing picture of life in Christ.

The true Gospel is fantastic beyond words. It starts with our physical and spiritual alienation from God and our crying need of reconciliation. And that reconciliation must be both physical and spiritual. It must not stop at mere nearness or amicability. It means and requires oneness. The divine answer to our need is to grant us the Holy Spirit of Christ in a real uniting. It is conversion, a literal change into a new creature and creation, through the willing death of the old one. It continues triumphantly with resurrection and glorification in union with God in the Spirit. The true Gospel is about reunion with God! It's about oneness with the Almighty! Shout, child, shout!

Our purpose and glorious future is the give and take of life in oneness with the Creator. We will serve God as his very own Body, as the living and holy Temple of the Spirit. In turn, he will share his very life with us, love answering to love within the very heart of God. That's the very purpose of the creation and of salvation (1 John 5:20). We will participate in God eternally in oneness, knowing good and evil, doing his will and rejecting what is not his will. It will be a mutual sharing in one another, within God himself (John 17:11, 20-23; 2 Peter 1:4). Yes, child, we will share as One in the Godhead! We will be his hands and feet, and also his volition, sharing directly in the very mind and self-awareness of God (1 Cor. 2:11-16; Heb. 5:14)! That's the true story of true glory. It is unspeakably marvelous beyond anything orthodoxy imagines.

In truth, every law is just an imaginary abstraction. So sin is imaginary too. It is the imaginary breaking of the imaginary abstraction that is Law. Nothing is actually broken. Have you ever seen anyone actually pick up the pieces of a broken law? Have you ever seen someone keep a law, perhaps in a glass bowl up on the shelf? It's all imaginary. Guilt is imaginary as well, the imaginary stain of having metaphorically broken an imaginary law, an idea. The stain is imaginary, as is the idea of washing it away. And the idea of breaking it is equally imaginary. The concept of deserving punishment is only imaginary too. Child, child, open your eyes. Can sin really be washed away by killing Jesus? If Tom is dirty, how can he be made clean by bathing Billy? How can killing Billy cleanse Tom, even if we crucify him?

The entire Law is but a gathering of shadows, a brouhaha whispering about Christ. And Christ, being the reality toward which the Law points, is the annulment of the Law, its fulfillment. Christ Jesus is the truth of the Law.

Orthodoxy has confused the metaphorical with the literal, the letter with the Spirit. They has unwittingly cast the Old Testament over the New Testament, while denying that they have done so. And none are so blind as those who will not see. Mistaking the imaginary for the real Gospel, they have wrapped the heavy chains of Law around the ankles of grace. But Law can never make a person acceptable to God. Forgiveness of sins in the Law cannot save anyone.

Killing a lamb or goat doesn't change anyone's nature. Only the Creator can create a new person. Even killing Jesus doesn't change anyone's nature. People must realize that forgiveness of sins is just a figure (Heb. 10:1-4). It isn't real. It points to its reality in Christ.

Horrendously, Christians are being taught to run to the shadows for protection! But even shadows of the Savior do not save. The Law is powerless. It can neither save, nor condemn. Only Christ Jesus can save.

Salvation is gained only through actual, genuine physical and spiritual reconciliation with God. It is by God's grace through faith. And grace has nothing to do with Law. Grace ignores the Law. It sets it aside. Forgiveness of sins under the Law is just a figure, just a shadow of true reconciliation. We must not confuse the reality of the new covenant of grace with the metaphorical shadows of the old covenant of Law. It makes no sense to trust in shadows for salvation. Mistaking metaphors as if they were real was the minefield in which Judaism lost both her arms and her legs. Now Christianity is unheedingly jumping around in the same field!

An Unreal Gospel

In the hands of the churches, the Bible has become a childish, magical morality play, with no intermission between the first and second acts, and no popcorn. Supposedly, God made perfect, immortal humans that would live forever. Strangely, he put them in Eden with a sly, talking snake, forbidding them to eat of a tree that he himself had planted there, smack in the middle of the garden. But inexplicably, although they were morally perfect and possessed free will, they were full of pride and rebellion and disobeyed.

This caused them somehow to fall from perfection, that is, to become imperfect somehow. Somehow, inexplicably, their free choice made them imperfect. And somehow they brought the whole universe down with them. Evil broke loose everywhere from nowhere. Death invaded, again from nowhere. The whole creation fell somehow. It all changed. They had ruined God's perfect creation, so God must have his revenge. He must punish them. He will kill them and torture them and their children forever and ever, to avenge his honor and satisfy his immaculate justice.

They didn't do things his way, so they deserve it. Yes, he will eventually save a few of them, but the rest can just go to Hell. In the churches of Christianity, God's justice is a savage, voracious and ever hungry beast that lives on human pain, and is never satisfied, ever, no matter how much agony he inflicts, or how long it continues.

But God is merciful and loving, so he eventually sent his own Son to suffer and die in their place, they say. Somehow, his justice (!) is satisfied by viciously punishing an innocent human, the only innocent human. This somehow washes away the sins of those who would receive his Son. He kills Billy, and somehow all of Tom's family is cleansed. For those already dead and for those who never heard, well, sorry, but it's too late. Let them suffer. Salvation is only for a few specially chosen humans. No use crying over spilled milk. Que será, será. At least some of them can be forgiven now to enjoy life, safe and away from the unending screams that cry out hopelessly from the hot flames of God's insatiable justice.

To take advantage of God's offer, they must say they are really, really sorry for having offended him, for not doing things his way, even though it was impossible. They must invite him into their heart through faith in his goodness, and try not to break his impossible rules any more. Now, they try to be godly like him. (!) They must please God by doing his will, which is to behave themselves and follow his rules. Then he will allow them into his heaven of happiness, to bow before him and sing his praises, playing harps, thankful for his love and mercy toward them.

The churches cannot see that their Gospel is a repeat of Law, a series of metaphors, inconsistencies, contradictions, absurdities, impossibilities, and downright blasphemies. It's an accumulation of imaginary abstractions, magic, and foul desecrations. Their Gospel is unreal, a childish fantasy, and their God is a fiendish monster. The shadows of Law have mutinied and have taken over the ship. The shadows are taken for the real, and the real has been thrown into the brig. Law still hangs heavy over believer and nonbeliever, because sins are still believed to be something tangible, the literal breaking of God's Law. Besides misunderstanding the Gospel totally, the churches have draped the Old Testament shadows over the New Testament, covering the Gospel with the Law. Orthodox, traditional Christianity has become Judaism with a change of clothes, a works religion cloaked with Christian terminology. The orthodox, traditional Gospel preached in the churches of Christianity is Law-based.

Grace has been re-defined and has become a reaction to Law. It is called forgiveness of sins, which are then defined as transgressions of God's Law. But if that is the case, then grace is in relation to the Law, and derives from it. The Law is still in force, then, because sins are the breaking of the Law. The churches are caught in a whirlpool of legalism and can't get out unless they recognize that the shadows are not real. The shadows called sins are not the reality. Alienation from God is what is real. Sins are merely its symptoms.

Mistaking the illustrations for reality is the bottomless pit into which Israel fell. They didn't realize that the shadows under which they were living were just shadows. They painstakingly read the words, but they could not make out the pictures. The pictures in the Old Testament were of Christ. He was the real Lamb, the manna from heaven, and so forth. Seeing only the shadows, and not recognizing them as shadows, they killed their Lamb.

Fulfilling that typology, the blind end-time churches of Christendom will kill the true prophets of the Lord, accusing them of blasphemy for claiming to be the divine children of God. This is not just empty speculation. Judaism is a foreshadowing of Christianity. The pictures are true, but like Judaism, Christianity is picture-blind. Christians too will choose Rome over Christ. They do not realize the implications of the truth that Christianity is the fulfillment of the shadow that was Judaism. Like the Jews, they too have failed to recognize the pictures. They're too engrossed with the letter, and the satisfaction they get from reading a text and then moralizing about it, in order to try not to sin, that is, not to transgress the Law. The walk of faith has been transformed into behaviorism, a kind of works religion. Rule keeping has taken over in many of the churches. Judaism has been re-bottled and sold with a new label called Christianity.

And they take the events of Genesis as their support. Let's go back there, then, and see what it really says. And steer clear of the shovel, please.

In the Garden

Even with the creation of Adam, God was not yet finished with the work of creation. He would work with archetypes. Like a skilled photographer, he had yet to pose the man, to form a picture for future generations to see. He must pose Adam in a way that would image God past, present, and future.

The work was delicate, so he must take special care. Skillfully, he must wield the sharp scalpel of a surgeon and perform an operation on the man. It would be a self-portrait, a revelation of the Creator himself. So, before putting the man to sleep, the Creator aroused in Adam an intense loneliness. Unlike the other animals, Adam had no companion. He was alone. Then God put him to sleep, and from that sleep, a figure of death, he created Eve. All of this was a reflection of God himself. Their creation was in his image. It was meant to show what God is like and what he is up to, and why.

The Creation of Eve

The creation of Eve is wondrous strange and extraordinary. God begins by depicting and demonstrating Adam's aloneness, stating that it was not good (Gen. 2:19-20). But Adam had not yet sinned. Why was it not good? Remembering that good is God's will, rather than a kind of law-based morality, we understand that it was not God's will then for the man to remain alone. Importantly, this original evil was not the breaking of God's Law, for the Law had not yet been given. Nor was it an Unknown Law that he had broken. Adam was still innocent, but in a condition that was not good, that is, not pleasing to God. Without Eve, Christ Jesus could never be born. That was not good.

This is a strong clue, no, it is well nigh an open declaration that the Law does not determine true good and evil. Law is merely a picture, a sort of preview of that which will surely come in due time. Its realization will be Christ in his fullness. Good has little to do with keeping the Law, then. It has everything to do with doing God's will. His will is Christ Jesus, revealed preliminarily by the Law. That is, the Law was a description and a promise of what life would be like in Christ. It revealed God's will. And that will, of course, was his Son, in whom he would be well pleased.

The keeping of God's Law is just a shadow of the true good. The breaking of God's Law is just a shadow as well. It foreshadows the true evil. Adam, like Israel after him, lived in the time of darkness when the shadows of night still covered their understanding.

Daylight would come with Christ. The archetype of light unto day would be repeated. Until then, the people walked in darkness (Luke 1:78-79). Adam was a preview of coming events, and of the main attraction. He was a figure of Christ. The Creator was looking ahead, making all the arrangements for his own wedding day. Events in Eden were like a kind of rehearsal.

The Creator intended to make of Adam a complex unity, a husband and wife together forming one flesh, imaging Christ and the Church. They would in fact image God himself as well. He's a complex unity, one God in whom there is differentiation, a singularity and a plurality. Adam points back to his Maker with one hand, and across the millennia to the Son of Man with the other. Later, the greater Adam will hang, his arms likewise outstretched, and cry, "It is finished!" God's positioning of Adam shows us what the Creator was planning. He was preparing a Bride for himself.

And he would grow a tree.

The Death and Resurrection of God

We can see, then, that Adam's aloneness was an echo of God's aloneness. Adam's heart was beating in sync with the heart of the Creator. The pulse of the music begins softly, a lonely, plaintive note full of pathos, a single solitary strain that strangely stirs our heart. We can feel sympathy for Adam. We can hurt with him. We know what loneliness is like, for we've felt it ourselves. And it hurts, deeply. We need someone to love us, and to love in return.

And Adam images God. In the beginning, like Adam, God was looking forward for someone to soothe his solitude. He wanted someone to walk with him, to help him fulfill his dreams and share his future. He would die for someone to love and to love him in return, to walk with him and share eternity together with him. To image and illustrate this, he put Adam into a deep sleep.

Adam's deep sleep symbolizes death. And in this, too, he is the image of God! His sleep reflects how the Creator himself died for the world. It prefigures the death of Christ as well, who is the true image of God (Coll. 1:15). Through his own death, imaged in its sharpest detail at the cross, God is creating for himself a Bride, and will no longer be alone.

How did this happen? Is God really dead? Yes, in the process of creation, God's Spirit was separated from his Body. That's what death is with God. It's not destruction. It's a temporary separation of spirit from body. Death cannot destroy him. Matter and Spirit are eternal, child, remember? With God, the separation between them is only temporary, just three time periods or dispensations, as illustrated by the death of Christ Jesus. To know God, we can look to Jesus. And Jesus' death lasted only three days. It was just a temporary separation between spirit and body. It was not destruction. And he is the very image and likeness of God.

And the death of a saint is like that of Jesus. It is just a temporary separation of the spirit from the body. And it, too, images God. Like our death in Christ, the death of God merely changed what God was, into what he becomes. The separation of the Spirit from the world at the creation changed him. But he remains, now temporarily separated from the world in holiness. God's death, the separation of his Spirit from his Body, could not destroy God. Nor can death destroy the saints, who are made in his image and who share his nature and destiny, and his kind of death. That's the message of the cross. It's the word of triumph over death.

Adam's prefigurative sleep of death did not destroy him either. It was just temporary, a foreshadowing. It was the process through which God would create Eve. Her creation is an upward step, hinting at how God is creating a Bride for himself, involving the Creator's direct, personal intervention. It looks ahead to God's creation of the Bride of Christ, the greater Eve, through the death of the Bridegroom. And it looks upward, imaging God. Adam's figurative death ended in a figurative resurrection, and together Adam and Eve became one flesh. The creation of Eve points with one hand forward to the cross and resurrection, and with the other upward to the Creator and his death and resurrection as well. Adam's figurative death pictured both the death of God and the death of Christ. It was part of the image of God. God works in archetypes.

Death, for God as well as for Christ Jesus and the saints, is just a temporary separation of the spirit from the body. This is the lesson of the cross, and of the death of Adam through which God gave him Eve. Death applies to God as well as to Christ and the saints. God, too, died so that the world could live. He is the divine Archetype. He died for his Bride, separating from the world at the Flood. Death was a central part of the manner in which Christ Jesus imaged God.

This theme of death and resurrection, begun in Eden, sings wistfully throughout the Bible and across history. It's a soulful melody that tugs at our heart, a throbbing love song that weeps with the loneliness of separation and death, but in the end finds gladness and exhilarating joy in blessed reunion. The song sings of the great Prince who willingly undergoes an agonizing death in order to save his beloved, a beautiful slave-girl, to elevate her to his side on the throne. It's the story of the heroic Son willingly dying for his beloved, of the true Adam dying for the greater Eve. And it's the story of God and his love for the world. He, too, died for his Bride.

In Jesus' honor, uncountable legions of angels will soon gather, and join their voices to sing and serenade these lovers reunited. Angelic choirs will thunder the leitmotif of God's love in mighty, heaven-shaking crescendos and earth-quaking hallelujahs. The entire creation will joyfully sound the arrival of the world's long-awaited reunion with its Creator.

Meanwhile, let us make our way carefully through Eden.

Events in Eden

The Serpent

Already, in those pristine scenes, there is trouble brewing. A serpent is on the prowl, hunting unwary prey. He is well hidden, and blends in well with his surroundings. You will not find him slithering in the grass underfoot, or sliding silently along in the overhanging branches. He is craftier and more cunning than that. He hides where he can't be seen. He coils cleverly in the dark recesses in the heart of this first couple. He is well-camouflaged there, within their humanity, in the part that seeks its own will, its self-fulfillment and survival. He is assertive, and sly. And he is a liar.

He is not a beast of the field. The text excludes him from that category. He is a continuation of the force that accomplished the initial differentiation of the world from its Creator. His work is to draw the world away from God. That was his job since the beginning of our world. In the Bible, he is personified as Satan. In humans he is the Serpent. Surprisingly, he initially was good, for he is the agent of God's separation from the world, God's holiness. But being who he is, he seeks to draw all things, including especially the humans, away from God. Being in and of the world, they are self-oriented. Their inclination is ever to do their own will, which is the manifestation of the Serpent spirit. This built-in egotism was part of their nature from the beginning. Being in the creation and of it, they were oriented toward self and away from God. The primal couple, like everyone after them and all the other animals, nurtured the Serpent inside. So they must die.

God willingly underwent death too, separation of the Spirit from the Body, so that our world could come to exist. His death became the life of the world. Christ Jesus repeated this theme, this archetype, dying in his humanity, nailing the Serpent of human selfhood to the cross (John 3:14; Coll. 2:15). And he graciously calls us to follow, to live the same story for the same glory (Rom. 12:1; Eph. 5:1-2). It's the archetype of death unto new life, instituted by God as a reflection of himself. The creation is a reflection of its Maker. And death is an act of creation. It is how God is bringing the new creation into being.

The Serpent was already within Adam and Eve from the start because they were children of the creation, birthed from the earth where the Serpent was already active, pulling with all his strength and cunning away from God. The Serpent was not a snake or an evil entity hanging from a tree. He was the voice of their very own heart. The Serpent spirit lies hidden deep within carnal, sinful humanity itself. He is part of us, the part that ever seeks to serve self, and does so when it can.

He was initially good, for his work was in harmony with God's intent to separate the world from himself. That was God's will, and his will is what determines what is good. The Serpent was the power with which the Creator extracted and separated the material world from himself, a sort of anti-gravity principle working everywhere in all material things. But the separation was only for a season. God's ultimate desire was to reconcile the renewed and remodeled world back to himself, as pictured by Eve's reconciliation with Adam, in which the two became one flesh once more. Reconciliation of the world to God is what Christ is accomplishing (2 Cor. 5:18-20). He is overcoming the anti-gravity principle, destroying the power of the Serpent, returning the world to its Creator. And because God now desires reconciliation, the anti-gravity principle is no longer his will. It has become evil, then, for working against his will. The Serpent is now Satan, the opposer. Here, friend, is the long wondered-about origin of evil.

With the coming of that first law in Eden, the Serpent crawled out into the open in Eve's consciousness and tempted her to serve self, to fulfill her thoughts and desires as she always had. The Serpent aroused the curiosity in Eve, raising doubts within her, questions about the fruit of that special tree. She went to it, testing, examining it closely. She didn't see any rottenness. It looked good. It was ripe and ready, right for a bite. What might it taste like? God had planted it. She touched it, and nothing happened.

The Temptation

Why had God said that they could not eat of that one fruit? Why? Had he really said it? The Serpent was playing with her mind, playing merry-go-round in her head. She was curious, thirsty for knowledge. She wanted to know the truth. Why would God forbid them knowledge, and such a luscious fruit? Did Adam really know what he was talking about? Did God really say what Adam says? After all, God had promised them both, when they were together, all the plants and trees as food, all of them (Gen. 1:29). She had heard it with her own ears. How, then, could Adam say that this one fruit was forbidden? Adam must be mistaken. I need to find out. I want to know.

God himself planted this tree, and it's a good one. Just look at it. Isn't it beautiful? And just look at all that luscious fruit. Why would God plant it here if he didn't want us to eat from it? Besides, God himself told us that we could eat from every tree. Adam must not have understood. I think I'll try it. Yes, I'll just take a little bite, and see. I want to know.

The Awakening

So she did what she wanted. She ate, and she didn't die! So she gave some to Adam to eat. And he didn't die either. Their eyes were opened, just as the Serpent had said! This was not their literal eyes. It was their understanding. They had served their own will rather than God's will. They understood, now, what evil was. Good was God's will, while evil was that which is not his will. Their actions had put them at enmity with God. They saw themselves now in their true nature and condition. They were at risk, vulnerable to the hungry terrors that watched and waited in the dark. They had disobeyed. They had done that which was contrary to what God had said. They had worked their own will rather than God's will. Woe! Woe!

The text says that they became fearful, upon seeing that they were naked (Gen. 3:10). It doesn't say that they fell. It says that their eyes were opened. Sight here means more than physical vision. It symbolizes spiritual awareness and understanding. Their nakedness was more than physical. It was spiritual. They had no righteousness with which to clothe themselves. They realized now their enmity against God. They became afraid, and rightly so. So they hid themselves. Their actions had shined a bright light on their true nature. They were self-oriented, naturally disposed to doing their own will rather than the will of God. And the will of God is what constitutes good, while not doing his will constitutes evil. They understood, now. But they were on the wrong side! So they hid themselves. Well, at least they thought they did.

But God sacrificed a couple of goats, and clothed the humans in goatskins. This was not to hide their sexuality. It was an object lesson in biology, to demonstrate and symbolize that they were indeed animals and naturally self-serving, but that nevertheless, God would cover up their shame and alienation. Hope of life would be available. God had a plan. Their animal nature would be re-clothed through a coming sacrifice, a necessary death. Their nakedness would be covered. But it would require more than just fig leaves. Humanity would surely die, yes, but in death there would be hope. And it would not be in Judaism, for fig leaves were not a sufficient or proper covering (Mark 11:13-14; Luke 13:6-9).

The goatskins given to Adam and Eve were to hide their shame. Their spiritual unworthiness inherent in their carnal, animal nature would be covered over. Adam and eve were animals. Yes, child, humans are animals (Gen. 1:20, 24, 2:7, 7:15, 22). Their new clothing meant also that new life ultimately would come through death of the animal nature. It was a message of hope even after death. It imaged being re-clothed with Christ. Later, when God gave

Abraham the sign of circumcision, it meant essentially the same thing. It meant that life would come through death. It meant that the human animal would be cut off and die. The Adam of earth would give place to the Adam of heaven. God had not lied. Earthly Adam would surely die. The Serpent had lied.

God's clothing of their nakedness was an informative peek into the future. It looked across the centuries toward the one who would be God clothed with humanity, or rather, humanity clothed with God. But before he would come, the lesson was repeated in the story of Jacob who, picturing the coming one, wore goatskins in order to win the birthright from his elder brother. That foreshadowing story showed that Christianity would supersede Judaism (Mark 11:13-14; Luke 13:6-9). The spiritual man, pictured by Jacob, would displace the man of the flesh, pictured by Esau. The spiritual would displace the fleshly by taking on flesh. It was a picture of the Incarnation of Jesus, which happened at his baptism. The same lesson would be repeated in the tabernacle, a symbol of God's Body, that was covered with goatskins to symbolize his coming humanity. With events in Eden, God was posing Adam and Eve for posterity. Looking back from the cross, we can understand how it was prefigured even from the beginning.

When their eyes were opened, the primal couple's knowledge of good and evil was awakened (Rom. 7:5-11). It was not a fall. Their disobedience did not separate them from God. Nor did it make them to be evil or sinful. It did not change their nature. It manifested it. Their new spiritual insight was a forward and upward step toward Christ and the new creation. Adam now knew good and evil (Gen. 3:22). Good is God's will, pictured by obeying his Law, and it brings life. Evil is that which opposes his will, pictured by not obeying his Law. It results in death, the kind of death that brings destruction. Their eyes were opened, and they understood. They knew now that, in their carnality, they were incapable of doing God's will. They must die.

Spiritual sight is always better than blindness. Why else would God plant the tree? Why else would he give them the Law? The purpose of the Law is to give spiritual sight (Rom. 7:7-11). God does not desire blind followers. Did you get that, child? God does not desire blind followers. Faith is not blind. It is based on solid evidence. We trust Christ Jesus not blindly, but because he has proven himself to be unswervingly faithful and true. He has proven himself.

Already in Eden, the path was being readied for the coming Son of God, in whom the knowledge of good and evil would be perfected. If acquiring this knowledge were a sin, then Christ Jesus was the chief of sinners. But that's not the case (Heb. 5:14). His superb knowledge of good and evil was part of the image of God (Gen. 3:22). He understood the Law, the symbol of God's will, but more importantly, he knew God's will itself, firsthand, personally. He was One with the Spirit.

We must understand that the sin of Adam and Eve did not make them sinners. Let's repeat that. Adam and Eve's sin did not make them sinners. They were already sinners by nature. That is why they sinned. They merely exhibited their true nature. Their disobedience did not cause them to fall. It opened their eyes to the nature of their humanity, to what they already were. This is what the Law does. It opens our eyes. The Serpent was already inside them, inciting self-centeredness. Adam could now distinguish between good and evil, but he was on the wrong side! He would die. He would have an end. The Serpent had lied. Adam needed help, desperately. He needed a new nature (2 Cor. 5:1-4). Humanity needed a savior.

Curse of the Serpent

The Serpent had told Eve that she would not die. She would be like God. That was not an evil desire. The desire to live and to be like God, who is good, is not evil. It's an excellent hope, the eager expectation of all his children. Indeed, it's the will of God, for he wants his children to bear his image. The tree was a good tree, planted by God, and its fruit was desirable and good. After all, it prefigured the cross. All the trees were good. And God had promised them all to this primal couple (Gen. 1:29). Yes, he had promised them the fruit of every tree.

And in fact the couple did become like God (Gen. 3:22). They came to know good and evil. But they also died (Ps. 82:6-7; John 10:34-38). To be godly, to be like God, involves death! The Devil is still telling the same lie in many of the churches today, as he did in Eden. He promises that people who receive Christ, who partake of the fruit of the cross, need not die to self. He slithers onto the pulpits

Seeds of the Future

and preaches passionately through the microphones that Jesus died in our place as our substitute. He hisses that we can partake of the fruit of Calvary's tree and become healthy, wealthy, and wise in this world, and thoroughly enjoy ourselves because Jesus suffered in our place for us. Because of the cross, we can now live in luxury and happiness and our humanity can thrive with God's blessings. All it takes is faith that this is so. And send us your money to prove your faith! These churches are serving the Serpent of human nature and calling it service to Christ Jesus!

The truth is that, in order to become like God, and know true good and evil, we absolutely must die to self. When we receive Christ it includes his death as well as his life. We receive all of him. The true Gospel is a call to take up our own cross and follow. Receiving Christ comes with a cross. And the cross has our name on it. A temporary death is part of the image of God, child. But do not fear. Death for the saints is merely a momentary separation of the spirit from the body. That is the lesson of the cross. Believe it.

Because of his deceptiveness, the Serpent was destined to crawl on his belly, and eat dust all the days of his life. There would be enmity between his seed and that of the woman, and he would come out on the losing end. Indeed, there is a hint that he would himself die with Adam, in the phrase, "all the days of your life," which is the same phrase God spoke to Adam. The Serpent will die with Adam the death that brings destruction. Humanity will take the Serpent to its grave. But the saints will rise again, freed from the Serpent's coils, and selfishness will give way to loving service of Christ.

The Serpent in Eden was not a snake. Nor do snakes generally eat dust. What it means is that he would share in Adam. He was the self-centered impulse that lives in all humans, and he was already squirming restlessly in Eve (Isa. 27:1). Many churches have taught by and large that it was a snake. That is ridiculous. Would God curse all snakes of every kind for the thoughts in Eve's mind? No, and neither do snakes talk, child. Well, Satan used ventriloquism, someone has said. Again, why would God curse snakes for what Satan said? And what of worms, and moles and gophers? No, it was the Serpent in humanity who spoke. Eve was talking to herself. She didn't believe what Adam had told her (cf. Gen. 1:29). And she would satisfy her curiosity.

God cursed the Serpent of human nature to go on his belly. The Serpent's food would be the dust of the earth, the same stuff of which Adam was made. Adam's food, too, would come from the ground. And the ground had come under the curse, like the Serpent. God was hinting that the Serpent would live and die with humanity. They would share the same destiny (Phil. 3:18-19). And that has been the case throughout human history. Our evil thoughts and desires come from our very own selves (Jas. 1:14-15). They do not come from a talking snake hanging from a tree (Mark 7:17-23; Eph. 2:1-3; 1 John 2:16).

Ultimately, according to God's word, the Serpent would be bruised on the head, and lose the strife to come between the flesh and the Spirit. Spiritual mankind would emerge victorious over the carnal Serpent nature. In dying, humanity would bring about the destruction of the Serpent. The seed of the woman, of course, is Christ and those who receive him. The seed of the Serpent is carnal humanity (Matt. 13:38; John 8:44; Acts 13:10; 1 John 3:8-10).

The seed of the woman would be epitomized in one man, Christ Jesus. It follows, then, that there will come an individual who will be a special seed of the Serpent, the epitome of evil, of all that is contrary to God's will. He will serve the will of the Serpent fully. And the will of the Serpent is the will of the flesh, of self-serving humanity. The coming Antichrist will embody all the world's antagonism toward God in its self-service. He will take humanism to its furthest limits, mixing a lie with the truth as in Eden, telling the people that they can receive Christ, partaking of the fruit of the cross, and not die. Instead of dying to self, they can fulfill all the possibilities of their humanity. They can climb the heights of human nature, and delve its deepest depths (Rev. 2:24). They can experience all the pleasures of human life to its full because of Christ. The cross was God's service to carnal man. So, enjoy yourself.

Is that not the health and wealth Gospel with its family and friends? The Antichrist will assure humans that they can partake of the knowledge of good and evil, and be like God, without dying to self. Indeed, in complete blasphemy, they will teach that Jesus' death was so that believers might in fact fully serve the self. The self is the Serpent spirit, child! They will promote Serpent worship, and claim the cross as its basis. The lie of the Serpent is that believers will not die. They can now enjoy life's riches and pleasures, provided that they have enough faith. God will bless their Serpent worship! Because of the cross they can now serve the Serpent of human nature and find happiness and self-fulfillment. The Antichrist will preach this false Gospel through nominally Christian churches. Thinking to serve Christ, they will unwittingly serve the Antichrist. And service to the Antichrist will take the form of service to the Serpent, calling it service to humanity.

The fulfillment of human potential will be the Antichrist's theme. He will serve and exalt humanity to the place of God. He will claim to be Christ's substitute on earth, Christ's vicar or stand-in. And in utter deception he will actually call the people to Christ (Matt. 7:21-23, 24:4-5, 24; Mark 13:6, 22). But it will be a false Christ, and a false Gospel. It will be a call to indulge fully in humanism, with Christ's blessing. He will speak from the churches of Christianity that have fallen away from the truth. And they all will have fallen.

The true Anointed One will triumph not only over this seed of the Serpent, but over the Serpent himself (Rev. 20:10). He will close the deep chasm that exists between God and humanity, and will return the world to its Maker. Self-centered humanity will surely die. Selfishness will die with their death. It will be the death of the Serpent, just as God predicted in Eden. The agent of separation will be rendered immobile and impotent.

The saints, on the other hand, will deny themselves in order to do the will of God. Jesus said that whoever seeks to save his life would lose it. He said that no man can serve two masters. He emphasized that we must take up our own cross and follow him. So, whom are we to believe? Shall we trust the Serpent, or, the Savior? Shall we serve humanity, or, Christ Jesus?

The Subjection of Eve

Because Eve enticed Adam into disobedience and death, she was made subservient to him. She was deceived by the Serpent, while Adam went willingly (1 Tim. 2:14). Why? There is a subtle hint that he sacrificed himself in order to be with her and to protect her. The text does not say this explicitly, so we must look at the picture. We must look carefully at the second Adam. The fulfillment of a promise can tell us much about a promise. The antitype can tell us much about the type. Since Adam is a figure of Christ, we can learn much about Adam by looking at Christ Jesus (1 Cor. 15:45-47). A look at Jesus will give us insight into Adam.

Because of his great love, Jesus willingly underwent death with his bride, who had been deceived by the Serpent. He died to be with her in death as in life because of his loving oneness with her (Eph. 5:25; Heb. 2:14). This shows us clearly that, as a picture and illustration of Christ Jesus, Adam ate from Eve's hand because of his love for her, and because they were one flesh. It was because of their oneness or communion. This first communion meal looked forward to another that would be celebrated by the greater Adam, and which would itself be a picture of loving oneness in death as in life. Surprisingly, Adam willingly sacrificed himself for his bride, not as her substitute, but because of their oneness. He was foreshadowing Christ Jesus. He died because of his love for her. These events were a foreshadowing of the cross. The Gospel was being preached already in Eden. God was posing them with skill and dexterity. Notably, Adam did not die as Eve's substitute. He joined her in death. Remember that, child.

Subtle hints of faith and salvation abound in this episode. It is not the sordid, sorry, and blasphemous tale of rebellion, treachery, and pride that orthodoxy has presented to us. It is a beautiful love story of courage, faith, and hope. Adam's willing death hints of his great love for Eve, and of his deep trust in God's goodness and mercy. It hints that he was, even then, at the beginning of our history, hoping against hope in the resurrection from the dead (cf. Heb. 11:17-19). He was trusting in God, whose power and goodness would prevail even past those dark portals. He foreshadowed Christ Jesus, the second Adam (1 Cor. 15:45).

Eve similarly had trusted in God's goodness. Contrary to what many churches teach, she did not purposely rebel against God. Her eating was an act of trust, of faith. It was God, after all, who had planted the trees. Surely it was not for their harm. And she was right. She ate trusting in God's promise and provision. After all, God had promised them the fruit of every tree as food (Gen. 1:29). She ate in faith, believing his word. The Gospel is evident even there, in God's first garden. Those early events whisper of later ones. In a certain death to come later there will be salvation through faith in the goodness of God, by eating from a tree in the middle of the Garden

Seeds of the Future

that God has planted. Eve ate in faith, foreshadowing the true Church.

Adam, for his part, was doing the same thing, trusting in God's goodwill toward them. When questioned, his response to God, and his reason for eating, was that God himself had given him the woman. Importantly, he was not trying to put the blame on Eve, or on God, as so many churches have mistakenly taught. He was not saying, "Well, you gave her to me, so it's your fault." He was saying, "Well, you gave her to me, and you are good. I trusted in your goodness." It was the response of a trusting son to a loving and beneficent father. It was an act of faith. We know that every good and perfect gift comes from the Father of lights (Jas. 1:17). God's gift of Eve to Adam was a good and perfect gift. Neither will a loving Father give his children a live scorpion, or a snake instead of a fish (Luke 11:11). Adam trusted in the goodness of the heavenly Father, and that's what he was implying in his response to God when he said, "You gave her to me." He had eaten in faith. And God's gift of the Church to Christ was of God's goodness as well.

Adam was, after all, a foreshadowing of Christ. He was portraying Christ Jesus. Was Jesus a sneaky, craven coward who would willfully sin and then put the blame on the Church, or on God? Would Jesus impugn God's goodness? No, and neither would Adam, who foreshadowed Christ, do such base and abominable things. Adam was portraying Christ, child. His answer was not a fearful and perverse effort to divert the blame either onto the woman or onto God. Would he blaspheme God to his face? Is that what Jesus did? Or, did Jesus partake of the cross trusting in God's goodness?

Adam's answer to the Creator meant, "You gave me the woman, and your gifts are altogether delightful and good. I love her, and I am willing to die to remain with her, for we are one flesh. I ate because I trusted that you would make things right somehow, even through death itself." He was foreshadowing Christ Jesus, the second Adam. God gave Adam the woman, and the woman brought him death. But even death itself, if it be a gift from God, is a good and perfect gift. And, like Christ Jesus, he willingly accepted death because of his love for Eve, and his oneness with her. It was an act of love. And love denies self in its concern for its beloved. It denies self. Is not this what Jesus did? And is this not how he overcame the Serpent?

Seeds of the Future

Our first ancestor was one of the unsung heroes of faith, a figure of Christ Jesus the greater Adam. Eve likewise was a heroine at his side. Human history began in faith and heroism, foreshadowing Christ, and imaging God. This is a story of love and faith and God's goodness, a prefiguring of the Gospel, not a sordid tale of duplicity and rebellion, and of a fall. Jesus did not fall when he partook of the cross! They both trusted, even as we do today, in God's goodness. Adam, like Christ Jesus and every believer who receives Christ, trusted that God was gracious, and powerful even in the dark. He was willing to walk into the very jaws of death for his bride, trusting that somehow God could make it right. And he was right.

God held nothing but goodwill toward them. Because of them the creation was very good. They would lead to Christ Jesus. And Christ Jesus was God's purpose for the creation. The prophecies that God pronounced upon the personages in Eden were not punishment. They were previews of their destinies. They were prophecies of how the Gospel would play out. The play was already written. The pictures had been posed perfectly. Their future would be in accord with the nature of each. And the roles that they each played in Eden's drama were in accordance with the roles they would play in history. They were figures of the future, and of himself. God was choreographing events. He was posing them, and painting pictures of a glorious future for humanity, for they imaged God. Take this to heart, child. The image of God is not cowardice, deception, and deviousness. It's not rebellion and fallenness. To portray Adam and Eve that way dishonors Christ Jesus and blasphemes God himself, for they image him.

All three personages had played their roles just as God had intended. Earlier, it had been the Serpent's assignment to separate the world from God. He was doing his job, fulfilling his nature. It is notable that the woman was not told that she would die. There is a subtle hint here of eternal life for the true Church, who fulfills the figure that was Eve.

Adam, like Christ, was intended from the start to rule. The woman was meant to be Adam's complement. The Serpent was the great liar, and the reason for their death. That is his nature (John 8:44). Each played their role according to their individual natures. Events in Eden would prefigure the Gospel and future history. The creation

Seeds of the Future

was not yet finished. Adam and Eve were still being formed into the image of God. They would foreshadow Christ.

The greater Eve, the true Church, is properly subject to Christ because he gave himself up for her (Eph. 5:24-28). Like Adam, he died willingly, because of his love and oneness with her. The dowry was his lifeblood. The greater Eve will live forever because of him. So, it is altogether appropriate for the Bride to serve the one who is her Savior. He was the reason for her creation (1 Cor. 11:8-9).

It was likewise in Eden. Adam gave himself up for Eve, because of his love and their oneness. Is it not appropriate for her to love him in return? And wasn't Adam the reason for her creation? Her subjection to Adam was not in order to demean her, but to bring her appropriately within his love and protection. After all, he would die because of his love for her. He foreshadowed Christ Jesus.

It is entirely right and proper for the Church to serve Christ, for he gave himself up for her, dying in order to save her, because of their oneness and his love for her. He died willingly for his bride. Without him we would die alone, forsaken and forgotten forever, just road kill on the highway of futility. Our surrender and service to Christ is not punishment, nor does it demean us. Serving the will of God in Christ is our joyous privilege, a superb honor. To walk in the light of his will, accepting the leadership of his Spirit, is an exhilarating stroll atop the scented heights of bliss and blessedness, and should be the earnest desire of every true saint.

Correspondingly, Eve's service to Adam was not a punishment. It was the appropriate and proper response to his loving self-sacrifice. It placed her under his protection and providence. Prefiguring Christ, he had given himself up for her, to be with her come what may, in life and in death, trusting in God and proving his love and faithfulness. The two were one flesh. To serve Adam would work her own wellbeing, then, for in serving him she would serve herself. Likewise, in loving her, Adam would love himself, because of that selfsame oneness (Eph. 5:22-28). Eve's relation to Adam, like that of the true Church to Christ, was an uplifting, honorable, appropriate, and beneficial relationship because of Adam's love and care for her.

This is a beautiful love story, not the conniving and rebellious power struggle and fall that the churches love to tell their gullible and undiscerning listeners. It's a story of valor, self-sacrifice, faith, and honor. It's a love story. In dying for Eve, Adam overcame his selfishness. In dying for her, he triumphed over the Serpent inside of him. It's the story of Christ Jesus, folks! A little later, Moses would lift up a serpent in the wilderness, and those who looked upon it would be healed. Still later, Christ Jesus would be lifted up on a hill called Calvary (John 3:14). The death of the Serpent of human nature was the ministry of Jesus. Adam foreshadowed him. Isn't it nigh unto blasphemy to teach that Adam was a coward who tried to put the blame on Eve, as so many churches teach?

The Typology of Marriage

Marriage, begun in Eden, is a living testimony of Christ with his Bride, but especially of God with the world. Adam was a figure of Christ Jesus, while Eve was a figure of the true Church. Because marriage testifies of the relationship between Christ and his Bride, a husband's role within marriage, then, is based upon being like Christ. His leadership should be exercised in a Christ-like manner, demonstrating their oneness and his self-sacrificing love for her. It should have as its purpose a Christ-like concern for her life and welfare, and their togetherness. Whenever he steps outside of that role, not being Christ-like or loving, he loses his authority over her. His authority comes in accurately and authentically taking the role of the Savior (Eph. 5:22-33). That is his role and his responsibility. In the marriage relationship, the husband images Christ (1 Cor. 11:7). Wow!

Likewise, a wife is to be a help for her husband and abide by his leadership as he seeks to lead in Christ-likeness. She is his helper and companion. Together they are symbolically one flesh, not two, and they image God in this. She complements Adam. She completes him. And together they image God. Whenever she steps outside of that role of helping him as he seeks to be Christ-like, she loses the right to his love and protection. And she fails to image the Church.

Would it not be improper for the Church to attempt to exercise authority over Christ, or to serve her own selfish and carnal interests and desires instead of serving him? The proper function of the Church is to serve Christ, bear him children, and teach them. Churches should be devoted to evangelism and spiritual growth, then. This in no way demeans or belittles them, and it did not demean or belittle Eve. Nor does it belittle wives. Men cannot bear

Seeds of the Future

children. Only women can do so. It's their role within marriage, and portrays the role of the Church. In the outworking of God's plan, the Church bears and nurtures his children as she receives his love, guidance, and protection.

This is why the Church must evangelize. Christ does not preach and witness directly. He does not send the angels to the work. He has sent his followers out to the task. The Spirit works through the saints. The Gospel is holy fire, and must be carried in holy vessels. The man Saul was told to meet with Ananias, remember (Acts 9:1-19)? Only the saints may carry the holy flame of salvation (Num. 16:1-40).

These roles and relationships present the original, ideal patterns and meanings of marriage that were demonstrated from the beginning. Marriage is a living picture, a testimony of God. Together, husband and wife testify of Christ's loving oneness with the Church, and of God's future oneness with the creation. Soon God and the world will be reunited. That's the Gospel. Husband and wife live daily the Gospel story. It should be an honest and true reflection of that story, honoring the One whom it images. It should be a good testimony, a good marriage.

But like the other things of the Law, marriage is not obligatory. Believers are free to marry or not, depending on the leadership of the Spirit. Begun in Eden, marriage is, after all, an institution of the Law. And the Law was just a shadow that disappeared with the coming of the light. The saints are not under the Law.

This is not to say that believers should cohabit without marrying, however. Although the Law is not binding, it is a divine lesson to learn how to live in Christ. All things must be done for his honor and glory. And marriage is an excellent way to testify of him. But it should be a good testimony, led of the Spirit. It should not portray Christ as an adulterer, or as unfaithful, or selfish, or anything that is not truly Christ-like.

Eve's pain of childbirth was not a punishment or a belittling of her. It was a prefiguring of what will come upon the true Church because of her place and nature as the Bride of Christ (1 Tim. 2:15). God's good pleasure, and salvation, will be as available to women as to men, even while woman's role within the biblical marriage relationship is to help her husband lead in Christ-likeness and bear him children, rather than to rule (Acts 2:17). But we must remember, also, that women in Christ are free from the Law. It has no authority to force them into a role contrary to the Spirit's leadership. The Law holds no authority over the children of God, male or female.

Because of this, the pattern of marriage in Eden is just that. It's only a pattern, non-binding on the saints. Like the sacrificing of lambs and goats, and other things of the Law, even marriage itself has been annulled in Christ. However, because of the weakness of human nature, usually it is best to marry anyway. A good marriage provides for the welfare of society, of the home, of children, and of the churches. It provides an excellent way to testify of Christ. A good marriage says good things about the relationship between Christ and the Church.

The pain of childbirth reflects the price of children being born into the kingdom of God (Rev. 12:1-2, 5). Zion's children are born through the immense suffering of the cross of Christ, and of the saints. The birth of the corporate Christ will come in the final day, when the Antichrist will have killed all the faithful witnesses. The pangs of persecution will run, each following ever closer and stronger behind the other, until the final blood-bath spills over the world. The blood of the saints will flood the earth, and the earth will give birth to the children of God, in an instant, in the blink of an eye (1 Cor. 15:51-55). These are a few of the lessons of Eden. There are more.

The Curse of the Ground

Another lesson can be learned from God's curse of the ground. It is notable that Adam was not cursed directly. The ground received the curse. But it involved him, because he drew his physical life from the earth. The Lord was introducing Adam to his destiny, posing him to depict it. His earthly life would consist of sorrows, hardships, and frustrations. It would be a lifelong struggle, a war that he would lose. What the Creator was telling Adam was that humanity had no lasting future. He would be cut off. He would surely die.

Adam was formed from the earth. The curse of the ground meant that the things that make up human life in this world would be fruitless and frustrating. He had no lasting future because he was incapable of doing God's will. And to serve God's will was the reason that God had created him. The Creator wanted for himself a

Seeds of the Future

new Body. But Adam was unserviceable for that purpose, as evidenced by his breaking of that first law. A self-serving humanity, serving the Serpent rather than God, would not do at all. It would be like a cancer in the Body.

Eating means more than to munch lunch. It unites the eater with that which is eaten. What eating meant for Adam now was that his participation in the fruit of the earth, which meant his humanity in all its strivings and aspirations, its toils and troubles, would be a dead-end street. The earth was cursed. His life would be a pile of dirt and a wisp of air. Human striving would have no ultimate purpose. The greatest human works would be mere sandcastles awaiting high tide. He would be no better than road kill on the highway of futility. What a stark, tragic picture of human life without Christ!

Adam would have to work, yes, but that was not his problem as some think. Hard work was not the curse. Work is good (Gen. 2:15). Indeed, God himself works, and left us an example. We are ultimately to be like him. Adam had sinned by eating, not by working. So, Adam would now have to eat of the plants of the field, for he could no longer reach out and pick the choice delicacies he so loved from God's organic garden. He would get heartburn, and ulcers, and acid reflux, and food poisoning. Flesh and blood could not live in Paradise and eat from the tree of life. Humanity had no lasting future (1 Cor. 15:50). Adam would fill out the remainder of his day, and die.

His frustration would last "all the days of his life," the same phrase God used with the Serpent, showing that they would share in a single fate, and a common end. They would live together and die together (Rom. 7:24). The Serpent would accompany him out of the garden. He would live off the man, eating at his heart. They both would partake of the same dust of the ground. They would be chained together in a common destiny (Rom. 7:24; Rev. 20:7-10). The Serpent would share Adam's grave.

Not only would Adam live estranged from God, eating in toil and trouble, but the land that he worked would produce thorns and thistles. This meant that in the fields of his endeavor, in this world of dead works, would grow harmful, painful, and profitless things that would stab and sting. Human life would be a carousel that went nowhere, a merry-go-round of madness full of hurts and heartaches. Adam would ride until he got dizzy, and then he would fall off.

His destiny of death would find its greatest fulfillment at Calvary. Jesus' crown of thorns signaled that he was taking on the full measure of Adam's thorn-filled fate. He bore all the pain, sweat, sorrow, and frustration of human nature, all of it, and fulfilled in himself the destiny pronounced upon Adam. It was heaped high upon him, a great mountain of pain and suffering, because he was the ultimate Adam, the epitome of all that was pronounced for humanity. The crown of thorns on our Savior's bloodied brow was a sign to alert us that the cross was the fulfillment of God's forewarning word to Adam.

Those great drops like blood that fell from our Savior's brow, that he sweated in Gethsemane, were signs as well. They too signaled that his horrible death was the fulfillment of God's word to Adam (Luke 22:44). The human Jesus did not evade the destiny that was pronounced upon humanity in Eden. Incredibly, to his unending glory, he experienced it full strength, willingly, without any anesthesia. He filled Adam's cup to overflowing, and then drank it down to the dregs. Glory to him! Thank you, Jesus.

Adam's life is a foreshadowing. God was drawing pictures for us to see and take to heart. He was posing the first couple, positioning them just right, for generations yet to come. The pattern of all creation is darkness before light. First comes the long night of waiting, and then the glad daytime of rejoicing (Ps. 126:6). If this world is sorrowful, it is only because of the great joy that awaits. Life will overcome. Faith will be confirmed. The fulfilling of the Gospel will be glorious beyond imagination (Rom. 8:18). Yes, Adam would die, but God had already hinted of the Gospel to them. Life was already in the wings, waiting. Death would sing its song, but life would have the encore, with full orchestra and chorus.

Despite the unrestrained horrors of the cross, the light of salvation was shining, and could not be extinguished. God is benevolent and good, and even the dark midnight of death cannot controvert his loving plans. Life comes in the morning.

Chapter Seven
Paradise Lost

Things had gone downhill for humanity. Cast out from the garden, destined to partake of the fruit of the ground in sorrow, and forced to play unwilling host to a treacherous and deadly parasite, their once so promising story had turned tragic. But it would get worse. Troubles would come in waves, each time higher, threatening to sweep humanity away. From the beginning, human history has been an intense drama, filled with suspense and uncertainty.

Outside of the Garden

Even after God drove the inaugural couple from his garden, he would not forget them. His plans and purposes for the creation were still in place. They had not changed. Events were moving along just as he had envisioned and planned. Their disobedience had not been unforeseen, nor had it wrecked his purposes. He continued to nudge events at key times, never overriding their precious freedom of choice. He was purposely posing them in ways that would portray the future, painting prophetic pictures in the dark that could be seen only after the divine light of understanding would come. It would be necessary to wait patiently until the one with eyes to see would arrive, the one who could interpret the meaning of the pictures.

Until Jesus came, the picture of God and his plans would remain hidden and undisclosed to human and angel understanding. But it was there, nonetheless, right from the beginning. The creation was a self-portrait. In due time the greatest and mightiest Son of Adam would wipe away all the centuries of accumulated dust and dirt from the painting, and reveal its true typological colors. He would reveal God in the brilliance of daytime and in the power of truth. Looking forward to those resplendent days, the Creator was planting seeds of destiny that would sprout when their time would come. He would plant them outside of Eden. The whole world would be his garden (Isa. 6:3; Hos. 2:21-23; John 20:15). He would nurture and cultivate it, and in due season the flowers that he was planting would bloom and fill the air with their many delightful fragrances.

East of Eden

God placed the cherubim, and the flaming sword that turned in all directions, on the eastern side of Eden, to guard the way to the tree of life. He had cast humanity out toward the east to fulfill their destiny and die. Yes, these strange, sometimes baffling events were seeds of God's planting. But what scented flower could bloom from their doom, from their being cast out of Eden toward certain death?

The garden, sometimes called Paradise, is the place where grows the tree of life. In the Revelation we learn that this ever-flowering tree grows within the holy city, New Jerusalem, which is a symbol of the temple and body of God. To enter this city, one must partake of Christ and resurrection. Eden's tree of life, then, is a symbol of the cross. With its fruit of eternal life, the cross is the tree of life foreshadowed in Eden. The garden in Eden, then, called Paradise and where was the tree of life, symbolizes the place of God's presence. Away from God's presence, barred from eating the fruit of the tree of life, Adam would die. This is extremely important. Adam's death came because he was excluded from the tree of life. It's a hint that eternal life comes from partaking of the fruit of the cross, and eternal death comes by being excluded from that fruit.

The sword that flashed fire and turned every which way, was a figure of God's word. In symbol, this said that eternal life would come only through the word of God. It also said that eternal life was off limits to humans in their animal, carnal nature. The cherubim would sheathe the sword only for Christ (John 14:6). Only the new generation, born of the Spirit, would partake of the tree of life, of the cross. Flesh and blood hides the Serpent in its heart, and can't get him past security. The x-rays of the Spirit catch him every time. Human nature cannot enter through the gates of the holy city of God's presence (1 Cor. 15:50). Humans must be transformed. A new living creature must be created. All in due time.

These four cherubim east of Eden will be seen later, covering the mercy seat and the Ark of the Covenant with their wings. The tribes of Israel encamped around the wilderness temple repeated the same symbolism. They pictured true Israel gathered around the throne in the true Temple in heaven (Num. 2:1-34; Eze. 1:4-28, 10:9-22; Rev. 4:6-8). But all of that will come to light only later. Looking at events in Genesis, it seems that humanity has no lasting future. Tragically, they must work the hurtful, thorn-filled fields of human endeavor until they return to the ground from which they were taken. Could such a seed planted east of Eden grow into a lovely flower?

Strangely, God had promised them the fruit of every tree bearing fruit (Gen. 1:29). No tree was excluded, except the tree of the knowledge of good and evil. And it had been forbidden only to Adam, not to Eve. Indeed, Eve had eaten of that tree precisely because of God's promise to them both. And the promise had not been contingent. God had given them every tree for food, yes, every tree. This included the tree of life. And yet God had run them off precisely so that they could not partake of this one tree. What had happened?

Had the Creator lied? Was he now taking back what he had given them, reneging on his promise? The idea is unthinkable. Sometime, somewhere, somehow, God would make good on his promise. The tree of life eternal would be in humanity's reach. Adam is a representative of the race. We are included in Adam. Even in the hour of darkness and death there is light, faint perhaps, but never put out. The darkness cannot extinguish God's candle. Everywhere, from the beginning, the light of salvation glows. The Gospel is present wherever we look. Yes, Adam must die, but death would not be the end. His story would continue. Death would become a blessing. There would come a son of Adam for whom the tree would yield its fruit in abundance. And he too must be planted in death. The loveliest and most aromatic flower of all would sprout and grow on a hill called Calvary.

The cherubim, as we've said, were figures of the tribes of Israel, which in turn were figures of the saints (Num. 2:1-34). There is a hint here, then, that the way to the tree of life and salvation, guarded by the cherubim wielding the sword of God's word, would be through the preaching of the people of God. It would be by his presence and in his power, following the guidance of the Spirit (Eze. 1:24-25, 10:5). The Word would become flesh. The Gospel of salvation would be proclaimed by the tribes of the new Israel (John

20:22-23). Did you get that, tiger? They would not remain silent (Rev. 11:5). They would not hide in the hush. And the saints are the new Israel. Does this include you, child?

Cain and Abel

Another seed that God planted is the story of Cain and Abel. Many know the story. Few realize that Cain (a spear) is a figure of Judaism and the Jews, while Abel (breath) symbolizes Christ and the saints. Fewer still are those who realize that when the Jews instigated the death of Jesus, and that foreordained spear pierced our Savior's side, it was the story of Cain and Abel re-enacted, or rather, fulfilled (Acts 2:23; Rev. 1:7). The story of Cain and Abel is the story of the cross. The seed planted in Genesis blossomed on the hill just outside of Jerusalem. It flowered as the fulfillment of this foreshadowing story of Adam's first two children.

It's a tale of two offerings too. Abel's offering was accepted, not because it was by blood, but because it was by faith (Heb. 11:4). Cain, the elder brother, offered the fruit of the soil. The soil, we recall, symbolizes human nature (Matt. 13:19). Cain offered from the soil of human merit. But ever since Adam's disobedience, the soil was under a curse. Cain's offering, the fruit of the God-cursed ground, was unacceptable.

Cain the elder son symbolized Judaism, vainly attempting to win God's favor by offering human behaviors, confusing this with merit. Like the Jews later, he felt that he deserved better. Overcome by jealousy and anger because God had accepted Abel but not him, he slew his younger brother. This portending story of murderous anger and jealousy is repeated in the Jews' treatment of Christ and the early Christians (Heb. 10:19, 11:11-14). Like Cain, the Jews rose up and slew the greater Abel. The blood from Jesus' spear-pierced side still calls to God from the ground (Gen. 4:9-13; Zech. 12:10; Rev. 1:7). And Judaism still offers the fruit of the ground although it no longer yields its strength to them (Rom. 10:19, 11:11). The glory is gone, Ichabod. Cain's offering is refused. The ground of human merit has been cursed, twice. Child, don't try to please God by good behavior, by being a goody goody, by following rules and regulations. Do it by following Christ. Let him lead you, directly and in person.

Paradise Lost

But what was the enigmatic mark that God placed on Cain? In those early days the letter Tau, or T, was often used as a signature mark to signify ownership. It was a foreshadowing symbol of the cross. God placed it on Cain to show that he was under God's protection. Whoever would kill Cain would suffer a seven-fold vengeance.

It seems strange that God would so protect Cain, a murderer. But these events were seeds of God's planting. They would sprout and grow into beautiful scented flowers in the last days. God's curious mercy upon Cain was a figure of God's unimaginable mercy upon the latter-day Jews. God will place a mark on the Jews, identifying them as his own even though they have murdered Abel, that is, Christ Jesus (Gal. 4:29). Whoever would kill the Jews will suffer a seven-fold vengeance. The number seven signals God. Seven-fold vengeance is God's vengeance. This speaks of the last days, and is a warning to the Antichrist. But he will not listen.

The Tau that God will place on them is the sign of the cross. In the End-time the Jews will receive Christ. They will be sealed unto the Savior (Zech. 12:10-13:1; Rev. 1:7, 11:13). The seal will be the sign of Jonah, the sign of the dove, a symbol of the Holy Spirit given to believers because of the cross. The Jews will one day undergo the true baptism of the Spirit. Then, when the Antichrist tries to destroy them, he will suffer the sevenfold vengeance of God, and will himself be destroyed along with all his followers (2 Thess. 2:8-10; Rev. 19:20-21).

Meanwhile, Cain has been banished from fellowship with God, and he languishes east of Eden, in the land of wandering. We remember that Cain had been a tiller of the ground. Now, for murdering his younger brother, his toil in the soil he so loved is cursed again. He spilled innocent blood on the ground, and so the ground will no longer yield to him its strength. The ground here, as in the story of Adam, is a symbol of human endeavor, of all works-based religions. And Cain, as we've said, prefigures the Jews. After the cross, after Cain has killed Abel, their sacrifices and offerings are unacceptable. Slaughtering animals, after all, does not make anyone righteous. No, child, nor does it procure eternal life. Their efforts to please God through human endeavor no longer yield their desired fruit. The ground is cursed and unfruitful.

Paradise Lost

What this means typologically is that the Jews, being in Judaism figuratively tillers of the ground like Cain, have lived by cultivating the soil of human merit. Children of the flesh, they have served the flesh. Their focus has been on blessings and prosperity in this present life in this present world. To be rich like Abraham, or David, or Solomon, has signified for them divine favor. Long life, prosperity, and lots of children have been their proof of God's good will toward them. But God's true good will came with Jesus (Luke 2:14). After the cross, Judaism has become a form of leftover ethnocentrism, of humanism directed toward themselves as Jews. Judaism now is humanism primping and preening in front of a mirror in order to impress God. It is a grasping for God's favor by offering him human behavior, wrapped tightly in laws. They offer the fruit of the ground that God has cursed twice.

Many Christian churches of today have followed their example and have become tillers of the soil too. God's blessings, they say correctly, are available to everyone who has faith. Then they add greedily that faith is the means of gaining health, wealth, and happiness here on earth. But that is not the Gospel. It's the error of Balaam, and will be the artifice of the Antichrist. These churches are following in the footsteps of the Jews, tilling the same doubly-cursed ground of worldly prosperity. But how much treasure did Jesus accumulate? How long did he live? How large a family did he have? How many wars did he win? Was not his focus on heaven rather than on earth?

Others take a verse or two of Scripture and moralize about it, as if the Bible were a text on how to please God through religious or social etiquette. They are fallen in the same bottomless pit as the Jews. Look at their shoes. Is that not behaviorism all over them?

Throughout their early history, God's favor upon Israel meant his presence among them. Theirs were the covenants and the promises, and the system of worship given them by the Creator (Rom. 9:1-5). His presence and favor assured them of victory in war, health in body, and material wealth and prosperity. But because of the cross, because Cain killed Abel once more, the soil of Judaism is blighted and under the ban. Their focus on the flourishing of the flesh no longer yields its strength to them. Their house was left desolate at Pentecost. Their fields are dry, waterless wastes devoid of the Spirit (Luke 12:35). God's blessings now no longer consist of health,

Paradise Lost

wealth, and protection from enemies. Humanism, even that which takes the form of Judaism, is under God's curse, child. The true riches are heavenly, not worldly (John 18:36). The children of blessedness now are not Jews, but new converts reborn into the kingdom of heaven, both Jews and Gentiles.

The history of the Jews reveals clearly that God's blessings and favor no longer guarantee prosperity in this world as it did with the patriarchs. Is not Jesus our complete and perfect example? The health and wealth Gospel is an attempt to revive Old Testament shadows. Its preachers are luring the unlearned onto land twice cursed by God! They offer drink from a chalice of poison, and then unashamedly ask for money, lots of it. Their own prosperity gained by fleecing the gullible then becomes the proof of their doctrine. The more people they can deceive, the richer they become. Their wealth is based on the number of people they mislead. And they promote the blasphemy that their prosperity and service to the Serpent of self is evidence of God's favor upon them! They implicate God in their deception. Material prosperity is a carrot that they dangle in front of the people, who then become infected with the same greed (Mark 10:25; Luke 16:13). Don't be fooled, fellow.

Jesus is our only true example for right living. He calls us to follow him, a man of sorrows, rejecting the crumbly pebbles of prosperity in this world for the sparkling, many-faceted diamonds of heaven (Heb. 12:1-2). He invites us to take up our own cross. The way to Paradise is not in the hot air balloon of worldly success, but on a *via dolorosa* carrying our own cross to our own Calvary. The fiery sword that guards the way to Paradise will puncture the balloon every time.

And the error of humanism has a companion in the false and insidious doctrine that Jesus died in our place as our substitute. So we don't actually have to follow him very far. Indeed we can't, because he was supposedly one-of-a-kind, the God-man, something we can never be. He didn't really say to deny ourselves and take up our own cross. Well, he did, but he didn't really mean it. He wants to bless us and make us rich, healthy, and happy. That's why he substituted for us.

Substitution is the flip side of the works righteousness error. Rather than trying to earn God's material blessings through human endeavor as in works righteousness, it supposedly accepts God's material blessings freely through faith and flattery. But the emphasis is still on this world. Rather than earn worldly blessedness as in Judaism, they expect God to grant it to them freely, if they have enough faith that he will and if they praise him sufficiently. They implicate God once more in their worldliness and humanism, in their Serpent worship. It is the same message that the Antichrist will preach.

And many churches love it and employ it, serving the people and promising them happiness and satisfaction. It draws huge crowds. People love to be served. And it gives them an excuse to indulge their carnal appetites fully, being politically correct and well hidden behind the smiling mask of religious piety. Swimming in materialism and carnality called prosperity, these churches can pretend that the hand of God's blessing is upon them because they grow large and prosperous. They serve humanity as if this were service to God. But they are actually serving the Serpent. They do not understand that the promotion of human welfare and prosperity is not the Gospel. They proclaim life, but it is merely the shadow of life, entirely animalistic. True life is in the Spirit, not in the flesh. They are pretenders tilling the ground twice cursed by God. What is that stuff smeared all over their shoes? And just look at the mess they leave behind them.

People must understand that the ground of Cain, which is Judaism and her look-alikes, has been cursed. You can't walk in it without getting humanism all over your shoes. And it's very slippery. If you slip and fall in it, well, you get the point. Not heeding the lessons of the past, many churches are working hard cultivating a field of cockleburs (Gen. 3:17-19, 4:11-12). They are spiritually wretched, miserable, poor, blind, and naked, but think that they are rich. They believe that material and numerical prosperity is a sign of God's favor (Rev. 3:17-18). What's your church like? Are you being led by a blind and naked church that thinks to serve God by serving the Serpent of human nature?

These churches are actually fulfilling the foreshadowings of Baal worship, whose worship consisted in sexual debauchery. Their programs are calls to come and indulge your carnality, called abundant living. Don't deny yourself. Enjoy yourself in the name of Christ! God wants to bless you with all the pleasures that this life offers. That, dear friend, is spiritual adultery (1 John 2:15-17). May God be merciful.

Nevertheless, as Judaism wanders in the wilderness east of Eden, far from the presence of the Lord, barred from the true temple and paradise of God by the cherubic sword, the Jews remain under God's watchful gaze. This, too, is a flower that will grow and perfume the air with its fragrance.

When Christ returns, it will be from the east, from where he left, on the Mount of Olives (Eze. 10:19, 11:22-23, 43:1-4; Acts 1:9-12). Olives symbolize those faithful ones who have been crushed so that the oil of the Spirit might flow. In the end-time, the crushed Jews will look repentantly upon him whom they have pierced (Zech. 12:10; Rev. 1:7). The blood of the greater Abel still calls to God from the ground. It calls for mercy upon his people. And it will be heard.

Perplexing Questions

If Genesis were easy to understand, there would not be so many unanswered questions about it. But long centuries have passed between our day and the writings. And with the centuries has come an intellectual distance between the ancients and us. Our language and thought processes are different. Our culture, and the way in which we look at the world and explain it are far removed from how they perceived reality.

As if that were not enough, orthodoxy has intruded her own misguided interpretations between the truth and us. She has strewn her misguided traditions all over the text. Thank goodness for shovels. One thing is for sure. We'll get lots of exercise.

The Long Lives

For centuries, people have wondered and debated about the long lives of the early humans. Is their longevity just mythology? How could they have lived so long when today, even with the most advanced medicines and scientific breakthroughs, we seldom reach even a hundred years? Some have speculated that it is because of

Paradise Lost

diet. Prior to the Flood, they say, people were vegetarians. Eating meat has caused the decline in longevity.

But where's the proof? Vegetarians today do not live for hundreds of years, even if they have vegetarian parents and grandparents. A vegetarian diet can affect our health, but it cannot extend our lives more than a few years, and certainly not several centuries. I have yet to meet a live eight or nine-hundred-year-old vegetarian. I doubt that you have, either. In fact, I'm fairly certain you haven't.

Others try to change the length of those early years, making them shorter than what we have today. For example, one of today's years can be said to equal ten of those early years. It's an interesting game for a while, but the fun doesn't last. Their months would have lasted just three of our days! That's kind of short, isn't it? Their days would have been around two-and-a-half hours (Gen. 7:11). And the Flood would have lasted all of four days and nights! The earth must have been spinning faster than an ice skater doing the whirlies. The air would have been blown away.

Seth would have been a father at ten-and-one-half. Enosh would have been married and a father at nine, and Mahalalel at the ripe old age of six-and-one-half! The game is amusing for a while, but not very credible.

Imagine putting in a day's work in an hour. That sounds good, but wait. Subtract lunch and two coffee breaks. You'd have three minutes for lunch, and forty-five seconds to gurgle your coffee down, go to the bathroom, etc. Dizzying, isn't it? You'd better hurry home right now, because you'll have less than an hour's sleep. Hurry. You've got just two minutes to get home and to bed. And tomorrow will be the same. No, changing the length of the year does not work.

Another large group thinks that the length of human life deteriorated because of the sinfulness of humanity. As humans became progressively more sinful, it affected their health and longevity. But if this theory were true, then human longevity would have continued to decline. The human race would have become extinct long ago! Is that the case? It doesn't appear so. We are not even on the endangered species list. Perhaps a bomb could do the job, or maybe a meteor. But sin? Eating apples? No. Eating pears? No. Pomegranates? No. Lemons?

Paradise Lost

Human nature has not changed, nor is it changing. Sinfulness has not gotten worse. Cain, only the second after Adam, was already a murderer, jealous and angry, and full of hate. Creation is no longer happening, so people are not changing. God is resting from his work on this creation, and we're still living in the original Sabbath of creation. Human nature is not running backwards, or forward. The gears of creation are disengaged. The world is parked, the motor is off, and the doors are locked. And only the Creator has the key.

Besides, true sinfulness consists not in the things we do, remember, but rather in our participation in createdness. We're not more created than the early humans. This world was meant to be temporary. And humans are of the world and worldly. Our createdness, not our sins, is what separates us from the Creator. People of today are just as much a part of the creation as were the ancients, and just as naturally wicked, but not more so. Remember, also, that sins are just ideas. Although our character can change to a certain degree, as well as our personality, our nature doesn't change when we have an idea, regardless of what the idea might be. Ideas and actions in fact express our nature. And much of the time it isn't very pretty, is it?

This is not to say individuals and societies cannot sometimes sink lower and lower into the quicksand of depravity. The level of morality in a culture or country can decline until they choke in their own corruption. People, after all, are people, and you know what that means. See how they walk, shoes heavy with immorality. Unable to stay upright for long, they keep falling drunkenly into the mud of humanism, fulfilling their human nature, and proud of it. The more of human life and its accessories that they can accumulate, the higher is their opinion of themselves. Their goal is more, ever more and more. Blindly, they have not learned Eden's lesson. The road of human endeavor is twice cursed, and leads to a very dead end.

And many have walked it. Such was the condition of the Canaanites whom God commanded Israel to dispossess. It was the same with ancient Rome. People can fall to such a level of rebellion that God will abandon them. God destroyed the ancient world with the floodwaters of Noah's day for working the ground. Working the ground symbolized human endeavor, including human fulfillment. And human fulfillment, child, is by no means godliness. Jesus counseled his followers to deny self, not to indulge its lusts (1 John 2:15-17).

The wickedness of the antedeluvians was not a change in their nature. It was the free, unbridled expression of it. Human nature is naturally predisposed toward success and survival through selfishness and pleasure-seeking. We have what some call egos, and are oriented toward doing our own will rather than doing God's will (Rom. 8:8). The antediluvian people grew in wickedness, yes, but this was not a progressive deterioration in their biology, or a change in their nature. It was in their behavior. It was the free expression of their nature. It was not a change in their genes, but rather in their culture and in their morals. It was the progressive expression of humanism, ever more wicked, which in its very nature is opposed to holiness.

We recall that good is the will of God, while wickedness is opposition to the will of God. The people were not breaking the Ten Commandments, because these had not yet been given. Nor were they breaking an imaginary, unknown commandment. Their wickedness was not in relation to a set of divine laws. It was enmity to God's will. Their manner of living was not in keeping with God's plans and purposes. The Creator was looking ahead, choreographing events so that they would lead to his Son.

As we have seen earlier, sins and guilt are just imaginary abstractions in the mind. They have no objective reality. They cannot be transmitted through our genes, as by magic. It is true that actions such as lying or stealing can affect our health. But honest individuals do not outlive dishonest ones by centuries. And greedy people live about as long as do generous ones, sometimes longer. Individuals who disobey the Ten Commandments last about as long as those who obey them. If you tell lies, it won't usually diminish your children's life span. And telling the truth won't add centuries to your life or to that of your children either.

The idea that sins affect longevity is an extension of the false, magical doctrine of the Fall of Man. Supposedly, the first sin caused death and deterioration to invade Adam's perfect and immortal nature, and he began the slow process of dying. Presumably, his children inherited this deteriorating physiology, which continues to deteriorate, because of the fall. But there was no fall. Adam didn't stub his toe, or skin his knees. He opened his eyes, not his toes or his knees or elbows. And there has been no consequent progressive physiological deterioration. Since the Flood, the elevator of human biology is stuck on the ground floor. Since the Sabbath began, creation in this world has ended.

The theory of deteriorating biology makes sins biological, literal and substantive, something real, whereas the Bible teaches that sins are intangible, imaginary things with no physical reality. Sins are ideas, blinking neon lights that go on and off in our minds. They are will-o'-the-wisps that exist only in the presence of Law. Where Law is nonexistent, it can't be broken, and sins can't exist (Rom. 4:15). Sins are only as real as people think they are.

You cannot make anyone live for several centuries by making it illegal to die young. Law has no power, because it has no life. The humans who believe in it are where the power lies. Not laws, but the people who enforce them wield the power. Law by itself cannot give life, nor can it take life away. The death penalty is not accomplished by a law, but by those who believe in the law. The long lives of the early humans, then, could not have been on account of obeying or not obeying a law, even if there had been a law. Their wickedness was not based on Law. Wickedness brought the Flood, it's true, but it did not cause the drop in longevity. Wickedness is merely the natural, self-serving state of humans. Laws exist only in the mind. Sin was not a butcher's knife that chopped human life expectancy into little pieces.

Law entered the world when God forbade Adam the fruit of a certain tree in Eden. But he disobeyed. Nevertheless, neither the law nor his sin killed him. He lived on for several centuries. The law was just an idea in his mind, an abstraction. He did not imagine or pretend himself to death. He died because of the Serpent inside him, eating at his innards. Death was already inherent within his mortal nature. It was a built-in part of his biology. To live forever, he needed to eat the life-giving fruit from the tree of life. But he couldn't get past the sword. So he died a natural death. Death is natural. Eternal life is unnatural, for it is holy, separated from this world.

Then later, when Moses was given the Law, it was for Israel alone, and had no great effect on Israelite longevity either. The life span of Jews or of present-day Christians is not a rubber band that can be stretched centuries long. The fountain of youth does not flow in this present world. And the tree of life grows only in Paradise. To get there, you have to get past the sword. The word of God keeps intruders out of God's garden. It's off-limits to uninvited humans. He doesn't want rowdies coming in and disrupting the party.

The End of the First Creation

We remember that the pre-Flood world was encased in a greenhouse. Humidity was much higher then, and the sun's rays did not bombard as they do today. It was a different world than ours. The atmosphere, the soil, and the weather were different. But most importantly, the Spirit had not yet withdrawn from the world. It would leave at the Flood (Gen. 6:3). Human life span plummeted only after the Flood. The great Deluge was the cliff from which human longevity jumped. It was because the creative, life-giving Spirit of God separated from this world.

There is no need to disbelieve the years of the Bible, or to make sins into real animals that bite. Sins are like piranhas, it's true. But they're just pictures of piranhas, not real ones. The things that are called sins are really the expression of human nature acting contrary to the will of God, revealed in his Law. Humans do not have real piranhas swimming around inside them, although sometimes they may have worms. The flood of Noah's day marked the turning point in human longevity because it marked the start of the Sabbath, when God began his rest. It was when God stopped his work of creating and withdrew his Spirit.

The end of the first work of creation was, of course, the beginning of the Sabbath. Having finished one project, God started on the next one. The Bible says that he rested from his work of creation when he had finished forming the first human couple. That seems clear enough. However, God continued to relate with them personally, positioning them, pulling them out from the pit of animal innocence with the rope of Law. And he kept up the conversation with others. Humans multiplied until the time of Noah, centuries later.

The end of this world can tell us about the beginning. The future is child of the past. Up until now we have been foreseeing the future by looking backwards. Now we will turn our heads and look at the future in order to understand the past. They relate as type to anti-type. History is God's poem. The beginning is a promise, and the end is its fulfillment. Understanding the fulfillment can help us understand its promise.

As we approach the light at the end of the tunnel, we see that the present world ends only after the new world is ready to appear. Before the coming new creation of eternal glory can be completed, this present creation must be transformed. Before the greater Noah and family can step out into the pristine new world of tomorrow, this present world must pass away. Like the first world, it will undergo a flooding, purifying baptism, this time a baptism of fire.

First has come the darkness. First is the night, and then the day. That's the pattern. And the pattern holds. This world will be recycled. The end tells us what the beginning has not told us. It gives us the rest of the story. What it says is that, in the end, or rather in the great and glorious new beginning, God's true Sabbath rest will come out and sing its song, but only after the present world bows out and leaves the stage. The world of eternity will enter the spotlight only after the curtain closes on this present temporal world. One world must leave before another takes its place. The shadows will disappear when the light comes. This present world will be transformed. This tells us that the first Sabbath, in which we are living today, did not begin until after the destruction of the antediluvian world, which happened in the floodwaters.

This bears repetition. The coming new world is standing in line waiting its turn. And God's true rest will not begin until after the passing of this present world. Correspondingly, God did not rest until this world of today, in its present state, had been fully formed. And significantly, the world in its present state did not arrive until after the Flood had destroyed the previous world of wickedness. God rested only after the Flood. Until then, creation was still happening. When Noah and family disembarked from the ark into the fresh new world of newly transparent skies, creation had stopped. The Spirit had departed. God had ceased from his work of creation.

Prior to the Flood, God looked upon the earth and saw its wickedness. He was sorry that he had made man. We must not take this to mean that God had messed up, or that he had not anticipated what would happen. It meant that God was about to effectuate a change, as when he said earlier that it was not good that man should be alone (Gen. 2:18). God was repenting.

But remember that repentance is change. It is not just an emotion. God's repentance meant that his involvement in the creation was about to change. Looking upon all the violence and wickedness in the earth, he declared that his Spirit would not abide in man forever, because man is flesh too (Gen. 6:3). After 120 more years, God's creative Spirit would leave. It was never God's ultimate purpose to live in rebellious, wicked humanity. His purpose was to live forever in the new creation that he would produce by transforming and glorifying carnal, sinful humanity. And Noah's new world was a shadow of it.

Pouring out his Spirit upon humanity gives life, while taking it away brings death (Job 34:14-15; Ps. 104:29-30). When God foretold in Genesis that his Spirit would be withdrawn, it meant that creation would cease. The Sabbath would begin. The Flood would come, and usher in a bright new world with clear skies and unobstructed vistas. God was painting pictures of the future. And the future verifies what the past promised.

After the Flood, because God withdrew and hid his face from the world, longevity plummeted. Prior to that time, God's creative Spirit was still roaming throughout his creation, filling it with life and vitality. Now, today, the world possesses only the spirit of this present age (John 12:31, 14:30; 2 Cor. 4:4; Eph. 2:2, 6:12; 1 John 5:19). The Spirit of creation is no longer operative as it was in the beginning, for the Sabbath has come. The dance of creation has ended. The band has struck up another tune, and another dance has begun. It's been a slow dance so far, but the music is getting faster.

God's holiness means that he is separate from this world. When God withdrew from the world, not only did he make the seventh day holy, but he also sanctified himself! Of course, like the other things of the Old Testament, it was only a shadow or portent of the future. It was partial and prefigurative. God's true Sabbath of holiness and separation from this world will happen when this world and all mankind are destroyed in the flooding glories of the coming consummation, when this world is changed and God makes all things new. He will reveal himself in his brand new body, which will be the new creation in all its marvelous grandeur (Isa. 11:1). This world will have been re-created. It will have been recycled.

The new creation will be the glory of the exalted Christ on the throne of heaven, a throne in which the saints will share (John 12:41;

Rev. 22:1-5). Yes, it's a flower planted from the beginning, a beautiful, sweetly scented grandiflora rose. The divine Gardener likes to plant in rows. He plants in patterns. And the patterns, even from the beginning, speak of his purpose of revealing himself fully in the glorious and perfect realization and manifestation of Christ. God's holiness and glory will be fulfilled in Christ Jesus and the saints.

Forbidden Intermarriages

Another of those places where the Gospel is hidden in history and in God's word is when the sons of God married the daughters of men, and had mighty, renowned children by them (Gen. 6:1-4). Who were these strange and mysterious beings? There has been speculation, staggering at times under a load of racial bigotry, that there were two strains of humans, one righteous and the other sinful, the sons of God being the righteous ones. A son of God in this scenario would mean a righteous person. The daughters of men, then, would have belonged to the unrighteous and evil tribe. It must have been that the righteous girls were ugly, while the bad girls were pretty. Good men married naughty but pretty girls, and their offspring were giants. Huh?

It doesn't work that way, does it? Neither obedience to the Law nor disobedience to it makes one's children more beautiful than the neighbor's children, or much larger. Beauty comes with the luck of the draw, not by telling the truth, or by obeying the Law. At least, that's how it is with outward beauty. Moreover, why would the crossbreeding between two tribes or lineages of humans produce giants, while their inbreeding among themselves would not?

If one group was righteous and the other unrighteous, what law was one group obeying, so as to be righteous? What law was the other group disobeying, to be unrighteous? There is nothing in the biblical account that even hints that God had given any of them any law. The Law of Moses, of course, was not yet given. We recall, also, that every law is imaginary. Righteousness and unrighteousness exist only when there is a law to obey or disobey. Righteousness is obedience to the Law, while disobeying it is unrighteousness. Both are purely imaginary, then, and could not affect biology or longevity.

Obedience to laws does not change human nature. Nor does it produce giants, child.

How can disobeying an imaginary set of laws make you taller and stronger? Can an idea cause human genes to mutate? Will your children be giants because you disobey an imaginary law? Will they be stronger and healthier if you are jealous, or greedy, or tell lies, and marry a naughty girl? The whole idea is ridiculous. This view again commits the error of making sins tangible and real, as if they could affect the reproductive process to produce a special strain of humans. Like a game show on television, the idea barks, "And now, ladies and gentlemen, here's 'To Tell a Lie!' Tell a lie and make your children more beautiful. The bigger the lie, the bigger your children. Who's our first contestant today?"

The intermarriage was not between two groups of humans, one righteous and the other unrighteous, or one ugly and the other fetching, but between angels and humans. The sons of God mentioned here are angels, not humans (Job 1:6, 38:7; Jude 6). What this passage means is that, in the days of Noah, before the Flood, some of the angels had impregnated human women. This was contrary to God's purpose (cf. Gen. 10:8-12; Jonah 3:2; Rev. 11:8). His purpose, of course, was Christ Jesus. Angelic crossbreeding with humans could not be allowed to continue (1 Peter 3:19-20). Christ Jesus would be a normal human, not a giant angel-human. He would be a real, genuine and true human. Get it?

The angels had perverted God's command that the creatures he had created should reproduce after their own kind (Gen. 1:11, 21, 24). That was the pattern God had initiated. Humans should reproduce after their own kind. They should beget humans, not giants or angels. The angels had jumped the fence. They had crossed the borders illegally. So God banned them to pits of darkness until the day of judgment (2 Peter 2:4-5; Jude 1:6-7).

In God's plan, Christ would be the asexual union of the Spirit with the flesh. It would be ordinary flesh. Get it? Humans would have the opportunity to receive Christ. Receiving Christ does not result in a race of giants. Nor was Jesus a giant. He was a normal, genuine human. Indeed, Israel's possession of the Promised Land required dispossessing the giants living there. Those giants that Israel dispossessed were symbols of the principalities and powers that work against Christ, the wicked angels that the saints dispossess in

Paradise Lost

Christ (1 Cor. 15:24; Eph. 1:10, 20-21, 2:2, 3:10; Coll. 2:10, 15; Heb. 1:7).

God's judgment and imprisonment of these overreaching angels, elsewhere called principalities and powers, and in our own day sometimes called natural laws, means that those original creative principalities and powers are no longer operative. A new race of humans is not forming. Creation has ended. It means, also, that Jesus was not born through the union of God and Mary. God did not impregnate Mary. He was not born God the Son. He was born as baby Jesus, fully and only human. The Spirit did not repeat the sinfulness that the wicked angels of the creation had done. Rather, the Spirit enabled her to conceive on her own. It was not God who was born to her. It was the human Jesus. He received the Spirit and became Christ the Anointed One at his baptism, at the age of thirty.

This raises an important question. What, then, of the traditional Christian doctrine of the Incarnation? The tradition implies that God somehow impregnated the virgin Mary, because in the tradition it was very God himself who was born to her. Mary is supposedly the mother of God. Implied in the doctrine is that God punished the angels for cohabiting with humans, and then he committed the same abomination as they did (Jude 6)! Is this what his being a jealous God means? Is the idea not blasphemous? Is the traditional doctrine of the Incarnation not blasphemous? Would God do such a thing, even if he is God? No, it is because he is God that he would not.

Orthodoxy teaches that the union of God and humanity was at Jesus' conception, rather than what the Scriptures explicitly show, at his baptism. For God to be the literal Father of Jesus, he would have had to materialize and somehow implant his seed within her. God would have had to enter her virgin womb. That would have constituted adultery.

With that doctrine, orthodoxy has made God into a cuckold, an incestuous hypocrite, and an adulterer. And the virgin Mary has been made into his willing accomplice. Mary has been made into the Mother of God! And yet she is his daughter, as well as his paramour. Confusing? It gets worse, for she was already betrothed to Joseph. Let's clear our way back to the truth of Genesis.

God employed principalities and powers, also called messengers of God and angels, in the process of creation. Today we sometimes envision them as natural laws. God employed some of these angels to effectuate the separation of the world from himself. Chief among them was the one called Satan. They were powers working in the creation. Some of them were employed to develop and generate the processes of reproduction. They were the agents God used in creating the various plants, birds, animals, and humans, each with their capacity for reproducing. Their orientation and influence was away from God, for they were under the head angel, the prime principality now called Satan whose work was to separate the creation from the Creator (Eph. 3:10, 6:12; Coll. 2:15). The life forces of all the plants and animals were oriented inward, then, toward self-preservation and propagation. Those forces of creation were still operative up until the Flood. The Sabbath had not yet come.

In response to the actions of these creation angels with human women, God declared that his Spirit would not always work or abide in man. It was a hint that he would leave, and that this would occur 120 years hence. With the Flood, God's creative Spirit withdrew from the world, and he rested, making the day holy. Creation ceased, and the Sabbath began. The angels of creation who had impregnated the human women were put in prison, that is, they were rendered inoperative and incapable of creating or materializing. With those original powers of creation figuratively imprisoned, creation in this world is no longer occurring (Jude 6).

However, the new creation is being formed. Mary conceived from her own body, and bore a son. It was by the power and orchestration of the Holy Spirit. It was in holiness, which is a rejection of this world for the next, a step toward the new creation. And God invites us now to live in that same holiness, rejecting the Serpent, the spirit of this world, in order to rest in Christ.

He empowers us through faith to conquer the giants of this world and to take possession of our heavenly Promised Land. Our inheritance includes power over all the giants, all the laws of nature, the principalities and powers that presently keep us in subjection. We will share in the very throne and majesty of God himself. The miracle-working power of faith is an inkling of our future. This is why he invites whosoever will to come and eat from the tree of life and to drink deeply from the living waters. He invites us to follow his example, and to be like him because our future is to share in him. The saints will share in the very nature and lordship and identity of

Paradise Lost

God! They will hold authority and power over the forces of nature even as God does.

God's Repentance

We have said that the stories of the saints image the story of God. With the coming of the first law in Eden, humans gained the knowledge of good and evil, making them like God (Gen. 3:22). Similarly, through the idea of Law, of the recognition that there are qualitative distinctions between behaviors, the saints too come to understand their sinfulness. Human sinfulness is the outgrowth of their creatureliness that is incapable of doing God's will (Rom. 8:7-8). They perform wickedness, that which is not God's will. They need help. So they repent of their wickedness by receiving Christ.

And remember that repentance is change. Their repentance is an actual change into a new creation. Is this process something that the Creator himself undergoes? The Bible nods in the affirmative, and says explicitly that God repented of what he had done. He had created humankind. He sighed over the sinfulness of humanity. He changed. Seeing their wickedness, he was grieved in his heart. The relationship between God and the world underwent a change. He would destroy the whole race, along with the rest of the air-breathing animals. He would undo what he had done. It was not a change in plans, but rather a reaction to human sinfulness. And it was part of God's original plan from the beginning. It was a purposeful prefiguring, a hint of the coming repentance that would come in Christ. Repentance is godliness, a characteristic of divinity. God repented. In this too, the saints image God.

Some churches have taught that God is immutable, unchanging and unmoving. Starting with that idol of stone, they must try to explain away his repentance. But are not humans the image of God? Are we not called to repentance? The Scriptures say explicitly that God repented. And repentance means change. What did that involve?

We must remember that the God of the Old Testament is prefigurative. Remember? His full revelation will be the Son in his fullness of glory. Since the God of Genesis is just a foreshadowing of the God of Revelation who will be fully revealed in Christ, then his repentance in the Old Testament must be just a picture of his true

Paradise Lost

repentance, just a foreshadowing. What, then, is true repentance? It is change, which means that it is creation. There's a new world coming.

In the Old Testament, repentance meant to change one's mind about something. It often involved feeling sorry about a turn of events that a person had caused or done. It was mental, a change of mind, an attitudinal or emotional turn around, and often resulted in a physical response or action. It was largely a feeling or emotion. One of the components of repentance was a feeling of guilt and remorse.

But such repentance is just a shadow, part of the old system that has been replaced. True repentance is more than mental images, feelings, or emotions. It is an actual physical and spiritual change and transformation. It's an act of creation, a step into the new world. Repentance is the result of a choice. With humans, true repentance involves the birth of a new kind of creature. It is not a repetition or renewal of the old, carnal nature. It is not a remake of what Adam supposedly was like before he supposedly fell. It is, rather, a step upward from being merely human to being human-divine, like Jesus.

Yes, amazingly, a person who receives Christ receives divinity, for Christ is divine. Astonishingly, we become Elohim (Ps. 82:1-8; John 10:33-36)! It is a real, literal change, not merely emotional, metaphorical, or attitudinal. Repentance under the Law, which was largely remorse and a change in thinking and attitude, was just a shadow. True repentance involves stepping upward into the very being of God. Don't be afraid to accept this truth, child. Remember that Jesus was human like you before he received the Spirit. He was the firstfruits of a huge harvest. And he calls you to follow him, all the way to the throne (Rev. 3:21).

God's repentance for having made humanity, then, is just a foreshadowing of the true, literal change in which God is becoming a new Person by reuniting with the new, transformed creation. God is changing. He made a choice. He is undergoing true repentance, which is actual, literal conversion. Did you get that? God is undergoing conversion. He is evolving, from the inchoate Old Testament God into the fullness of Christ. And in Christ he asks us to follow him in true repentance. We too, like him, must be converted. We must be literally changed.

God's story is mirrored in the lives of the saints, who are being created in his image. The bedrock of the Gospel is that the saints receive Christ. Is that not something that God does as well? Yes, Calvary was Christ's offering of himself to God, bodily. And this greater Abel was gladly received. God, too, received Christ. Jesus the man received the Spirit of Christ at his baptism, while God the Spirit received the man Jesus. Then, after the cross and resurrection, the reunion was made complete. This is how God and humanity are reconciled. Both God and humans receive Christ, and they become one Body and one Spirit. Jesus was the firstfruits, which means that the rest of the crop will be like him. He is the firstborn as well. Reception of Christ brings a literal change in nature and in the manner of existence. It changes both God and humanity. It's not just a change in attitude. True repentance is an actual change in both body and spirit.

Receiving Christ signifies death for the saints (Rom. 6:3-4). But death is not destruction for them, as it was not for Christ Jesus either. It is a step into holiness, into separation from this world. Eagerly, they look forward to the resurrection, and to their new, glorified bodies. This, too, images God's future and eager desire. Like the saints who image him, he is waiting with anticipation his own resurrection, for his new, glorious Body. The divine Spirit and Body are now separated for a while, differentiated since the creation. God has died. But death destroys neither his Spirit nor his Body. Death for him, as imaged by Christ Jesus and the saints, is just a temporary separation between Body and Spirit.

It merely changes what he was, into what he is becoming. He is forming for himself a temple made metaphorically of living stones (John 14:2-3). He is changing. That is true repentance, and he asks us to truly repent as well. He asks us to be like him! True repentance is godliness. To truly repent is to be like God. To be truly godly, we must repent. Our own repentance, like that of God himself, leads to our work and inclusion in the temple of his delight (Rom. 12:2; 1 Cor. 3:9; 2 Cor. 6:1; Eph. 4:22-24).

Noah and the Ark

Another one of these interesting and informative stories is the epic, world-changing story of Noah and the ark. Let's consider it next. God's garden has many exotic and fragrant flowers. This is one of them, one of the most eye-catching and spectacular.

The story of Noah and the Flood is one of the best known stories in the Bible. We need not repeat the whole thing here. What we will do is focus on its foreshadowings. Like the other stories of Genesis, it has a prefigurative function. It's a flower that will sprout and grow in later times. Instead of reading the whole account, let's look at the pictures, and smell the flowers.

The first picture we come to shows God's repentance and his decision to change his relationship with the world. It would be a step into holiness, for his Spirit would separate from the world. He would destroy the world with a flood, but he would save some of its parts. He saved Noah, and instructed him to save two of every species, so that they could multiply and replenish the earth.

Does it not sound strange that God would take this approach instead of, say, creating a whole new and different world? After all, this world had already shown its corrupt nature. According to the doctrine of the Fall of Man, Noah and his crew had the same corrupt, depraved nature as Adam and Eve and the rest of humanity. And the animals were the same as they had been before the Flood. What was the sense in saving them, unless things were going according to plan? Did God have something more in mind? Actually, God did indeed create a new and different world. But he saved some of it. Get it? He saved some of the world.

Could God not have fixed that entire pre-Flood world without having to destroy it? Was it beyond repair? In actuality the Flood is strong evidence that God did not create from nothingness, for if God could create from nothingness, why would he take some of the old, broken parts of that antediluvian world and use them on this new, post-flood world? Why not, rather, just send that broken world into nothingness and create another one, from nothing? Of course, we already know the answer. God does not work that way. He recycles everything. He likes to work with patterns and archetypes. Rather than throw this world away, he would recycle it, and create a better one more to his liking.

As we've seen, his creative work continued until the Flood. The creation account is the story of how our own world of today came to be. And the world of today is itself a picture, a shadow of the coming new world that's being formed even as we speak. In fact, our speaking in the Spirit is part of the divine command that there come about this brave new world. It will be a new and greater humanity,

Paradise Lost

thoroughly washed and rinsed in the waters of the Spirit, to come out sparkling clean. Our testimony is dynamic and powerful. Our speech in the Spirit is creative, for it is God speaking through us (Matt. 10:40; Luke 10:16; John 13:20). God will recycle this world through his word of unopposable power. It will be through his creative Word, spoken and repeated by his saints as they live and speak in the Spirit. They must not remain silent.

Those who insist that God created from nothingness should be extremely glad that they are wrong. If God would create from nothingness, there would be no reason for him to save them. It would have been much easier to just start over from scratch rather than to go through the whole process of creating a new world out of this present corrupt and depraved one. And then the shame and agony of the cross would not have been necessary.

The truth lies in the fact that this world did not fall when Adam and Eve disobeyed. It is not a fallen world. God did not blunder, nor did Satan outmaneuver him or destroy his perfect plan. Satan was in fact the agent that God used to bring about God's holiness. Satan's work was to separate the world from God. And he's still working at it, in opposition to Christ Jesus.

The world-changing story of Noah and the Flood gives us a wide-screen look at God's reason for creating in the first place. This world was just a prototype, just a temporary mock-up of God's future home. Its watery destruction in order to begin anew was part of that prototypical purpose that tells the future, vividly and full colored. It's a pattern for us to recognize, understand, and take to heart.

The destruction of the antediluvian world tells us what's coming down the pike straight toward us. The Bible prints the future in archetype. First is darkness, then light. First come the shadows, then the reality. Everything is going exactly according to plan. The new creation of celestial clarity will be formed from this present dark and nebulous one. This world will be recycled. It's what the Flood tells us. Like the first creation, the future world of unlimited vistas will not arise from nothingness. Everything is on schedule. God's train is not running late. Nor is it on the wrong track. And it won't be derailed.

The traditional but false doctrine of the Fall of Man says that all nature fell with him, inexplicably, magically. Supposedly, it fell from perfection. That's a metaphorical, magical way of saying that everything changed, without explaining how. The Fall would mean that God reconstructed the post-flood world with faulty parts. He built this new car using rusty bolts with stripped threads, a blown-out engine, and a scratched and dented body. Every single part that God used in rebuilding his new car was faulty, every single part, because the whole creation supposedly fell. The Creator's new car has bent rods, torn gaskets, broken lights, burned-out wires, a slipping transmission, and a cracked block. The doctrine of the Fall makes no sense at all.

In order to build the coming new and perfect world, the Creator will have to replace every single part, and every part of every part. He cannot use any broken or imperfect components. Every single molecule, every atom, every dash and dab of reality must be renewed. But if the entire creation is fallen, there are no good parts to salvage! Every dash and dab has fallen, and it can't get up. Nothing, absolutely nothing can be recycled. The world is just a pile of junk, a total wreck, fit only for the junkyard. The whole thing needs to be just thrown away, all of it. God must buy a brand new world straight from the showroom of never-never land.

This idea of total depravity denies salvation then. If humanity is completely fallen, then strictly speaking it is impossible to save anyone. There is no part of us that is not fallen. Consider, dear one, that salvation means that some aspect of our present person will continue. That is what salvation means. Salvation requires that you save something. But according to the doctrine of the Fall, there is no part of us that is uncorrupted, so no part of us can or should be saved. That would be like putting broken spark plugs in a cracked engine, or like putting anti-freeze into the gas tank.

It would repeat the failures of the past, like saving Noah and his family to populate this post-flood world, hoping they would somehow behave themselves properly. But is that the history of Noah and his progeny? Is the world of today free from violence and corruption because God saved Noah? What will the new creation be like if God saves you and me? Friend, are you totally depraved?

But he will change us, the churches object. That is true. But if he changes us totally, then we will no longer exist. A totally new person will exist. We will be gone. We will not be saved. Every smidgen of our existence will cease to exist, and a new smidgen will take its place, from nothingness. Supposedly, every atom in us is fallen, as well as every part of every atom. Salvation will not have happened. In fact, the totality of who we are will have ceased to exist. We will go into nothingness. That is not salvation. It's the complete and total denial of the true Gospel. It's the anti-Gospel.

The orthodox doctrine of the Fall has tripped over the truth that Law and its children are just images. They're just ideas. And ideas don't change anyone's nature. Adam didn't fall. He opened his eyes. That's what the Bible says. The Law was a means of opening his understanding. It was the tree of knowledge, remember? That's what the Law does. It shows us our need of salvation. That need is what the true Gospel preaches. It offers salvation. Part of us will survive the coming change. Is total destruction salvation? No, it's insanity. Not the creation, but the doctrine of the Fall is itself fallen. Leave it there, child. Let's just shovel it to the side, and continue.

The true Gospel says that a part of us will remain beyond the destruction of this world. God will recycle. He can reuse some parts of this creation in building the new one, because the creation did not fall. He can save humans because we are not fallen! We are not totally depraved. We are his creatures, made in his image and destined to be like him. He made us with freedom of choice. He can save us by faith because we are creatures that can make choices by faith. Those who receive Christ will be saved. Those who don't receive him will not survive the change in which this world evolves into the new world of unimagined splendors.

Salvation is by faith, not by magic. Dear child, true faith does not call you to blindly accept absurd and groundless myths. Faith calls you to the truth. And truth is logical, rational, and understandable. The truth is never inexplicable or incoherent. If your church calls you to accept magic or nonsense in order to demonstrate your faith, run, child, run. And scream as loud as you can.

Water Colors

But let's get back to the Flood. In the Flood, God was drawing pictures of the future, in water colors. The floodwaters are a picture of baptism, which in turn pictures death and new life. The new world will arise from the passing of this one. Like Noah, the saints will emerge from the baptismal waters of death into the fresh new world of unobstructed vistas. This pattern of death into life is everywhere repeated. It is the pattern of creation, and of all reality. God is the Creator. He makes new things out of old things.

After the Flood, the animals could now be eaten, but not with their blood. Blood symbolizes life. We remember that eating something means to assimilate it. The forbidding of animal blood means that Noah and family, although they could eat the animals, were not to assimilate or participate in their life. This was a hint that in the coming new world, humanity would not partake of animal life. Humans would no longer be just animals. Eternal life will not be for the animals, including the human animal. The first Adam, the animal, must die, but another Adam will be born and reborn. In rebirth he will be more than human. He will be the God-man. And he will not remain alone. He will have countless brothers and sisters.

These pictures in Genesis tell us that the saints will be provided for in the new creation, and their lives will no longer consist of the animal nature. The saints will have survived the baptism of death that will flood the world, and will have risen to new life incorruptible. You will no longer be an animal, pilgrim. Again, we can see that the Gospel echoes and re-echoes in these watery scenes. Its colors, layered over with the dust and grime of time and church tradition, are washed and renewed to their original luster and clarity in Christ.

Jesus did not die on the cross to save all humanity. He died to save those who would receive the Spirit. There will be no more sea in the new creation (Rev. 21:1). Humanity will have gone the way of all the earth, cast into the symbolic lake of fire and brimstone. None of the animals, including the humans, will survive. Humanism is ground twice cursed. Its death sentence is certain and cannot be repealed.

The Covenant of the Rainbow

Another beautiful flower in the garden of God is the covenant that he made with Noah. It was a picture of the new covenant in Christ. God's promise that the waters of death will never again destroy the earth is a promise for both this present world and for the next. The floodwaters can never again overwhelm our world because there is no longer a bubble of ice enclosing it that can melt and rain down

Paradise Lost

upon it. However, that does not mean that this world will go on forever. God has spoken its transformation. The unquenchable fires of judgment and of holiness will burn it up along with its works, in a baptism of fire. The new creation will be formed from it. This world will be recycled.

The covenant of the rainbow is a picture of God's unchanging faithfulness. It is strong, unbreakable assurance of life in the new world of salvation and light. The angel of death will be banished, along with Satan its master, and the other angels that serve him. The saints will be secure forever, and their bliss will be without limits. They will bask contentedly in the Creator's watchful care, millennium following upon millennium, for as long as eternity rolls. It will be a time of eternal day, of knowledge unrestrained and divinely empowered.

Of Human Blood

After the Flood, God declared that human blood must not be shed (Gen. 9:4-6). The reason given was that man was made in the image of God. Contrary to what orthodoxy has taught, this image is not anything in humanity's biological makeup. We carry no God-gene within us. The image of God is the typological function that humans play. The shedding of human blood is a figure that points to the crime of Calvary. It's a shadow of the cross. God will avenge it. All the innocent blood shed on earth from the blood of righteous Abel to the blood of Zechariah will be required of this generation of the flesh (Matt. 23:34-36).

The shedding of the blood of one made in the image of God, like the other things of the Old Testament, is a shadow, warning against shedding the blood of Christ Jesus. God will require the lifeblood of his Son, the one made in his image. He required it of the Jews, and he will require it of the Christian Church, when she kills Christ once more, in the person of his martyrs who are made in his image.

Of Heavenly Eyes and Windows

With the Flood, the earth buckled, opening the "fountains of the deep," pushing up the waters that were in its underground (cf. Gen. 2:5-6). The "windows of heaven" were opened as well, when the encircling globe of ice above the atmosphere melted. God reached out and opened them, and the cold upper waters fell to the earth, which buckled further. Mountains were thrust upward as whole continents pushed and shoved each other under the slashing winds and the numbing cold (Ps. 104:5-9). Various seas were formed. The intensely vaporous atmosphere cleared and the clouds dissipated, to display the world with a sudden new clarity and light. A rainbow now arched across the sky. With the new open heavens the seasons of seedtime and harvest began, cycles of heat and cold. This is how the world that we know today was formed. This is how God's model prototypical creation was finished, and the moment in which he finally rested from working on it. It was finished, and it was enchantingly beautiful.

The creation all happened under God's direction, and was written down so that in due time we might believe in Christ. Waters are a symbol of peoples. What the Flood tells us is that the floodwaters of humanity will cover the earth for forty days, that is, for one generation. When this generation of the flesh will have dried up, the saints will step out, like Noah, into the fresh new world of unclouded sight and limitless vistas. They will know as they are now known. The new creation will stretch far and away into the newly opened heavens with incredible transparency. Wondrously, the saints will share in the mind of God (1 Cor. 2:16)!

Those who have exercised faith in Christ and who have received his Spirit will be transformed as they walk out from the ark of salvation onto Zion's Shekinah-lit mountaintop where the translucent air allows unobstructed sight and crystal clear understanding. They will gaze with eagle eyes into the infinite openness, looking out upon the possibilities of God's ever-beckoning, open future. They will share in the very life of the Creator endlessly, yes endlessly. But the forty days of this present period must fulfill their time. The generation of the flesh must pass away. The flood of humanity must subside.

As the flooding waters subsided in Noah's day, he began to think about leaving the ark to go out into the fresh new world. Astoundingly, Noah now becomes a picture of God himself. His actions are intensely typological and prefigurative. He sends out the raven, symbolizing God sending out the human spirit. It does not return to him. The raven is still flying to and fro in our own day, caw-cawing wherever it goes.

But Noah sends out the dove also, a symbol of the Holy Spirit, white and gentle, and it does return to him. It could find no place of rest, for the waters still covered the earth. The waters of humanity are still flooding over the earth unto the present day. Before the new world appears, before the dove of the Spirit can enter into its place of rest, the waters of humanity must dry up. Meanwhile, the Spirit waits.

Seven days pass, being a shadow of the times of the Law, the seven raven days of the human spirit and of Judaism's favor. Then he sends the dove out once more, and it returns with an olive leaf. The times of the Law and Judaism's favor are ending. The Spirit has been to Gethsemane.

The olive leaf signals the great Olive of Israel. It was not by chance that Jesus suffered in that garden, the place of the olive press. He was the Branch broken from off the tree of Israel. The garden was situated on a whole Mount of Olives, a symbol of the kingdom of God, where grow the olives, symbols of the saints. With Christ Jesus, the Gospel times have arrived. But God is waiting yet seven more days before sending out the Dove again, while the days of the Gospel run their course, until the waters are completely gone from the earth. The saints will then step out from the ark into the brave new world of unclouded clarity. They will be filled completely and permanently with the Spirit. God will have become One with the world again. The Dove will have found its resting place in the saints, in the corporate Christ. It will begin the true, long-expected Sabbath of God's eternal rest.

Three "days" are reckoned for the world. God's present "death," his separation from the world as was imaged in the three days of the cross, will last for three time periods or dispensations. And two of those days have already passed! The seven days of the first creation, followed by the seven raven days of Israel's favor and of the human spirit, have ended. We are living now in the third day, which holds within it the seven olive days of the Gospel, the dove days of Christianity's favor. It will end with the Resurrection. When these Gospel days of the olive leaf in which we are living have passed, when the olives have been fully crushed to release the oil of the Spirit, then the time of consummation will arrive. Noah (God) will send out the Dove, and it will not return. It will have found its resting place in the saints. The eternal Sabbath will have begun. Noah's Spirit-filled family will step out onto the mountaintop where the air is clean and crisp, and you can gaze deep into eternity.

As we've seen, the picture stories of the Flood tell and retell the Gospel tale, glorious beyond telling.

The Nature of Sin

To understand what humanity's problem is, and its solution planned from the beginning, we must clearly understand the true nature of sin, and how it affects God's plans. In the beginning, nothing is said of sin. It comes together with the Law. How so?

A Sinful Nature

Except for that first sin in Eden, there is nothing of sin and punishment in these stories, because the covenantal Law was not yet given. That Law came later, with Moses. Nor will the Law scowl and curse and grab at everyone in the bright new world of tomorrow. It won't smile there either, because it won't be there. The saints will share in the divine freedom, in oneness with the Creator. There will be nothing of sin and punishment in heaven. And except for Eden, there was no Law in the antediluvian world either. Yes, there was no Law, and yet the Bible says that the antediluvian world was wicked and filled with violence. In what did their guilt consist, if there was no Law?

The answer is that they were not in conformity with God's plan for the world. Wickedness, at its core, is nonconformity with God's will. Their wickedness issued from their creaturehood, from their animal nature that was in its character self-centered and therefore not in harmony with the long-range purposes of God. Humans are animals, child (Gen. 1:20, 24, 2:7, 7:15, 22; Eccl. 3:18-21; Ps. 49:12; 2 Peter 2:12). Their wickedness was the human impulse itself, called the Serpent. This inward orientation toward self-will is opposed to God's will.

Later, God gave Israel the Law in order to reveal this to them. It was a symbolic revelation of his will, and a hint of his plans of

Paradise Lost

Christ. It also revealed their incapacity to comply, for they were incapable of keeping the Law. This incapacity to do God's will is what causes humans to transgress it. Every transgression of the Law is sin (1 John 3:4). The Law demonstrated openly the human self-centeredness that makes them unsuitable for the Body of God. Sin, at its core, is this incapacity to do God's will. It's the true sin that the Law reveals. It's the true wickedness. And it's how humans were created. In keeping with the purpose of the creation, which was to separate the world from God, all the animals including Adam were made as self-centered creatures. And this is the reason why the antedeluvian world was destroyed. Their wickedness was the acting out of their very humanity. It was humanism let loose. Humanism is animalism.

Worldlings cannot do God's will, that which is good, because their inward orientation ever makes them do their own will. They ever serve the self. And in the antedeluvian world there was no Law, no word that would reveal God's will. They all did what they wanted, when they could. Is that not a picture of our world too?

The Law, with its rules-keeping, was never God's long-term goal. It is merely symbolic, merely a lesson. Its purpose, even in Eden, is to reveal that humans are incapable of doing God's will, and so are under sentence of death. His intent is to create for himself a Body, also called a Temple. This is why the Gospel is all about the change called repentance. Just as true sin is the incapacity to do God's will, true righteousness is the capability of doing God's will. The Spirit will give believers the capability of doing God's will, for they will compose the Body of God. This ability is presently only partial, but it will be made complete in the resurrection.

His will is ultimately accomplished not as compliance with rules or laws, but as participation and sharing within his own willing and volition (Rom. 8:6-8). God's will is known and done only in oneness with him (Rom. 10:6-10). Take that to heart, little one. God alone wills his will. Apart from him, you cannot know his will, or do it. You can try to follow his rules, his laws, but in Christ he expects more than that. To do his will, we must have his Spirit willing through us. We must live in union with Christ, we in him and he in us (John 10:38, 17:21-23). Otherwise, it's our own will that we do, even when we want to please him. It's our own desire moving us.

But what he really wants is for us to deny self and follow him, not in imitation but in oneness. He wants to share his identity with us.

Just as we cannot love in the place of God, neither can we will for him. When we try, it becomes that old lie called substitution, and quickly becomes idolatrous. Don't make an idol of yourself, child. Don't pretend to take God's place! And don't think that you are doing God's will by following a list of rules. His will is that you allow him to will in you and through you.

Humans do evil, that which is not God's will, naturally. Being self-centered, their nature and bent is to serve themselves. It's not their transgressions of laws, but rather their nature itself that is the reason that they must die. Sins just reveal their natural condition. That is one of the lessons that the Flood story tells. Self-centeredness and self-will puts humans at odds with God's will. They are then unsuitable to serve in his Body (Rom. 8:6-8). They'd rather do what they want, rather than what God wants. They can't help it. A new generation capable of doing God's will rather than their own must be born.

Humanity's problem is not the result of the Law. The problem is not just what we do, it's who does it, and why. Your problem, child, isn't what you've done. It's what you are. You can't do God's will because you're human, and your very nature impels you to want to do your own will. And you do it, when you can. You're self-oriented. We all are. Ultimately, only God performs God's perfect will. To do his will we must become One with God.

This is hard to see because we confuse the outward act of complying with a rule with the inward event of desiring or purposing it. God's will is like his love. It must be a live, in person appearance. If God's love is to be manifest, he must be present. It's like your own love. No one can do it in your place. A stranger cannot love in your place. Not even a friend can do it. Would you want what is called your love to be just a lip-sync performance by someone else, a stranger pretending to be you, hugging and kissing your children, and your spouse, in your place? No. Neither does God want a stranger taking his place. God's love is direct and in person. Otherwise, it's substitution. And a substitute for God is an idol.

His will works in the same manner. It's direct and in person. Remember that substitution is always false. A substitute will is fraudulent. To will is to wish or desire, and only God can wish for himself. Separated from him, humans cannot desire in his place. Substitution is make-believe, and is always false. Substitutes for God are idols, all of them, even if they have good intentions. Such substitution is the very nature and character of idolatry. Yes, substituting for God is the very nature and character of idolatry. Don't try to substitute for God by loving or willing or acting in his place, child. Let him will and love and act in and through you.

Think about it. Can another person will or desire for you as your stand-in? No, and neither can anyone will for God, or substitute for him. Our compliance with a rule is not identical with God's desiring. Even our compliance with what we think God desires is not the same as God's own desiring. When people claim to be doing God's will, many times it is mere compliance with what they believe he wants. But that's not what he wants. He desires more than mere compliance. He wants to actually live within us, and we in him (John 15:4-5, 17:21-23). To actually do God's will, God must be present and willing through us. Our will must be in oneness with God's will. We must not dress ourselves up as idols. We must let God re-clothe us as saints.

Of course, usually what people mean is that they are acting in harmony with what they believe to be his will. They believe that they are doing what God wants. That is a first step, but it can quickly become mere law-keeping or ritual if it goes no further. It can become a clone of Judaism. We must live in the Spirit. If we preach, it should be in the Spirit. If we write books on theology, it should be in the Spirit. If we read those books on theology, it should be in the Spirit. God wants to live through the believer, and for the believer to live through him. The will of God is that his children walk in the Spirit, for that is their future in glory for which they are being prepared. His will is that they learn to do his will as he wills within them. Our goal as believers is to meld our own wills with that of the Spirit so completely that we can actually do his will, that is, his willing, because he is willing through us. To put it in different terms, we must learn to merge our ego with that of God. It happens only in oneness with Christ.

The attempt to do God's will by following a rule or command is precisely the weakness and inadequacy of Judaism. It tells us that we should do God's will but it does not enable us to comply. Obeying a command is only the shadow of doing his will, at best a testimony, at worst an imitation. And an imitation of doing God's will is not God's will, child. Obedience of a law is just the shadow, just the first step. We must not confuse God's desiring with our actions in following a law, even God's Law. Law is ever at arm's length, never in oneness. God wants us closer than that. Our behavior in harmony with Law is not his will, unless he is willing our behavior. God earnestly desires that we take the next step, and follow his Spirit. We must step out from the shadows of legalism. After all, did not the Pharisees and other leaders think they were doing God's will by following the rules? And aren't these rules-keepers the very ones who crucified Jesus? Remember how Paul persecuted the first Christians, thinking to please God? Rules are subject to interpretation, but the Spirit's guidance is inerrant.

Jesus never once commanded blind obedience to laws or rules. He invites his followers to listen to him, to his very own voice (Ex. 15:26; Deut. 6:4-9; Jer. 3:13, 7:21-22). Never does he call us to the Law. He calls us to oneness with himself. The true Gospel is reconciliation, not legalism or behaviorism. Laws are just temporary road signs to Christ. Once we have found Christ, there is no longer a need for the road signs, except when we wander off and must find our way back. In Christ, we have arrived. We must listen to him, directly, personally, in oneness with him. Leaving the shadows of Law, we must go on to perfection.

Christ is not a list of rules or commands. He's a real, live person, present as the Holy Spirit within every true believer who has received him. The Spirit works to replace the Serpent of self-will. The voice that we must learn to follow is the voice of the Spirit within us who would will through us, just as he would love through us, and work through us, and speak through us. We are, after all, his Body, and we share in his Spirit. We must learn to live within that oneness, he in us and we in him, speaking, loving, and living the will of God (John 17:21-23). We must know his will directly, personally, because it is our own. That is, after all, the reason for our creation and the purpose of our salvation.

To Serve God's Purpose

Because sin and punishment are so ingrained and real in our thinking, it is helpful to re-emphasize the truth that sins under the

Law are just the symptoms of that primeval separation from God that originated during the process of creation itself. Because this world is separated from God and temporary, and we participate in it, we must die. To prevent death from being our destruction we must be re-created. It follows that forgiveness of sins is as much a figure as is washing them away. Sins are just ideas, just actions or inaction out of harmony with laws, which are themselves just ideas. Sins are ideas about ideas about how to live, child. Their reality is our innate separation from God.

That's hard for people accustomed to living by Law to grasp. But salvation is by faith, not by trying unsuccessfully to live in harmony with the Law. There is no Law that can save us (Rom. 8:3-4). Then, after being saved, we should walk in grace, not under the yoke of Law. Our leader and guide should be Christ himself. Salvation is not by legalistic behavior falsely called righteousness. And condemnation is not based on the things we do contrary to the Law that are called sins. Neither salvation nor condemnation are based on the Law. Life and death are based on God's eternal plans and purposes. His intent is metamorphosis into a new Temple and Body. Anything of this world that does not serve that bedrock purpose will eventually be destroyed. To escape the coming destruction, we must serve God's purpose. We must receive him into oneness with ourselves and learn to do his will within that oneness.

Yes, it's true that acts of lawbreaking called sins do not condemn anyone, or keep anyone from eternal life. Neither does keeping the Law save anyone. Only the true sin of remaining separate from God causes one to miss out on eternal life. Salvation comes by receiving Christ and being rejoined to God in the Spirit, thereby escaping from the transience of this present world. God wants a body that is healthy, strong, and well coordinated, with good balance, good reflexes, and excellent manual dexterity. He wants a body that will do his will well.

Sins are not Inherited

Our shovel has been quite handy. But we'll need to keep shoveling. We must keep it in hand here and carefully clear away more misinterpretations. Some churches teach that humans inherit Adam's sin and guilt. But that mistaken notion is entirely refuted by the truth

Paradise Lost

that sins are just ideas. And ideas are not inherited. Ideas of sin are not encoded in our genes. That mistaken notion arises largely from a passage in the apostle Paul's writings (Rom. 5:12-21). The passage in question develops the argument that both Adam and Christ display commonalities, because the one is the type or foreshadowing of the other. Adam is a foreshadowing of Christ. But the passage is extremely difficult. In order to bring out its truth clearly, we must examine it minutely.

In the passage, Christ is the second Adam, and they correspond to one another, especially in the fact that each relates to a group, called the many. Adam is a typology of Christ Jesus. That is the point of the passage. Although each is just one person, both Adam and Christ affect many people. They each have a relationship of one-to-many.

Throughout, the gift that is mentioned is the gift of reconciliation, of joyous life in oneness with God (Rom. 5:10-11). The togetherness of men in Adam, and the corresponding togetherness of men in Christ, is the jumping-off point for Paul's argument, as the following translation will show (Rom. 5:12-19).

> **(12)** Accordingly, in the same way that sin entered into the world through one man, and death through sin, even so death passed to all men, for that all sinned — **(13)** For until Law sin was in the world; but sin is not imputed when there is no Law. **(14)** But death reigned from Adam to Moses, even upon those who had not sinned in the likeness of the disobedience of Adam, who is a type (foreshadowing) of the coming one. **(15)** But (shall) not as the offense so also (be) the free gift? For if by the transgression of one the many died, much more did the grace of God, and the gift in grace which is of one man Jesus Christ abound to the many. **(16)** And (shall) not as by one who sinned (be) the gift? For indeed the judgment (was) of one unto condemnation, but the gift (is) of many transgressions unto justification. **(17)** For if through the one offense death reigned through the one, much more (will) those receiving the abundance of grace and the gift of righteousness reign in life by the one Jesus Christ. **(18)** So then as by one offense (came) condemnation to all men, likewise also by one (act of) righteousness (came) justification of life to all men. **(19)** For as by the disobedience of one man the many were designated sinners, likewise also by the obedience of one shall the many be designated righteous. (Rom. 5:12-19; the author's translation from The Greek New Testament, Third Edition, United Bible Societies, 1983. Cf. Interlinear Greek-English New Testament, Hinds & Noble, 1897, reprinted 1978, Broadman Press).

Understanding the Passage

The passage begins with the simple and obvious truth that sin entered the world of humanity through one man, and death entered through or because of sin. Then, death spread to all men in the same manner that it had come to Adam, as all sinned (v. 12). It was not as though death did not already exist. It entered the world of humanity when Adam died, since he was the primal man. He died because of his sin. Then, death spread to all humanity in the same way that it came to Adam, because they all sinned. As with Adam, their sin was the reason for their death.

The passage clearly shows that death spread to all men in the same way that it came upon Adam. The reason and manner of their death was the very same as that of Adam. But since their death was not because they broke the Law, we can see that Adam's death was not because he broke the Law, either. It was because he could not keep it. He could not live in accord with it. Adam was the first sinner. The first imputed sin came with the first law. Before that law, disobedience did not exist, for there was no law to disobey. The important point here is that all died in the same way, for the same reason. All died because all sinned.

Death came through Adam's sin. But note carefully that it doesn't say that his sinning caused Adam's death in some sort of biological process of deterioration. It doesn't say that he fell, or that his knees were skinned. He died because he was denied access to the tree of life. He was denied access to that tree because he was a sinner, not because he sinned. His sin was not the cause of his death. It merely revealed his sinfulness, which was its cause. Death came to him because of his nature, which caused his sin. His actions were the result of his nature. Adam's sin did not kill him. Denial of access to the tree of life is what did it, because death was part of his nature. Keeping him away from the tree of life allowed the natural processes that were at work in him to fulfill their function. That is why he died. And it's why we all die. Death is natural.

Importantly, it doesn't say that all men died as a direct consequence of their sinning either. It says that they died in the same manner as Adam died, and for the same reason. It doesn't say that sin is the immediate cause of death. It says that death is the ultimate result or consequence of sin, both Adam's and everyone's. Death happened apart from Law. And sin is the transgression of a law. Get it? Adam did not die immediately, nor was his nature changed. He died because he was denied access to the tree of life. We all die like he died, and for the same reason. If we could eat from the tree of life, we would live forever. That's the lesson we must understand. It's the Gospel.

Death is not because all humans share in Adam's sin. It's because they cannot get past the sword which guards the way to the garden of God. All die because, like Adam, they can't get to the tree of life. Death is inherent in our nature. Like Adam, we are mortal. The human animal was never meant to live forever. Immortality has ever been only in Christ. It was never in Adam.

The sinning of those antediluvians was apart from the Law, Paul says, so it was not the sin of disobedience, for as yet there existed no law which they could disobey (Rom. 4:15, 7:8). Sin, of course, means "to miss the mark." Here, it does not refer to lawbreaking. It means that they acted in accordance with their nature, in ways contrary to God's will. Their sin resulted from the natural condition of all humanity. Their nature itself was contrary to God's will. There is nothing here, then, that says sins are inherited. They did not inherit Adam's sin. They inherited his nature and condition of separation from God. They died because of their own sinfulness, which basically is self-centeredness. It was inherent in their very nature.

Notably, sin was in the world before the Law (v. 13). That's important. It was already here before Adam received the first law and disobeyed, and it was here before Moses received the Law and disobeyed (Rom. 7:9). Although the sin of disobedience is not imputed when there is no law, Paul says, all who lived from Adam to Moses still died. They sinned without breaking any of God's laws. This shows that sin, as we've said, is more than transgressing a law. Sins, and death, are a result of the natural human condition.

Death too, comes from something other than breaking the law. Death is inherent in Adam's nature. Why? Adam is incapable of doing God's will. He was never meant to live forever. Death was a built-in feature of human life right from the start. Only the man of the Spirit, Christ Jesus, was capable of accomplishing God's will, for his will was merged with that of the Father. He was fully indwelt by the Spirit. The Spirit helps the saints know and do God's will as they

Paradise Lost

submit to the Spirit's leadership. The Son, not the picture of the Son, not Adam, was ever God's goal.

The passage says explicitly that, from Adam to Moses all died, apart from Law. So, breaking the Law did not cause their death. And their death was like that of Adam. They died not because they broke a law, but because they were by nature at enmity with God's long-term purpose, which was Christ. They were self-centered.

Sins do not kill us, as if they had a palpable, substantive, physical character. They're just ideas. Our nature itself kills us. We self-destruct. This is why neither salvation nor condemnation are by works. It's why we must receive Christ and a new nature. This transformation will not be completed until the resurrection. Until then, life is a struggle against our human nature, which serves the Serpent within us, which we all inherit from Adam.

Adam was a type of Christ, the apostle adds (v.14). This statement is the key to understanding the passage, which is a comparison of type to antitype. Paul is comparing Adam and Christ, and shows their correspondence to one another. They share commonalities, and demonstrate similarities. This would seem strange, except that he is showing Christ to be the second Adam, the antitype or fulfillment of the first Adam' foreshadowings. Paul is pointing out their resemblance to one another. The key to the whole passage lies in their similarities. We must remember that. Adam and Christ are similar. To inanely interpret the passage as if Paul is contrasting the two, as if they were different from one another, misunderstands Paul's point, as if the second Adam were not like the one who imaged and foreshadowed him. It would be as if the mirror image of the one is different from the other.

The first sentence of verse fifteen is misunderstood almost universally as a negative statement. It should be understood as a question. The sentence is not a negative. It does not say, as it is usually misunderstood, "the free gift is not like the transgression." That translation contradicts the whole passage, and denies the very correspondences between the type and the antitype that Paul is developing. It directly contradicts the point of the apostle's whole argument, which is about their similarities. Absurdly, it says that Adam and Christ resemble one another, but they don't look alike. It's as if the image in the mirror is of someone else. That's impossible.

The sentence is a question that asks, "is not the free gift like the transgression?" Literally, it says, "but not as the offense, so also the free gift." The key to a correct understanding of the sentence is the word "also." Put a question mark at the end of the sentence, and nod your head. It's a question that calls for a yes answer. The trespass and the free gift are indeed similar. If not, the typology becomes nonsense. Paul compares Adam and Christ, and finds that they resemble one another. Each manifests the same relation of one-to-many. He is not contrasting the two. He is comparing them, and shows the one to be the counterpart of the other. For example, we can say that "Crows are black. Is that not true?" It asks for an affirmative answer, does it not? This is how Paul should be understood. In response to his question we must nod our heads. Yes, they are alike. Moreover, the free gift and the offense are alike, in that they both operate irrespective of the Law. Both life and death bear a relation of one-to-many.

By the one transgression many died, he says. But by the grace of God the one free gift brought life to many. The free gift is like the transgression, in that both the one transgression and the one free gift affect many (v. 15). The second Adam bears a strong resemblance to the first Adam. That's Paul's point. Both have a relationship of one-to-many. They are similar. But the free gift in Christ is much more abundant and marvelous, he adds.

Then, continuing the same thought, he poses another question, admittedly difficult to translate (v. 16). Literally it says, "and not as by one having sinned the gift." End this one with a question mark too, and nod your head yes once more. Is not the gift through one righteous act like the sin? Are they not similar? Judgment and condemnation fell on the many through one sin, and the free gift of justification came to the many by one act of righteousness. Yes, they are similar. Paul's point is that the relation of one-to-many applies to justification as it does to condemnation. Both salvation and condemnation fit into the same mold. The pattern holds. This is a true typology. And Paul does not ridiculously contradict himself.

Continuing, Paul adds that, if death reigned by the one offense of one (man), then much more shall they who receive the (one) gift of grace and righteousness reign by the one, Jesus Christ (v. 17). The pattern still holds. If death reigns over many through Adam, much more will life reign in many through Christ. The apostle continues developing this same point. Christ is the antitype of Adam, and his one act of righteousness corresponds with Adam's one sin, but is much more abundant.

As by one offense condemnation came to all men, in the same manner by one act of righteousness justification unto life came to all men (v. 18). Paul ever emphasizes the same thought, like a drumbeat, like a metronome, that Christ is the second Adam. The relation of one-to-many is a characteristic that both Adams share. Adam's rope lassos the whole herd of humanity, while Christ's rope lassos the whole herd of the heaven-bound. But Christ's rope is much, much better.

For, as through the disobedience of the one man (Adam) the many were designated or accounted sinners, through the obedience of the one (Jesus) the many will be accounted righteous (v. 19). Jesus is the antitype of Adam. This typology is Paul's point throughout the passage. What could be clearer? To deny their similarities misunderstands it, and contradicts the apostle. And it makes nonsense of the Gospel, as if sins could be inherited.

Because of Adam's sin the many were barred from the garden of God and the tree of life. So they died like Adam, even though they didn't break the law that Adam broke. Their death was not from a magical solidarity in Adam's sin. Happenings are not inheritable, period. Neither are ideas. That the many were put in the place of sinners refers to the consequences of his sin. Like Adam, they too were barred from the tree of life. His sin was not magically transferred to them. His nature and destiny were, but not by magic. The many were put in the place of sinners by being placed outside of the garden. It was because of their nature.

Likewise, because of the righteous act of Jesus, the many were set in the place of the righteous. We do not inherit Jesus' death on the cross. But we may receive its consequences. And always, the relation of one-to-many holds. The magical idea that sins can be inherited is nowhere to be found in this or any other passage. It was hiding naked behind the bushes, afraid to come out. But we've shined the light on it, and it has fled. Let it go.

Reconciliation with God is not just make-believe, not just a forensic declaration that the many are righteous, pretending that they are so. The Gospel is not sham and pretense. Believers are literally placed within Christ. People are in Adam, barred from the tree of life, or they are reconciled to God in Christ, having full access to its fruit. God has blown the Spirit of life into their nostrils and has placed them in the garden of God, to dress it and keep it (John 20:22). Those in Christ are no longer barred from Paradise. Wonder of wonders, they have eaten of the tree of life, just as God had promised (Gen. 1:29). He did not lie. They have partaken of the fruit of the cross. Yes, they have indeed died, but death has no power over them. They will rise again.

Paul does not argue that sins or salvation can be inherited. He argues the similarity between Adam and Jesus. We inherit Adam's sinfulness, his self-serving orientation and his separation from God and from the tree of life, but not his sin. Correspondingly, in Christ we receive reconciliation, which is a place in God. We inherit the benefits of Christ's righteousness, but not his past obedience. We inherit the consequences of his obedience, which is free access to the tree of life, just as we inherit the consequences of Adam's sin. In Christ we dodge the sword God placed east of Eden. But we don't inherit the things that Christ did. Actions are not inheritable. Just as we do not carry a God-gene within us, neither do we carry a sin-gene.

The Law was given so that sin might abound, so that grace might abound even more (v. 20). Sin causes grace to grow ever greater. The greater that sin becomes, the greater is God's grace in his mercy and love toward us. Adam's sin was very great, but Christ's obedience dwarfed it and scrunched it. Nowhere does this passage, or any other, teach that sins are inheritable. Sins are just ideas about actions, neither of which are passed on biologically.

Sin Apart from Law

We must receive Christ. Separated from him, we can't know his will. At most, we can only attempt to do his will haphazardly, on occasion, by trying to comply with rules and laws that we think are his will. But such compliance with laws is but a shadow. And God does not want us to chase after shadows, or to walk in them. He would have us walk in the light. You cannot do God's will by noncompliance with his will, child. People and churches that attempt to do God's will by following the Law in the place of listening to the indwelling Spirit are rebelling against his will. Even great zeal in following the Law cannot please him. Remember the apostle Paul, when he was Saul? Zeal in law-keeping can never substitute for walking in the Spirit.

God does not will through us if he does not live within us. If God's will is not our own, we can't serve his desire to provide for himself a useable Body, so we will not be saved. Everywhere we look, we see that the true sin that condemns is to be separated from Christ, unable to know or do God's will. Transgression of the Law was a figure or picture of that natural, self-oriented alienation from God. Sins under the Law are dark shadows that point to the outer darkness of oblivion outside of Christ.

A new creation is being spoken into being. A new Adam is being formed. The Spirit is moving over the waters, separating light from darkness. The bright Sun of righteousness has appeared in the heavens. The waters of humanity still cover the earth, but the breath of the Almighty is blowing, and will dry them up. The mountains are once more rising above the waters. Soon the Christ-covenanted saints will be given their foreshadowed blessings.

These stories of Genesis are like fossils that must be dug up and studied to reveal the secrets of ages gone by. But unlike the bones that human archeologists study, and that reveal only the mummified past, these bones reveal our future. They come to life when the divine breath of the Spirit blows on them. They dance and sing for us. And their prophetic song is ever Christ.

Chapter Eight
Christ in Early History

As we have seen, the tales that Genesis tells have a strong family resemblance to the final days. One would guess they are brothers and sisters, or at least first cousins, of future events. But the stories speak in a strange tongue. They talk in typology. The tongues of Genesis must be interpreted, as we've been doing.

The stories speak mysteries in the language of prophecy, to be fulfilled in the end-times. In the Bible, the past promises the future by resembling it. The end is in the beginning. The past is a prophet. The wedding in Eden, for example, was a rehearsal of a greater wedding in a greater Eden. But as we've seen, the stories do not all have happy endings. The Gospel has a flip side. Adam and Eve were cast out of Eden. Cain was cursed. The world was destroyed with a flood. So, what will we find at the tower of Babel? Will it be treasure, or tragedy? What tale will Babel tell?

The Tower of Babel

The story of the tower is almost as well known as the story of Noah. But we must bear in mind that the bones of Babel are not just sinking and decomposing relics of the buried past. They reveal things about our own day and beyond. Their story has a point. The sound and fury signifies and foreshadows coming events. The past points its bony finger toward the future. Babel will be repeated twice more. Each time, it will speak in a strange tongue, the tongue of typology. It can only be understood with bowed head and open mind.

By learning this strange language and understanding its mysterious typological meanings, we can find wise counsel and encouragement for living in our own day, and for tomorrow. But we must understand it and apply what we've learned. Otherwise, if we knowingly reject its truth, it will not benefit us. We must not close our ears or become stiff-necked if the truth that the tower tale tells conflicts with our beliefs or desires. We must keep our shovel in hand.

The Babel story is more than just an interesting tale about how the variety of languages in the world came to exist. It's a rose bush with thorns. God himself purposely confused the languages and instituted the diversity of tongues, to show his displeasure with the people's intentions. Their humanist plans for a central religion, government, and language were not in harmony with his own plans. Oneness would be achieved in Christ alone, not in human endeavor. Diversity of languages rather than uniformity is God's will for the present. He will speak and prophesy the Gospel with the voice of many waters.

The Creator likes harmony. But harmony is not a monotone, nor even unison. The music of the creation, and that of the new creation, is sung by many varied voices. Its harmony builds with mutually integrating and reinforcing strains that blend together into one song. They all sing the same song, but they have differing parts. The song of salvation is many-voiced and many-tongued. Each voice adds its distinct and special notes to the rising and falling tides of melody. That's the kind of music the Creator likes. He likes harmony.

Because the diversity of tongues is God's work and will, the variety of voices in the world cannot be silenced until the last, final gasp of the saints is wheezed out. When the harmony ends, when the song is finished and the heartbeat of the Gospel flatlines, it will bring the death rattle of this world. Human history will stop in its tracks, and lie down right there in the middle of the road and die. And Babel was a foreshadowing.

As at Babel, the foolish ambition to establish a one-world religion and government with a universal tongue will once more arouse God's displeasure (1 Cor. 15:24-26). He will again come down to see what the children of men are doing. It will be the final inspection of this world, the last judgment of the creation. Christ will return, to the utter terror of the Antichrist. Babel is the type. It tells us much about its antitype. The beginning foreshadows the end. The past is a prophet. Let's listen as it speaks.

The story begins reasonably enough. The whole world, still a relatively small population, spoke the same language. As they spread east, they came upon a plain in Babylon, and decided to settle there and build. They made bricks of mud and, using tar as mortar, they began working to build a city and a tower. Their intent was to establish a name for themselves, a common identity. They were working toward oneness, lest they be scattered. Their song would be a monotone.

Then the Lord came down to see their work, and it displeased him. It was wicked, that is, not according to his will. So he confused their language, so that they could not understand one another. Their project was frustrated. They had to quit building. He scattered them, directly contradicting their plans. His purposes, not theirs, would be worked out in history. Notice that God would not allow them to unite into one government, people, and religion, all of one tongue. Such a union would come about only through Christ. The imitation of Christ would flop.

Those are the bare bones of the story. Let's see if we can put some meat on them. Let's see if we can flesh them out, and call the Spirit to breathe on them, so that they might live. Maybe they'll dance and sing for us. At the least, they will prophesy.

The Goal of Oneness

But, as might be expected, we'll need to shovel away some false traditions and clear the dance floor. First, the tower builders didn't literally expect to build high enough to get into heaven. That's a childish interpretation. Heaven here is a word like our word skyscraper today. It is alliterative. A tower high as heaven is just a very high tower (cf. Deut. 1:28). Heaven, in those early times, was the atmosphere, not a spiritual place where angels fly and where God sits on his throne, as is imagined today (Gen. 1:8). They were attempting to build a high, impressive structure that would serve as the center of their religious, cultural, and political life. All of one language, they had big dreams, a rousing religion, and proud, inflated ambitions. Yes, they were thinking big, and preparing for the future. But they were wrong.

They were looking, as some do even today, to preserve their identity as one united people living peacefully together under one government and religion. You might say that they were humanists. In fact, go ahead and say it. They were humanists, centered on themselves, working at oneness. Their goal was their own prosperity and preservation. They were not irreligious, or atheists. They were religious humanists working to preserve their religion, character, and identity, with a universal tongue. Get it? A universal tongue.

Heading East

They were heading east. East is the direction of the morning sun, which is a figure of the coming and rising of the great Sun of righteousness (Isa. 60:2-4; Mal. 4:2; Luke 1:78-79; Rev. 1:16). The story hints, then, that these events will have their counterpart in the days of the rising Sun, the days of the Gospel. The story hints of the time of the approaching second advent, when the eastern sky will be lightening, and Christ is readying his return.

This tells us that in the last days, people will again become religious humanists with high hopes and grandiose, human-centered pride. Rebellious in their ambitions, they will attempt to establish a oneness of identity, with a world religion centered in a central city, tied to a world government that will seek to enforce uniformity. Underneath and supporting their work will be a common tongue. Does it not sound like the ecumenical, charismatic movement of today?

But the coming Babel, like its ancient foreshadowing, will be counterfeit, a mocking imitation of God's city, authority, unity, and word. It will be displeasing to the true Sovereign and Lord of harmony and truth. The coming Babel will be a direct rebellion against the will and wishes of God, an imitation, a phony. It will imitate the oneness of Christ and the saints. Imitation is ever Satan's ploy. He has fooled uncounted millions with this same old timeworn trick.

Imitation is substitution's twin brother. They are the children of wishful thinking and make-believe. They love to join hands and dance idolatrously around the truth. They're liars. All four; imitation, substitution, wishful thinking, and make-believe, never tell the truth. And scandalously, many central doctrines of nominal Christianity are built on what these four nimble-footed dancers say. They have pulled the wool over orthodoxy's head.

Do not the churches teach the imitation of Christ? Do they not preach that Christ is our substitute? People, that's wishful thinking, making believe that one thing is another. Can one thing be another, ever, even if it's shouted from behind a pulpit with great emotion? Let's move on, but watch where you step.

East of Eden lay Babylon, the land of Shinar. Babylon is a cipher for Roman Catholicism and her friends (1 Peter 5:13). Let's say it clearly. The Tower of Babel prefigures the ecumenical Church of the end-time headquartered in Rome. There, we've said it. Now you know.

The one language of Babel is a figure of the rebellious practice of tongues-speaking and all its attendant behaviors and doctrines, through which the Church will seek to enforce the end-time oneness of ecumenism, directly opposing God's intended desire for the diversity of tongues. The city will be the center of the one-world government that humanists dream of building. It will be united with the one-world church of the Antichrist. The Roman Church will prostitute herself to the reborn Roman State. And the Protestant churches will join with them, equally deluded.

In the early days when the Gospel first started to spread, the Spirit expressly forbade Paul from going eastward, for it was not yet time for these prefigurative events to come forward and show their rouged faces. Until the time of the end, the Gospel would face westward (Acts 16:6-10). When Christianity turns eastward, when the eastern sky begins to lighten in expectation of the coming day, it will herald the imminent advent of Christ. Today, the east is getting brighter. And Rome is wanting to rise again.

As the ancients headed east, they found a plain in Shinar, which is Babylon. It is worth repeating that the antitype of ancient Babylon, called Babylon the great, is the Roman government in league with the Roman Catholic Church and her daughters, the various Protestant and other churches and religions that will make league with her. It will include all of nominal Christianity (1 Peter 5:13; Rev. 17:5). In the End-time they will come under the influence and authority of Rome. This is the rebellious fallen city, the great whore from which the great Pretender will rule, speaking ex cathedra from his seat in the Roman temple, idolatrously substituting himself for God, pretending to be Christ's vicar (2 Thess. 2:3-12).

Going to Genesis once more, we read that they found a plain. This hints of false religion. In the final days, the people will embrace a pious religious humanism masquerading behind the mask of nominal Christianity. Their religion will be like a lofty tower, a manmade monument to human pride and arrogance. True religion is a mountain made without human hands. It is Mount Zion, high as heaven itself (Dan. 2:34-35; 44-45; Rev. 21:10). False, humanist religion is a tower reaching toward heaven, but set on the shifting sands of human self-service, and held together with the black tar of human labor. In the end, God's fiery breath will blow on it, and the whole building will burn (Isa. 11:4, 30:28-33).

Because there was no mountain, no true religion there on the plains of Babylon, they decided to make their own mountain. They would build a tower that would be their temple in which to practice their religion. Because they had no stones, their temple would be built of manmade bricks, burned in order to harden them (Isa. 2:12-17, 30:25). Did you get that, pilgrim? Their temple would not be built of living stones, for they had none. It would be the work of human hand. They must gather the mud and harden it, for they lacked the Spirit.

What a scathing figure of end-time Christianity! Built on the sand with hardened bricks rather than living stones, the government religion of the end-time will be utterly fallen, the haunt of demons and evil spirits, and howling, screeching things of darkness (Rev. 18:2). Like the original tower builders, their primary orientation will be inward. It will be to make a name for themselves and to be one people with one religion, one government, and one language. It will be a religion of humanism, with a counterfeit oneness. Remember that humanity holds the Serpent in its breast. Don't be fooled, little one. To serve humanity in the place of Christ is to serve the Serpent. Do not fall for the Antichrist's lie.

Pretending to worship God, like many churches of today the people of Babel were in reality serving their own human desires for worldly prosperity, seeking health and wealth for themselves and calling it God's blessings. Their goal was a socio-political religion. Their method was to wed politics and religion, secular kingship and priesthood, and call it good.

Later, pathetic King Saul repeated the same folly, joining kingship with priesthood. And he lost his kingdom (1 Sam. 10:8, 13:8-14). In the end-time, when the Antichrist joins the two ministries of government and religion in himself, it will again draw God's ire. These two ministries are joined legitimately only in Christ (Zech. 6:13). Babel's uniting of church and state was a mocking imitation of the kingship and priesthood of the true King. In the future, when the Beast and the False Prophet are wed in the Priest-king of Rome, it will incur God's wrath once more (Rev. 13:11-13).

Like the rebels of Babel, the seed of the Serpent that is called the Beast will deceive the nations and will draw them under his authority and dominion in a misleading mimicry of true baptism and communion (Rev. 13:14-18, 16:13-16). The mark of the beast, and the abomination of desolation, will be the practice of tongues-speaking, with all its attendant doctrines and traditions, which the Antichrist will promote when he takes his seat in the temple (2 Thess. 2:11). As at the tower in the land of Shinar, the babble of tongues-speaking today is not a sign of blessing, but of condemnation and imminent judgment (Isa. 28:9-13; 1 Cor. 14:20-21). It warns of God's displeasure, and portends disaster.

The Second Babel

Babel is a foreboding, foreshadowing warning for the last days. And the last days are already with us. They began when Jesus walked the earth (Acts 2:4-36). The tale of the tower was repeated in the ministry of the Savior, and the spread of the Gospel. Like their counterparts of old, the builders of Judaism had wanted to make a name for themselves too. They wanted their religion and their government to be not only a jewel in the crown of the earth, they expected that it would be the crown itself. Jerusalem would be the center of a world government and religion. The Jews would be kings and priests, holding dominion over the Gentiles in the name and authority of God. They would have a name and fame high as heaven. They, too, were building a city and a tower.

They expected that when Messiah came, he would liberate them from their shameful subservience to Rome, brought about because of their neglect of the Law. They must get back to keeping the Law, so that God would be pleased and come to be present among them again. They failed to see the prefigurative nature of the Law, and of their own chosenness. So, following the example of Babel, they strove to preserve their identity, tied to their religion of the kingdom. Their city of Jerusalem, they thought, would be the seat of world government, high as heaven.

Alas, the exact opposite happened. Their prime city became the seat of Satan, prefiguring the end-time cathedra in the Roman temple of Christianity where the Antichrist will squat (Rev. 2:13) They did not recognize the time of their visitation. God had come down once more to see what these children of men were building. When he came, they crucified him, through the agency of Rome. Echoing the past and prefiguring future events Caiaphas and Caesar, priesthood and kingship, joined in unholy league, bringing heaven's condemnation down upon the Jews.

They did not understand that God had come down from heaven once more to see the city and tower that they were building. They did not expect or understand his displeasure. On the day of Pentecost, they had no inkling that they were being rejected. Even Jesus' disciples wanted at first to remain in Judaism. They thought Jesus was for Jews only (Acts 1:6, 5:42, 6:14, 15:1-29). It took special revelations to Peter and to Paul for the Jews to accept the reality that the Gospel of salvation was for every nation. In trying to make a name for themselves, the Jews were at complete odds with the will of God. Their tower of human works was not God's will. Christ would build his temple with living stones on the highest peaks on the mountain of God.

When God multiplied their languages on the day of Pentecost, it was so that they would leave off building the tower and religion of Judaism. They were not to turn inward upon themselves, but were to multiply and spread into all the world with the good news. The Gospel song was to be sung in many languages. Its joyful music would ring out in multi-voiced harmonies, in many tongues. It was for all peoples.

Many Jews still jealously protect their identity today, and still await the Messiah to come and give them the dominion. They're still scrounging around in the rubble, picking up broken pieces of brick, gathering up fragments of tar, still looking to rebuild their tower. It will never happen (Deut. 34:4; Mal. 1:4; Gal. 4:30).

Pentecost was a repetition of Babel, same song, second verse. The believers that day began to speak in different tongues because God was displeased with Judaism. The time of judgment had once more arrived. Judaism had been weighed in the balances, and had been found deficient. The Jews were rejected on the day of Pentecost, for a new people of God who later were called Christians.

The Bride of Christ was born that day. A nation was born in one day, from the blood and water that had flowed from the second Adam's side as he slept. Life in the Spirit was now in the world, which had become the fertile, Edenic garden of God. The Judaism of Jesus' day was the second tower, and God's second witness. There will come a third witness, one more tower, and one more visitation.

The Last Visitation

The builders of Christianity, like the Jews who prefigured them, will not recognize the time of their visitation. They will be eating and drinking, marrying and giving in marriage, churches uniting with other churches, feeding the Serpent. Drunk with humanism, they will think that their unity, worldly prosperity, and growth are a blessing from heaven. The Antichrist will revel among them, squatting in the temple in Rome, pretending to be Christ's vicar, exercising both governmental and priestly authority illegitimately and speaking in tongues in order to deceive all Christendom. This supposed universal language will be his tool of deception by which he will unite all tongues-speakers in a counterfeit universal communion (Rev. 13:4-7). He will seduce the people into building a Christian State. He will call them to a false Christ, to an imitation, a substitute (Matt. 7:15-23, 24:5). He will promise the nations peace and prosperity. And the peoples will flock to him, eagerly and blindly, seeking peace and prosperity.

It will be a direct, frontal attack on God's plan and authority, rejecting the harmony that God so loves, for the sake of unison. It will deny individuality and freedom for the sake of sameness. Church will join with State in crucifying Christ once more, when the true saints refuse to bow before the abomination squatting in Rome. But Christ will call his people, the Jews that remain until the end, out of Babylon as he once called them out of Egypt (Isa. 32:4; 2 Thess. 2:8). Babylon will be destroyed forever (Isa. 11:15, 33:19). The blasphemous babble of tongues-speaking will be silenced in the waters of oblivion (Ex. 11:7; Rev. 18:21).

God has twice called his people out of Babylon and her abomination of tower-building that brings desolation (Matt. 6:7; Jas. 1:22-23). If the people will not listen, they will justly partake of her judgment. The leaning tower of end-time Christianity, built like Judaism on the shifting sands of humanism, will fall.

Chapter Nine
Recycling the Creation

There are other, continuing stories in Genesis, and in the Bible. And they all have meaning for us today. The Bible is a picture book. And the pictures portray Christ Jesus and the Gospel. But this present book cannot tell them all. We will pause for now, step out into the fresh air, set our shovel aside, and leave with a few parting thoughts.

The first thing that comes to mind is that recycling is godly. That's surprising, but wherever we look we can see this principle at work. The whole creation recycles at every point. Reality builds upon itself. That which is, comes from that which was. Recycling is the signature of God. It's how he works. It is a reflection of himself. It's what creation is all about. Nothing is ever wasted, nothing is thrown out. All things just change into something new. That which is, has been recycled. That which will be, will have been recycled. And at the center of it all is God the Creator. The new creation is the old creation recycled. The new believer is the old unbeliever recycled. The God of creation will be the God of the new creation. God, too, is renewing himself. He is not the immutable God that so many churches blindly proclaim.

Recycling is indeed the truth of our salvation. Salvation means that we will be recycled. It disproves forever the Calvinist doctrine of total depravity, for if some part of us is saved, then the so-called depravity cannot have been total. The false doctrine of total depravity unwittingly denies salvation and the Gospel. Recycling is at the very core of the true Gospel of salvation.

The truth also denies the erroneous, magical doctrine of the Fall of Man. And when I say magical, again I don't mean it in a good way. Perhaps I should say sorcerous rather than magical. Magic and sorcery, called witchcraft, are abominations.

The Gospel is about resurrection to glories undreamed. Resurrection too, puts the lie to Calvin. Resurrection means that we will receive new bodies recycled from material that already exists.

Spirit and body will come together. Salvation and resurrection both prove irrefutably that Calvin's total depravity is itself depraved.

The reason for all things is God. And he recycles. This is evident throughout nature, and in the Gospel. Recycling is, in fact, creation. Creation means to put things together in a new and different way than they were. Creation is change. And it's the character of all reality that we know. Everything changes.

And in the process of continual change that composes our world, the Creator repeats some basic patterns. The patterns are not perfect matches, however, which would deny newness. They're not exactly alike. The antitype is never a perfect clone of the type. But they are sufficiently similar that we can discern similarities and see that they complement one another.

God is a poet. The world itself is a divine poem. God's later work rhymes with his earlier work. But like Hebrew poetry, it is not the end-sound that is repeated. It is the idea. Knowing this, we can see that the darkness evolving into light in the beginning points to the future. It will be repeated. It hints softly that the present spiritual darkness will evolve into light. The night will spin into day. Prophecy will become fulfillment. The old world will give way to the new. And in all of it, we can discern patterns by which the new repeats the old, in a new way, like Hebrew poetry. The new rhymes with the old.

Surprisingly, as the world changes under his direction, as it moves from shadow to fulfillment, from darkness to light, God too is changing. God himself is transforming. Metamorphosis is in the very nature of God. It's the expression of himself. It's who he is. The great I AM is the One who WILL BE. He is changing into the fullness of Christ (Rom. 11:36; 1 Cor. 8:6). He is the Creator.

And because he is eternal, change itself is eternal. Change is the very framework of reality. Everything changes. Always has, always will. Everything testifies of its divine Maker. Stasis is just imaginary, a trick of our mind. It doesn't exist in the real world. Everything moves. Everything evolves into something new, always, everywhere.

The recycling that is creation is godly. Recognition and acknowledgment of the Creator's method helps us to know the Creator himself. He himself is evolving, reconciling the world back to himself. It's how he works, how he expresses himself and displays his purpose for this world, which is being transformed into a new world. It helps us understand the true Gospel, which involves a real, literal, physical and spiritual return to God. This return to God requires that the creation, and the saints, be made suitable for him. It requires transformation. Under God's direction and care this world will be changed, with the purpose and goal of serving as his divine temple. And the saints will be the living stones that make up that temple of his Body. They will be changed and made suitable to serve. They will be recycled.

Having finished the work on this present creation, God rested, making the seventh day holy. It is holy because God is no longer working to create this world. Now he is busy creating a new world, which will itself come about from the recycling of this present one. This is the work to which he invites whosoever will to come and join him in. The work is holy, that is, not of this world. His invitation is a call to enter into his own holiness, to leave this world to join with him in creating a new and better one. The saints are co-creators with God, as they speak his word and testify of him with their lives. Like him they are being changed even while they are helping to create the change.

The Creator is evolving into the fullness of Christ, in whom every saint shares. Christ's fullness is the revelation, goal, and destiny of God and of all his children. This is why, even now, his children have begun to share in the divine life, and repeat his archetypal story with their own lives and with their word of testimony. Like God, who speaks his will into being, the saints are learning to speak the words of faith, which are words infused with the Spirit, for they issue from Christ within them. Their words then become the all-powerful and creative words of God. The stories of the saints are short, condensed versions of the epic, all-encompassing story of God. Their lives reflect and harmonize with the One who is creating them in his image. The pattern holds. The Archetype of all existence is manifested in all his works, everywhere.

The saints must shine the bright light of truth over the darkness that is Darwinian evolution. God, not blind happenstance, is the Creator of this world and the next. And his purpose is Christ in his full, magnificent and divine splendor. Toward this purpose the Creator differentiated himself from the world temporarily, to be re-integrated in the Body of Christ. And the Body will include the saints, who will receive glorification together with their Savior. This is why they must learn godliness. It is their future.

Creation too is godly, for it is God's way of working, and of expressing himself. The world is the expression and reflection of its Creator. His nature is to create. Creation is the process of change that God determines and guides, and in which he manifests himself. And wondrously, he invites the saints to join him in this never-ending journey of newness and exploration, not just here in this present world, but throughout the endless cycles of eternity. And he enables them for the work, sharing his Spirit with them. He invites them to tell the truth, of the past, the present, and the future.

And the world itself is godly, because of its past and its future. It originated in God, and will be returned to him in Christ. Infiltrated by his Spirit it gave birth to all the plants and animals. And it sustains them. The world's creation somehow separated it from God. Matter was differentiated from Spirit. It is now called a dead world because it will be destroyed. It will be recycled and reconciled back to the Creator in and through Christ, in a second wave of creation, as the Spirit again fully re-integrates with the newly transformed world.

Humans in Christ are godly too. They are images of God, and repeat his story. Infiltrated by the Spirit, they share in the divine nature, and compose Christ's Body, which is also the growing Temple of God. Their place and destiny is to take dominion over the new world in the name of Christ, as prefigured by Adam's dominion over the first creation. They will command the natural forces of the future even as God now commands the principalities and powers of this present world. They are learning to take dominion over the giants, the opposing principalities and powers, in order to take title to the holy land of their promised inheritance.

Gloriously, they will be co-creators with God, making his will and desire come to fruition. Even now, as they preach the Gospel in the Spirit and new souls are saved, the saints have a part alongside God in creating the bright new world of eternal day!

This is why the saints must learn to walk in the will of God and in the indomitable power of faith. Faith in action is creative. On the other hand, humans outside of Christ are not holy. Like Adam, they are just animals, and share in the animal nature only. Human life apart from Christ lies totally within the first creation, which is unholy and destined for destruction. However, humans have a degree of freedom. They have the ability to create. They have the capacity for abstract thinking, to make plans and work toward their accomplishment. They can understand Law, and can know the difference between good and evil, between that which is God's will and that which is not his will. They have the ability to determine their actions, and their future, by this knowledge.

This knowledge of God's will is gained first by their meeting with the Law, and then in a truer and fuller manner by receiving the Spirit and walking therein in direct, personal knowledge of God's will. Eventually they will come to share fully in the mind and will of God. They will share fully in the divine consciousness.

True holiness, then, consists in separation from this present world, and is accomplished not by human works, but by participation in Christ in the new creation. Sanctification is separation from this world. God's holiness consists in his separation from it, which is the result of the primeval process of creation. Creation ended at the Flood, which was when God's Spirit removed from the world. The new creation, even now in progress, will end in another flood, this time in the end-time fires as God's word fulfills itself. This present generation of the flesh will be burned up. The saints are separated from this world and sanctified by their reception of Christ and their walk in him. It happens through the word of God. They become holy, as God is holy. Presently they are in the world, but not of it.

The Law, as we saw, is only imaginary. This truth can cause an upheaval in Christian thought. It goes directly against orthodoxy and the teachings of many or most of the churches, if not all of them. It means that sins and guilt and forgiveness are imaginary too. They are just ideas, just pictures like the rest of the Law. And the Law has been annulled in Christ. Shockingly, even forgiveness of sins is just as imaginary as is the Law itself. It means, also shockingly, that condemnation is just as imaginary. Having no substantive reality, sins and guilt cannot be passed on genetically. The reality that sins and guilt picture is separation from God in the creation, which is a dead end street. Death comes not because of people's sinning, because of their having broken the Law, but because that's how this world was made. It was purposely meant to be temporary. Humanity, like the rest of the menagerie, was meant to be temporary, and do not and have never possessed eternal life in themselves (1 Tim. 6:15-16).

Death did not enter the world because of Adam's sin. It was already here. Death passed to all humanity because humanity in itself is just the first step in a larger process, and is incapable of doing God's will. Death happens to us naturally. Eternal life is only in Christ. Adam and Eve did not possess eternal life. They did not have a God-gene. Their imaging was their typological, illustrative function or quality. They did not fall from perfection. Rather, their eyes were opened to their need of a Savior. That is precisely why God gave Adam that first law in Eden. It was to open their eyes. The Law has the same function today. It shows us our need of a Savior.

The creation's natural separation from God was not caused by bad behavior, and cannot be remedied by good behavior. The separation can only be healed by receiving Christ and in him receiving reconciliation with God. Reconciliation is a literal physical and spiritual re-joining with God. It is the glory which forgiveness of sins pictures. Guilt is the realization of our inadequacy. We need help. The Law leads us, if we will, to Christ, who alone can help us.

The true Gospel, then, is this present world's origin in God, and its return to God in Christ. Salvation means that the saints will share in that reconciliation, and will survive the destruction and recycling of this present world. Salvation, then, is not based on the Law of Moses, which dealt with sins and guilt and punishment, and was given only to Israel. Judaism, in all its rites and rituals and its system of sacrifices, was just a preview, just a picture of the true Gospel of salvation for all people. The true Gospel of salvation is a story of estrangement followed by reconciliation, rather than about breaking God's laws followed by forgiveness of the punishment due for breaking them. That would make punishment utterly unjust, for no one is able to keep them. Moreover, laws are only ideas, and cannot literally be broken, or kept.

Judaism, a religion of Law, was a shadow religion. Its forms, structures, and history are figures foreshadowing their fulfillment in relation to Christ. Even the God of Judaism is but a shadow. God's complete revelation will be in the fullness of Christ, when Creator and creation are once again joined together as One. He is the reason for the creation of this world, and the goal of the new creation. Christ is what the forms and figures of Judaism prefigured, and what the stories of Genesis tell us. But we must listen.

So then, Christian life does not consist of being led about through the nose by a list of rules. True Christianity is not behaviorism. Nor is the Bible just a fountain of moral platitudes. True life in Christ is divine freedom. Yes, child, life in Christ is freedom even from the principalities and powers that govern this present world. True freedom is to share in the mind and body of Christ, and in his dominion over all things. Miracles are an inkling of this, and of our future. In the new world, that which is counted miraculous today will be commonplace. It will be the normal state of affairs. The saints will command the powers of nature by the irresistible authority of God. Their words will be the very word of God. Their actions will be his actions, their dreams will be the dreams of God! And a hint of this exhilarating, mind-boggling freedom is already available to every saint!

The miracles recorded in the Bible are hints and intimations of the saints' irresistible authority and power that they inherit in Christ. And incredibly, this breathtaking power is already ours to take, as much as we can handle. It is the power of faith, of walking in the Spirit, and of speaking the powerful and creative word of God. This is why the saints must learn to let God have his will in them, and speak through them. It is their life, their future, and their glory!

These truths and more are hinted in the stories of Genesis. Its stories are like a row of prophets that line up one after the other to prefigure and foretell the Gospel, and God's purposes. They are never silent. They speak. They use words to paint pictures. And the pictures tell us about Christ Jesus and the glories he has prepared for us. Every story adds another sentence or two to the divine promises.

The first begins by saying that the way things are in this world is because God made them to happen as they do. Another tells us that life originated from the earth itself, because of the Spirit's presence within it. A following one gives a rough sequence of how the earth and heaven came to be in their present form. The next one tells us that the man of the flesh holds within him the Serpent, which is an orientation away from God in self-service. Incapable then of doing God's will, he will be cast out from God's presence to his death, to be superseded by the man of the Spirit. Another story tells us that the man of the flesh is a murderer, and will not prosper. The same story also tells of a righteous one whose offering is accepted. A fourth story steps forward, smiles reassuringly, and tells us that God will

Recycling the Creation

give Eve another son, another Abel. Following that, a stern-faced story wrings its hands and warns that because of the wickedness of humanity, God will destroy this world, and will bring about a bright new world in which the true Sun himself will shine unobstructed in the cloudless expanses. The stories of Genesis are foreshadowings of the future. They will be repeated. The pattern holds. The poem rhymes.

Babel warns against building a humanistic state religion and an ecumenism based on tongues-speaking. It will be the final abomination, the last rebellion that will bring God's judgment crashing down. When the world finally and totally rejects the Spirit of the Son and kills the end-time saints, shedding the blood of those made in the image of God, it will be the blasphemy against the Spirit that will never be forgiven. The sharp sword of the Lord will then fall swiftly upon the necks of the wicked.

But the pattern and archetype of all creation is recycling. Recycling means salvation! Upon the destruction of this world the curtains of the heretofore unseen will open and the spectacular new creation will take center stage. The saints will be changed into beings of light, transformed into a divine rainbow of life, fully baptized within its resplendent glories. From the ashes of this present world the shining new phoenix of unfettered life will arise, taking form as the Creator has long desired. The saints, eagles of the new creation, will gaze, wondrously and far, into the ever-beckoning future of uncharted possibilities. Exultantly, they will spread their wings and take flight into those vast, infinite and uncharted skies. The world will step out from its cocoon and begin to sing, pulsing with the heartbeat of God, dancing to the melodies of his will. Unnumbered saints will shout the joyful song of salvation, exuberant in their divine, unfettered power, experiencing life together with God in the full freedom of unhindered creative expression.

Not understanding these truths, the mainstream churches preach Judaism's God, calling him Christ Jesus, but keeping the chains of Law wrapped tightly around his ankles. They preach legalism coupled with behaviorism, a Gospel of sin and forgiveness, keeping God and the creation forever separated, unwittingly serving the Serpent principle. And this is true even of growing, friendly churches. Taking the metaphors for the reality, and the reality for metaphors, the churches have unwittingly placed themselves under the Law of Moses, and have become slaves to things that should be their servants. They have become slaves to the Law while claiming to have been freed from it. But their freedom is only from its punishment, not from the Law itself.

Those churches that realize that the Gentiles have never been under the Law of Moses invent for themselves the Unknown Law! They must have something for which to feel guilty of and be forgiven for. The truth is, orthodoxy's doctrinal shoes have idolatry and blasphemy all over them, and it's gotten all over her white robe. But these chains of Law cannot bind the true Samson. The Law was just a shadow, just a thread.

Believers must proclaim the true Gospel and the true God. They must open their eyes to see the truth, and their mouths to speak it, loudly. In order to do this, they must recognize and reject the falsehoods that the churches have promulgated for centuries. They must understand the truths of Genesis. The end was already there in the beginning, printed boldly in archetype, told in typology.

They must recognize and understand the true image of God in them, and reject the satanic notion that we are fundamentally and forever separated from God. He wants us more than near. He longs to merge with us, and share together unimaginable wonders and unthinkable glories. So he calls us to join him in holiness, leaving the vanities of this world for the joys of the new. Our hearts should beat for heaven, then, where thieves cannot steal from us, and the moth cannot eat away at our white robes of righteousness.

We must stomp down hard on the false Gospel of humanism, and cultivate our creative freedom to serve rather than be served. We exist to serve God, freely and willingly. We must learn to serve him directly, in oneness with him, having nothing intruding between us. And he is the Creator. His word is creative. As we speak his word in oneness with him, it too is creative and powerful. As we speak in the Spirit, it transforms hearts and minds, and the world itself. It gives life to the dead. Our inheritance in Christ is marvelous beyond belief. In him, the principalities and powers that govern this world are but servants. The saints must see the enormity and grandeur of their standing in Christ. Christ is God, people! Christ is God! In receiving him we become One with the Creator! That is the story that the creation tells.

Believers must proclaim these truths, everywhere. They must not remain silent. Like the past, the present can be a prophet too. We must not hide in the invisibility cloak of silence. We must rouse the words in us and send them out with the good news. And should we not sing them, loudly, in the song of salvation?

About the Author

Pastor John writes to show believers the greatness of glory denied them by the central doctrines of mainstream Christianity. Here he focuses on Genesis, providing a different and startling explanation of the first things, and how the beginning previews the end.

www.ingramcontent.com/pod-product-compliance
Lightning Source LLC
Chambersburg PA
CBHW020649300426
44112CB00007B/300